Acclaim for Antonia Fraser's

Must You Go?

"Entertaining and ultimately touching in its determination to recapture lost time, to portray a younger, more carefree self and to bring back a lost loved one, if only on the page."
—Francine Prose, *The New York Times Book Review*

"A stirring celebration of what Fraser, reflecting near the end of Pinter's life, observed as a union 'to the infinite degree happy beyond all possible expectations.'" —*The New Yorker*

"Fond and touching. . . . A crisp, clear-eyed portrait of a shared life of creative work, political activism, wide-ranging travels, family. . . . Theirs was a fine romance, and Fraser shares that with us." —*The Seattle Times*

"Extraordinary by any standards. . . . It is simultaneously a love story, an intimate portrait of a great writer and an exercise in self-revelation." —*The Guardian* (UK)

"Immediate and absorbing. . . . In creating such a finely wrought picture of a man who was both one of the great playwrights of the twentieth century and the love of her life, she deploys her own talents." —*San Francisco Chronicle*

"It takes a daring biographer to turn her sharp eye on her own life as Antonia Fraser does so movingly and beautifully in her —Tina Brown, *The Daily Beast*

Antonia Fraser

Must You Go?

Antonia Fraser is the author of many internationally bestselling historical works, including *Love and Louis XIV, Marie Antoinette,* which was made into a film by Sofia Coppola, *The Wives of Henry VIII, Mary Queen of Scots,* and *Faith and Treason: The Story of the Gunpowder Plot.* She has received the Wolfson Prize for History, the Norton Medlicott Medal of Britain's Historical Association, and the Franco-British Society's Enid McLeod Literary Prize. She was made a Dame for services to literature in 2011.

Must You Go?

ALSO BY ANTONIA FRASER

NONFICTION

Mary Queen of Scots
Cromwell, the Lord Protector
King James VI of Scotland, I of England
The Lives of the Kings and Queens of England (editor)
Royal Charles: Charles II and the Restoration
The Weaker Vessel
The Warrior Queens
The Wives of Henry VIII
Faith and Treason: The Story of the Gunpowder Plot
Marie Antoinette: The Journey
Love and Louis XIV: The Women in the Life of the Sun King

FICTION

Quiet as a Nun
The Wild Island
A Splash of Red
Cool Repentance
Oxford Blood
Your Royal Hostage
The Cavalier Case
Political Death
Jemima Shore's First Case and Other Stories
Jemima Shore at the Sunny Grave and Other Stories

ANTHOLOGIES

Scottish Love Poems
Love Letters

Must You Go?

MY LIFE WITH HAROLD PINTER

Antonia Fraser

Anchor Books
A Division of Random House, Inc.
New York

FIRST ANCHOR BOOKS EDITION, OCTOBER 2011

The Library of Congress has cataloged the Nan A. Talese/Doubleday edition as follows:
Fraser, Antonia, 1932–
Must you go? : my life with Harold Pinter / Antonia Fraser.—1st American ed.
p. cm.
1. Pinter, Harold, 1930–2008. 2. Dramatists, English—20th century—Biography.
3. Authors, English—20th century—Biography. 4. Fraser, Antonia, 1932– I. Title.
PR6066.I53Z6457 2010
[B] 2010007374

ANCHOR ISBN: 978-0-307-47557-2

www.anchorbooks.com

Printed in the United States of America
10 9 8 7 6 5 4 3 2 1

CONTENTS

Part Three

Preface

The subtitle of the book declares its contents: this is 'my life with Harold Pinter', not my complete life, and certainly not his. In essence, it is a love story and as with many love stories, the beginning and the end, the first light and the twilight, are dealt with more fully than the high noon in between, described more impressionistically.

I have based it partly on my own Diaries; these have been kept since October 1968 when I suffered from withdrawal symptoms after finishing my first historical biography *Mary Queen of Scots*, the centre of my existence for so long. I have also used my own recollections, being careful to distinguish between the two, immediate reactions (I always write my Diary the next morning unless otherwise noted) and memories.

On the whole Harold did not read these Diaries (although he was free to do so: they were not kept secret). I have noted the rare occasions when he made a comment or scribbled something in it himself.

I have also quoted Harold where he told me things about his past, once again noting the source, and have occasionally quoted his friends talking to me on the same subject. Looking back at the Diaries, I see that I always paid special attention to any green shoots where Harold's writing was concerned. Although it was not a conscious process, I suppose this was a consequence of a biographer living with a creative artist and observing what went on first hand.

Harold and I lived together from August 1975 until his death thirty-three and a half years later on Christmas Eve 2008. 'O! call back yesterday, bid time return,' cries one of his courtiers to Richard II. This is my way of doing so.

Must You Go?

PART ONE

Chapter One

FIRST NIGHT

I first saw Harold across a crowded room, but it was lunchtime, not some enchanted evening, and we did not speak. I was having lunch in the Etoile restaurant in Charlotte Street; my companion pointed to a trio of men lunching opposite us. They were in fact Robert Shaw, Donald Pleasence and Harold; they were discussing Robert's play, *The Man in the Glass Booth*, in which Harold would direct Donald. My companion admired Robert Shaw intensely: the handsome red-headed star who was said to do his own stuntwork and embodied machismo. Apparently I said thoughtfully: 'I'll take the dark one.'

On the next occasion I heard Harold's voice, once aptly described by Arthur Miller as his 'awesome baritone', before we met. There was a recital about Mary Queen of Scots at the National Portrait Gallery, based on my book. Harold's wife Vivien Merchant took the part of Mary, an actor took all the male parts and I read the narrative. These were professionals and I was intensely nervous; a kind friend in the audience told me afterwards that my knees were visibly shaking in my natty white trouser suit which had perhaps been the wrong call as a costume. Nevertheless things were running along smoothly – Vivien was an accomplished reader who gave Mary the correct Scottish accent – when suddenly there was some kind of interruption, a man's voice raised, at the back of the gallery. Afterwards I enquired rather crossly what had happened. 'Oh, that was Harold Pinter,' I was told. 'He attacked the attendant for opening the door in the middle of the recital.' 'I didn't hear the *door*,' I muttered, having just learned that the projected LP of the recital would have to be abandoned due to the disturbance. Later, when I was introduced to Harold, I asked him if it had indeed

3

been him. 'Yes,' he replied with satisfaction, 'I do that kind of thing all the time.' In similar situations in the future, I sometimes reflected wryly: 'I can't say I wasn't warned . . .'

And so to the evening of 8 January 1975 when I went to the first night of *The Birthday Party* at the Shaw Theatre, directed by Kevin Billington, husband of my sister Rachel. The author was of course there and there was to be a dinner party afterwards at the Billingtons' house in Holland Park.

At this point, Hugh and I, Harold and Vivien, had both been married, oddly enough, for exactly the same period almost to the day: that is, eighteen years since September 1956 when Harold and Vivien got married in a Registry Office in Bournemouth (they were in rep there) while I dolled myself up as Mary Queen of Scots and Hugh wore a kilt at the Catholic Church in Warwick Street, Soho, with a full sung Nuptial Mass. Hugh and I had six children; Harold and Vivien had one. Hugh had been a Conservative MP since 1945; Vivien was a celebrated actress. I was forty-two; Harold was forty-four.

I considered myself to be happily married, or at any rate happy in my marriage; I admired Hugh for his cavalier nature, his high spirits, his courage – friends nicknamed him 'Fearless Fraser' after some 1930s trapeze artist – his independence, his essential decency and kindness. I even admired him for his detachment, although his lack of emotional intimacy – he once told me that he preferred families to individuals – was with hindsight probably what doomed us. I on the other hand was intensely romantic and always had been since early childhood; the trouble with romantics is that they tend to gravitate towards other like-minded people, or people they choose to regard as such. So there had been romances. But I had never for one moment envisaged leaving my marriage.

Harold, I learned much later, did not consider himself to be happily married. He too had had his romances, perhaps more than the world, which cast him as the dark, brooding, eponymously 'Pinteresque' play-wright, realized. Later he also told me that he had never been in love before, but had once loved Vivien very much, her essential vulnerability inspiring him with a wish to protect her, before other matters drove them apart. They led essentially separate lives in an enormous stately six-storey house in Regent's Park Terrace; but he too had never contemplated leaving his marriage.

8 January 1975

A very enjoyable dinner party at Rachel and Kevin's house in Addison Avenue: a long and convivial table. I was slightly disappointed not to sit next to the playwright who looked full of energy, with black curly hair and pointed ears, like a satyr. Gradually the guests filtered away. My neighbours Richard and Viv King offered me a lift up the road. 'Wait a minute,' I said. 'I must just say goodbye to Harold Pinter and tell him I enjoyed the play; I haven't said hello all evening.' They waited at the door. I went over to where Harold was sitting. 'Wonderful play, marvellous acting, now I'm off.'

He looked at me with those amazing, extremely bright black eyes. 'Must you go?' he said. I thought of home, my lift, taking the children to school the next morning, the exhausting past night in the sleeper from Scotland, my projected biography of King Charles II ... 'No, it's not absolutely essential,' I said.

About 2.30 in the morning, poor Rachel and Kevin were visibly exhausted, and we were the last guests. In the end, it was Harold who gave me a lift home, in a white car with a driver (he never drove at night having once been found 'weaving' in Regent's Park). I offered him coffee. I actually gave him champagne. He stayed until six o'clock in the morning with extraordinary recklessness, but of course the real recklessness was mine.

We sometimes speculated later what would have happened if I had in fact answered: 'Yes, I really must go.' Harold, convinced by then that I was his destiny, would gallantly reply: 'I would have found you somehow.' But we had few friends in common: Edna O'Brien was one, and the producer Sam Spiegel another. But fundamentally we lived in different worlds. The night of 8/9 January was the chance and our chance.

Subsequently the tabloids made much of our different backgrounds, the working-class Jewish boy from the East End and the Catholic aristocrat with her title. But we were, in our early forties, a long way from our backgrounds and, as usual with the tabloids, these descriptions were more for headlines than accuracy. Although Harold was technically born into the working class – his father worked in a tailoring factory – ever since the success of *The Caretaker* in 1960 he had been extremely well-off by most standards: he was able, for example, to retire his father, worn-out with his labours, to salubrious Hove where his parents would live happily for another thirty years.

Again technically, since my father was an earl and my mother a countess, I could be argued to be an aristocrat. But my father, born Frank Pakenham, only succeeded to the Earldom of Longford when I was nearly thirty; my childhood was spent in a modest North Oxford house, my father, with no private income, teaching at the University. My mother, being a Harley Street doctor's daughter, was in any case convinced (and thus convinced us) that the middle classes were the salt of the earth whereas the aristocracy was feckless, unpunctual and extravagant, an assumption that our beloved father's attitude to life did nothing to discourage. I had no inherited money myself, and had earned my own living since the age of twenty-one, first working for a publisher and, after marriage, by journalism and books.

After the publication of *Mary Queen of Scots*, an unexpected bestseller in 1969, I found that for the first time in my life I had money to spend. Most of it went on the delightful task of renovating Eilean Aigas, our house in the Highlands on an island in the River Beauly, which gave the impression of being untouched since the '45 rebellion. Our finances had been so perilous before this, since Hugh was entirely dependent on the then modest salary of an MP, that he had actually sold the house to a cousin by the previous Christmas – providentially the cousin's finances proved to be equally perilous and he reneged on the deal just in time for my windfall. To give only one example, I put in a heated open-air swimming pool round which the New Year celebrations regularly made the welkin ring. The truth was that by the mid 1970s, both in our different ways successful writers, Harold and I belonged to the same class: I will call it the Bohemian class.

13 January

While I was away, Harold had apparently called home on the public line; on Monday morning he called on my private line – I'm not sure how he got the number. We met for a drink at the Royal Lancaster Hotel in Bayswater ('an obscure place' he said truthfully) at 6 p.m. The bar was very dark and at first I couldn't see him. That made it all the more like a dream. But 'so it *wasn't* all a dream' was the verdict of us both at the end. Told me of numerous obsessional phone calls – no answer – often from the famous Ladbroke Grove telephone box opposite Campden Hill Square. Had evidently told Kevin Billington about the *whole* thing! I began to guess this and he then admitted it. Can't say I care. 'I am loopy about you: I feel eighteen' was the general theme; I said I preferred the word 'dippy' . . .

The truth is that Harold has mesmerized me. Kept waking all night on the subject of a) him b) Benjie's departure for boarding school at Ampleforth. But a) has quite taken my mind off the horrible sadness of b). (Our third child and eldest son, aged not quite fourteen, was setting forth for his father's old school.)

23 January

Met Harold at 5.30 in the Royal Lancaster Hotel (he has telephoned daily). Parted at 11.30 to our respective matrimonial homes. We never left the bar, just talked and talked. Discussed among other things *No Man's Land*, his new play – to open at the National in April – and how he started to write it. At first he thought he was echoing himself ('What, two old men together *again* . . .'), then he thought: 'You are what you

7

are.' He had sent me the typescript after our first meeting. I liked the character of Spooner, the failed poet. So I asked him: 'Did Spooner get the job?' On the whole he thought: No. 'But Spooner is an optimist and there will be other jobs.' I said I would have to stop my ears at the first night for the dark of the ending: Winter/Night forever. But I liked 'I'll drink to that' at the end. 'That's the point,' Harold said, delighted . . . I am quite obsessed by him when I am with him. He tells me he is quite obsessed by me all the time – the days spent waiting to telephone, etc. . . . Described his life as a kind of prison, how, when can we meet, ever?

26 January

Taken to supper with Anthony Shaffer, author of *Sleuth*, by an old friend. The fashionable doctor for artists, Patrick Woodcock, warns me quite innocently against playwrights: 'They're the worst.' Thought of Harold. I suppose I'm in love with him but there are many other things in my life. Yet: 'oh, oh, the insomniac moonlight' in the words of the Scottish poet I like, Liz Lochhead.

30 January

Harold called. He asks: 'Does it make you happy that we met? You wouldn't rather we hadn't met?'

1 February

I knew it would be a good day. Harold rang up in the morning and said, 'Tea is on', having said two days ago 'the situation is fluid'. Went at four, discreetly parking the car in Sussex Place. The house in Regent's Park Terrace is vast, on first impression, and extremely sumptuous. I suppose it would not be so sumptuous if ten people lived in it. But with three, it is. A lot of large beautiful modern pictures in huge quiet rooms, apparently unlimited in number. Harold made tea. We went upstairs to the greeny-grey drawing room, vast pictures, few objects, greeny-grey light, enormous quantity of chairs and low sofas.

'I will show you my study presently.' And he did. At the top of the house, sixth floor in fact, we went up and up, like Tom Kitten. A marvellous room, much space, also less hushed. A desk with windows overlooking Regent's Park and the other way, roofs. A chaise longue. A few chairs. Lots of books, novels and poetry. Harold presented me with his poems. 'I would make a good secretary if you ever needed one,' I said, seeing the accommodation. He said: 'the same thought had already crossed my mind.'

9 February

Joyous, dangerous and unavoidable – Harold's three words to Kevin Billington about us, quoted by Harold to me on the telephone. Not bad Pinteresque words.

19 February

Period of crisis. On Sunday Harold called to say that Vivien was very ill (pneumonia) in Hong Kong, with the dreadful possibility of not being able to go on and film *Picnic at Hanging Rock* in Australia – something she really wanted to do. He is racked with guilt. 'Something of her own that I didn't write. That's what she wanted.' Much strain of cancellations and late-night calls. Nevertheless we met for drinks in the bar of the Churchill Hotel (twice).

21 February

Bought works *about* Harold at Foyles to feed my obsession. Seems to be in the class of Shakespeare judging by the nonsense that is talked ... gave me a buzz all the same.

22 *February*

Harold in Hong Kong has written me two poems, one short, one very long, which he read to me twice: 'I have spent the evening in my hotel room writing poems to you.' The long one began:

> My heart is not a beat away from you
> You turn, and touch the light of me.
> You smile and I become the man
> You loved before, but never knew

It ended:

> You turn, and touch the light of me.
> You smile, your eyes become my sweetest dream of you.
> Oh sweetest love,
> My heart is not a beat away from you.

This was the short one:

> I know the place
> It is true.
> Everything we do
> Connects the space
> Between death and me,
> And you.

It subsequently became a favourite poem of Harold's to mark this stage in our lives and he often recited it. However, when the poems arrived on the pale banana-coloured paper of the Peninsula Hotel, I protested about the comma after 'me' which divided us and left him on the side of death and it was eliminated (although not put immediately after 'death' as I wanted!).

22 *February, cont.*

He really seems mad with love. Diana Phipps, my confidante, on the telephone: 'What happens when he asks you to pack your bags?' Me: 'He *won't*. That's the great thing. He isn't a marryer. He has been married as long as I have.' Diana: 'Don't count on it.'

In spite of that, thank God, she is wrong. Our relationship is more likely to bust out of passion because he won't be able to bear it, not at that level anyway. His love letters, leaving aside the poems, are extraordinary. From time to time he writes in his large, clear unmistakeable handwriting: 'I'm calm. Calm.' and then he bursts out again, now with a big love letter, now with a poem – an extravagant poem, accompanied by a note: 'This came out of the lonely middle of a desperate night thousands of miles from you, your image thudding in my skull. Don't be alarmed by it.'

24 *February*

Kevin Billington came round, thanks to Hong Kong calls ad infinitum, and we had an extremely intense conversation; beginning of course with much embarrassment as up to that point we were friendly but not close. 'It's very serious for Harold,' he said and added: 'I speak as Harold's friend and not because of our family relationship.' Me: 'It's quite different for me . . . I haven't known anything like this before or perhaps once years ago but ever since I have tried to guard myself.' Kevin: 'I'm very glad.'

25 *February*

Drink with Edna O'Brien at her request. She looked like a beautiful fortune-teller in her shawl by the fire, me her client. 'He's much enraptured,' she said. Then: 'I'm glad this is happening to him. Last summer when he was writing *No Man's Land* in that cottage I almost

thought – well,' she hesitated. 'He says he was waiting for death,'
I replied.

28 February

The last call from Hong Kong. No more contact for the next week. But
lots of poems have arrived on the banana-coloured hotel paper. I keep
them in a clutch in my handbag and read and reread. One of them is the
strongest love poem I have ever received.

———

Harold came back, with Vivien, on 10 March. He was in a terrible state
when I didn't answer my telephone, also when I did. Explained later it
was jet lag edging on panic that he had lost me.

11 March

Everything is now all right. But first I went to the Memorial Service for
the murdered Ethiopian royal family who had helped me on my visit
there in 1964. Deeply moving with the noble young Asfa Kassa, son of
my patron Aserate Kassa, in charge: the grave and beautiful Crown
Princess, a few other Ethiopians. I wept when Asfa read the lesson of
Solomon and the Queen of Sheba in Amharic. ('And Solomon gave the
Queen of Sheba all that she desired.')

Back here to wait for Harold. A knock. He was there. He clutched
me and we clutched each other. At first it was almost desperate, he had
suffered so much. Finally he said: 'I feel like a new man' (as perhaps
Solomon said to the Queen of Sheba).

12 March

Beautiful white and pink and green orchids from Harold with a note:
'My heart.'

13 March

Day transformed at six when Harold rang up and said he wondered what my evening arrangements were. They had just finished testing leading ladies for the film of *The Last Tycoon*, produced by Sam Spiegel, for which Harold had written the screenplay: Harold read the Robert De Niro part. Met at the Stafford Hotel. We talked and talked. Harold back on the kick of saying he's going to tell Vivien sooner or later. 'I should like to go away with you. Maybe Antarctica? But would you follow? I would like to be married to you when I'm eighty.' 'I'll be seventy-eight.' Where is all this passion leading, I ask myself. The trouble is – when I am with him I don't care about anything and when I am not with him I don't care much either as I am always thinking about him.

14 March

Drink with Harold on his way from the National at the Strand Palace Hotel. Naturally he has told Peter Hall who was directing *No Man's Land*, 'I've fallen in love', because of the need for an alibi.

16 March

Harold caused me a great deal of heart-beating terror by announcing he was going to tell Vivien: 'I don't want to pretend I'm on a lecture tour.' I suppose I'm used to being on that lecture tour and it seems a perfectly good way of life. But Harold's force is burning me up and fascinating me all at the same time.

22/23 March

Weekend of considerable tension. Harold rang up Sunday evening and said he had told Vivien on Saturday: 'I've met somebody.' Her rage at his dishonesty in deceiving her (for two and a half months). Vivien says about me: 'She's a very bonny lady.' But – with whisky and nightfall more rage at the deception.

———

I did not know at this point that Vivien was on her way to being a serious alcoholic; a condition which would lead to her death in her early fifties. Nor did Harold discuss the subject with me at this point, either in extenuation of his own behaviour or out of guilt. There was the odd oblique reference which I did not understand.

24 March

In a way it is unfair for Vivien to pick on the deception as opposed to Harold's feelings, as he has always wanted to tell her; he couldn't before she went away and certainly couldn't when she was so ill. But nothing is fair in love (or war) whatever they say. For the first time I faced up to what another life would be like and whether it could ever exist. Or would be right. Right for whom? Never right for some. Diana Phipps: 'Everyone must feel the temptation to leave their life behind. Don't forget that in fact no one ever does leave their life behind. You take it with you.'

In the meantime, as they say, I always wanted to be in love. Ever since I was a little girl. And I always wanted to know a genius, which I suppose Harold sort of is, but that did not lure me to him in the first place. I was lured, compelled by a superior force, something drawn out of me by him, which was simply irresistible.

27 March

Last day before Scotland for the school holidays. It is snowing and I went for a snowy walk in the park. Nevertheless there were wet heaps of grass to be seen where some incurable optimist had started to cut it. So, through the snow and blustering wind came the unmistakeable smell of summer: lawn mowings. Met Harold at the Royal Lancaster as once before. He gave me the first bound copy of *No Man's Land* with such a romantic inscription that I shall hardly be able to leave it about. The situation seems very fraught in the Pinter home and I honestly don't know how it will turn out. Mingled fright and excitement.

6 April

Horror has struck at the periphery of Harold's life. Mary Ure, wife of his buddy Robert Shaw, died the night after Robert had been out with Harold. Robert's guilt – and his own. In the end after a lot of talk and guilt, we both went round to see Robert Shaw hidden in the Savoy with his children. Harold in a fearful state. The Shaw daughters full of fortitude. His son, the image of Mary, infinitely touching.

The rest of April passed with me toing and froing between London and Scotland during the school holidays, while being extremely active in campaigning for Public Lending Right (I was Chairman of the Society of Authors). Vivien left Hanover Terrace for a while; Harold continued to attend rehearsals of *No Man's Land*.

14 April

Harold came to lunch before rehearsal. Now very gloomy about the play – just because Sir Ralph Richardson can't happen to get the words in the right order. This is torture for him. But says he is a little bit in love with Ralph all the same. Me: 'As he is a man and seventy-two, that's okay.' Harold and Sir Ralph: the perfect actor for him except for this one fault which could utterly ruin everything Harold conceives the play to be, in terms of rhythm and poetry.

20 April – Sunday morning

Hugh asked: 'Are you in love with someone else?' I don't think he expected to get the answer 'Yes! I am madly in love with someone else.' After a bit I told him who it was. Hugh, grimly: 'The best living playwright. Very suitable.' Then: 'How old is he?' Me: 'My age.' Hugh: Well, that's also very suitable.' I had dreaded this moment so much, thought it would never come, because it never could come. Then it did come, suddenly, in a twinkling of an eye, and *in a way* it was perfectly all right. Except as Harold pointed out about his own situation, nothing is ever the same again.

———

The next weeks were agonizing for all concerned with a few bright moments which did not relate to personal relationships.

23 April

The great Public Lending Right Demo Day in Belgrave Square outside the Ministry. Wore spring-like suit to LBC Radio at 8.30 a.m.; frozen by 11.30. We hustled importantly on to a traffic island in Belgrave Square, media actually outnumbering the authors. But Angus Wilson came all the way up from Suffolk, good sweet man that he is. Bridget Brophy magnificent and large in a white princess-line dress, Maureen Duffy in a mauve frilly shirt with her trouser suit, running the show with her loud hailer. Gave interviews to TV, having been told by Frank Muir not to smile: 'Look grim and defiant.' Natasha (my fourth child: the others were Rebecca, Flora, Benjie, Damian and Orlando) said: 'You looked like someone who wanted to have her own way. Like a queen, but cross,' she added kindly.

Met Harold for lunch and gave him my lucky agate to hold in his sweaty palm at the first night of *No Man's Land*. Went with Rachel and Kevin, and my brother Thomas to the theatre. Drink in the upstairs bar. Suddenly Harold walked in. Transfixed. Both of us. Could hardly speak or look at him. 'Hello, Antonia,' and hand outstretched: a very deep gravelly voice.

Then the play . . . In the interval Milton Shulman, there as drama

critic of the *Evening Standard*, asked innocently: 'What's it all about?'
Revealed that he had been asleep in the first half. Critics!!! Me: 'It's
about the creative artist locked in his own world. Gielgud as Spooner
is shabby reality trying to get in.' Milton: ??? Me: 'Well, I'm only trying
to help.' Later we four went to Odin's. Harold telephoned me from
the first-night party at Peter Hall's flat in the Barbican. Harold: 'I was
happy with it.' He went on: 'I watched you when you walked across
the front of the stalls going to your seat after the interval. I liked your
dress. You looked so beautiful.' (I still have the dress.) Me: 'I just
couldn't speak in the bar.'

24 April

Vivien told Harold: 'The myth of the happy Pinter marriage is
exploded. It hasn't really existed for many years.' She had not come to
the first night; Harold took his son. This morning the *Daily Mail* blew
the gaff, talking of 'a literary friendship'. So that's what they call it
these days!

25 April

Harold is leaving Vivien for Sam Spiegel's flat in Grosvenor House 'So
that murder shall not take place.' It's difficult to comment on this
because up till the other night I had thought their marriage a happy one
(albeit not *perfect* . . . because perfect marriages if they exist are immune
from late-night romantic encounters). So I don't understand anything
at the moment.

28 April

Harold moved into Sam's flat. Tried to liken it to a ship: large for a
ship. Actually quite large for a flat. But the point is really, the grimness
of anyone leaving their home where everything is arranged to their
satisfaction, to live in a place where it isn't. Harold very low. The

prospect of Paris seems to cheer. But I'm sure the missing of home remains an eternal thing.

5–15 May

In Paris at the Hotel Lancaster. What can I write? (I'm back in London.) However, here goes. We had our suite, Harold's famous emphasis on suites! A sitting room, *très charmant*, a large bedroom and another one for me, I insisted on that for telephonic reasons. Harold met me at Charles de Gaulle Airport, I floated up in the new moving passageway as in a dream towards him. Chauffeur-driven car (another great obsession). Thereafter we lived in our suite and went to restaurants and never really did anything at all for ten days. Very restful that, doing nothing. We did take very small walks in the truly wet and freezing weather (I bought two umbrellas when I was in Paris) ending fairly rapidly in bars. Like Hirst in *No Man's Land*, Harold drinks a hell of an amount. Mostly we talked, sometimes good talks, sometimes 'a good talk' about the future. Occasionally Harold whirled into jealousy about the past.

We met Barbara Bray, the translator and literary critic with whom Harold had worked on the Proust screenplay for so long, Beckett's girlfriend. Despite avowed Women's Lib feelings, Barbara maddened Harold by looking and talking all the time to him, never me. I didn't notice so wasn't maddened. Finally she said: 'I should be interested in you as a writer because you're a woman, but of course it's Harold I'm interested in.' 'So that's two of us,' I said. Much more fun was the ravishing Delphine Seyrig who failed to turn up as a cool blonde as I had hoped (see *The Discreet Charm of the Bourgeoisie*), but emerged as a frizzy red-haired biker holding a helmet. She was nevertheless delightful, very warm to me, and her beauty could not be quenched.

On Sunday evening Harold said we were swimming nearer and nearer the sea, in a series of rock pools. The ocean was ahead. Someone I adored was Harold's translator Eric Kahane: a kindred spirit. (We became lifelong friends.) Once back, Harold went to Sam's flat at

Grosvenor House, me to Campden Hill Square. But Harold found a lawyer's letter from Withers & Co. informing him that his wife was suing him for divorce, the cause being his own admitted adultery with me. This was the one thing we were sure would never happen, even though Vivien had written to Paris to announce what she would do if he didn't return. Harold to me: 'Tell your husband that my intentions are strictly honourable.'

16 & 17 May

Harold in a terrible state about money although he seems to me to earn a fortune, enough anyway not to worry. I think worrying about money is a substitute for worrying about the future. Harold has written me a magic poem called 'Paris': it ends 'She dances in my life.' I cling to that. What will happen next?

PARIS

The curtain white in folds,
She walks two steps and turns,
The curtain still, the light
Staggers in her eyes.

The lamps are golden.
Afternoon leans, silently.
She dances in my life.
The white day burns.

Chapter Two

PLEASURE AND A GOOD DEAL OF PAIN

22 May

Long, long talk with my mother at her Chesil Court flat about everything. She showed much brilliance, unlike some, in achieving her objective, which was to keep me approximately married to Hugh. 'You note I am *not* talking about sanctity of family life.' Tells me meaningful stories of her friends whose lovers chucked them for younger women, and is annoyed when I smile.

Harold has returned home to Regent's Park to be with his son while Vivien is in Crete. Harold: 'I want you to know that the way I am thinking is that I want to live with you, that's the way my thoughts are.' Then: 'In twenty years' time, we wouldn't have this sort of crisis, because we would be sixty-four and sixty-two.'

Me, thinking of Lady Longford: 'What about younger women?'

Harold (furious): 'I like mature women, doesn't she realize, I am a boy at heart, ever eighteen, so naturally I like mature women.'

28 May

Lunch with Mark Boxer at Neal Street Restaurant. Physically, a curious mixture of Harold's looks, the dark curly hair and black/hazel eyes, but less force in his appearance. We had not met for some time.

Mark: 'Do you remember when I brought a cricket side to the Hurst Green Cricket Club against your father?'

Me: 'How odd! Of course I do. And I was telling somebody interested in cricket about it only the other day.' I had indeed attempted to establish my cricket-loving credentials with Harold by telling him about this match against my father's village. Of course Mark, who was always up for any gossip, got the reference immediately.

Mark, meaningfully: 'Would SOMEBODY "interested in cricket" like to play in a match for the *Sunday Times*?' I blushed. Mark told me he had been thinking aloud of cricketing stars for this match in Surrey, then of stars who played cricket. He asked the Surrey Chairman: 'Would Harold Pinter do?' Explained he was a playwright. Man from the club, affronted: 'We have heard of Harold Pinter in Surrey!'

30 May

Took Harold to dinner with Diana Phipps. Diana seized a moment alone to hiss: 'He's marvellous. I revise all my advice. You must marry him as soon as possible.' Really! She's worse than Mummy in her advice.

The next night we had dinner with Sam Spiegel who simply could not understand why Harold had told Vivien: 'You could have had all the pleasure and none of the pain.' Ah, the Viennese!

2 June

I love Harold, I adore him, but I wonder whether I am *capable* of uprooting myself for anyone? Do I have the courage? I am quite a cowardly person, I know. Whether I have not finally and carefully constructed my own very pleasant prison from which emotionally I can't escape. If only we could just go on and on being lovers . . . I fear for the effects of everyday life on love.

I was photographed for the *Sunday Mirror* in connection with a book *Scottish Love Poems* I had chosen and edited for my friends Angus and Stephanie Wolfe Murray to launch their new Edinburgh imprint, Canongate Publishing. The photographer took me into the garden. It was very cold and rather silly. I should stop fooling around with hats and roses.

Vivien is back from Crete, much calmer but steadfast that she will cite me in the divorce.

7 June

I worked on *Charles II* and felt rather happy for a change. Letter in *The Times* about the naming of the characters in *No Man's Land* for famous cricketers. I remember remarking to Harold in Paris that Hirst was evidently Jewish (I have some Jewish friends called Hirst). He said indignantly that he was named for the Yorkshire cricketer. Now he states: 'The names were appropriate. That is to say, Spooner could never have been called Hirst.' Harold tells me I am his 'joy' before going very joyfully off to cricket.

11 June

Coffee at Grosvenor House with Harold. Very hot day. Wore new white piqué dress with pink and blue stone necklace. He has now heard definitely from the lawyer that I will be cited and soon. I need a lawyer. Harold hugged me. 'I love you and want to marry you.' (He had not used those exact words before.) Afterwards I question it, the whole idea. Harold firmly: 'No, I like being married. I think we had better get married.' I said nothing although it is quite like being in a car of gathering speed going to the sea and still not quite making up my mind whether I intend to bathe or not. Exhilarating. And frightening. Later that evening Harold said: 'I proposed to you today and you said you would think it over.'

12 June

Went to Edinburgh for the launching of *Scottish Love Poems*. I am intensely proud of this book: it seems to set the seal on my Scottish

life. Splendid party included twenty poets. The men were either old
and hoary (Hugh MacDiarmid, with his thick, thick head of white hair,
Sorley MacLean) or young and drunk. The poetesses were grave and
gentle, Liz Lochhead bright-eyed and laughing. All were very nice to
me.

Confided my situation to Stephanie who was clear and helpful on
the subject. This was in my bedroom at the North British Hotel. In the
lift on the way down I decided: 'Yes, I will do it.'

13 June

It was 'a summer's day of unusual heat' – one of Harold's favourite
quotations from T.S. Eliot. Harold, in a very jolly mood and elegant
in his black silk shirt and biscuit-coloured suit. I wore my favourite
biscuit-coloured lace dress which made Emma Tennant say, when we
visited her, that we had clearly decided to dress alike for the foreseeable
future (no way!). He seems to have guessed that I will say Yes. We went
to the Belvedere Restaurant in Holland Park, a room looking over the
iris garden. I took a deep breath and with a kind of heat in my face
rather than a blush: 'What I am trying to say,' I began, 'is that if you
asked me to marry you now, I would accept you.'

14 June

The next day I had to tell Hugh. It was beyond anything ghastly,
beginning with the moment when I fetched him inside from the
thunderous garden where he was smoking and reading the *FT*. It now
thundered inside. In the end I summoned Harold round. He drank
whisky, Hugh drank brandy. I sat. In a surreal scene, Hugh and Harold
discussed cricket at length, then the West Indies, then Proust. I started
to go to sleep on the sofa. Harold politely went home. Nothing was
decided.

16/17 June

My mind is strangely blank about the past days. Just as well perhaps.
I do remember I went to the I C A to hear Harold read Philip Larkin.
His deep voice has been one of the things I have loved about him from
the beginning. My heart turned over when he read an early poem: 'Love,
now it is time for us to say goodbye.' Drink in the pub with the poet
Ian Hamilton, man with a sympathetic and even beautiful face but not
saturnine as I had imagined. (Harold is saturnine.)

19 June

Lunch with my mother at Chesil Court, having written her and my
father a long letter so that they would understand that we could not
discuss 'Whether' only 'Why?' and 'When?' She said it was a good
thing such a letter had been written (I knew that was the right approach
because she is after all a writer and currently studying Byron). At the
end she told me she would not come to Marylebone Registry Office,
'but I will do anything else'.

20 June

Told Thomas: known as my 'Irish twin', being a mere eleven months
younger than me, and my closest person since his birth which, as
I sometimes pointed out, ruined my status as a happy only child.
Thomas said: 'I have always thought ever since playing tennis with
you in Norham Gardens (during our shared North Oxford childhood),
that you would be very difficult to be married to.' Pause. 'I myself am
very difficult to be married to.' Then he talked at length about himself.
Restored to the point – me! – he said: 'You have a special problem. You
are a woman and a strong character yet you want your husband to be
stronger. Women with strong characters who want to dominate are
always fine because there are plenty of weak men around. Also plenty
of strong men for weak women. But yours is a special problem.' 'Come

off it, Confucius,' I said. But actually he's quite right in a maddening way. Hugh's superior age – fifteen years – and experience in the war had blinded me at the age of twenty-three to the fact that although he was certainly a strong character, he was essentially a loner.

George Weidenfeld (my publisher, also my oldest adult friend, ever since I worked for him aged twenty-one) very charming to Harold at dinner, which pleased me.

———

Terrible weeks of strain followed, compounded by Harold directing Simon Gray's new play *Otherwise Engaged* with Alan Bates. In the end Sam Spiegel persuaded Vivien to withdraw the divorce petition for the time being. With his usual worldly bluntness, he told me that it was entirely in her own interests to suspend proceedings as if she doesn't want to go to law, Harold may change his mind, but once she has, he never will. I didn't comment. I knew that Sam, to whom we were both devoted, thought all this romantic talk about marriage was nonsense; why couldn't we just have an affair like everyone else?

23 June

Had lunch with my hero the urbane and brilliant Charles Wintour (editor of the *Evening Standard*) and told him that for 'personal reasons' I must resign from the *Evening Standard* Drama Panel where I had been the lay critic very happily for seven years. I refer to a 'serious relationship' with Harold.

Charles: 'It is honest of you to raise this.' Later he says: 'I must say that I admire your nerve.' I thought he was perhaps referring to his own situation. As in most resignation meetings, however, I ended by not resigning. All this of course was about *Otherwise Engaged*, which would inevitably be considered by the panel.

Charles: 'We must rise above it. No one would think your critical judgment impaired.' Me: 'No, no.' Thinks: not half. Took Marigold Johnson to the theatre: Michael Frayn, pleasant and extremely funny.

24 June

Mummy takes the opportunity to say that she will now write me a letter to say that what I am doing is wrong: 'The trouble is, darling, that the charm and charisma of your presence is such that one begins to feel a bit happier and even sound approving.' This flattery gets her nowhere. I put down the telephone, I think. Or maybe it's a wee slam-down. For heaven's sake, I'm in my forties! She never took so much interest in my love life when I was sixteen: she did not encourage confidences so I did not make them. I was perfectly happy with that: I loved being so independent. But it is a bit late to alter our relationship twenty-five years later.

25 June

Harold exhausted by the strain of his home life, coupled with rehearsals. Though he did manage to dictate a new scene for Jeanne Moreau to Sam Spiegel and director Elia Kazan for *The Last Tycoon*. Me: 'It's WORK that is another country, not the past.'

26 June

Gave the prizes at St Philip's Sports Day. Narrowly missed being extinguished – of all things – by a cricket ball. Ironic. Saw my lawyers, suggested by George Weidenfeld, in the morning. Mr Leslie Paisner seemed immensely wise, which is needed. Harold Paisner, his son, extremely young-looking, seemed sympathetic to what I am doing. To him it was romantic and dashing. But Mr Paisner *père* did implicitly warn me of possible dangers ahead. Also left me with some very sage words which I quoted verbatim to Hugh that night: 'If two sensible, educated, civilized people can't reach agreement about their own children, it is unlikely a court can.'

It was advice that Hugh and I took to heart. As it happens, our respective styles of parenting had always dovetailed: they continued to do so successfully for the nine years Hugh had to live.

Hugh was a devoted father. He was also someone who had chosen to base himself in his mother's house until his marriage at the age of thirty-eight – because that way he could enjoy the free social life of a very popular bachelor. Of his new existence in which he reverted to this kind of life, one relation observed later: 'In many ways the life of a bachelor with six children really suited him.'

27 June

Pat Naipaul came to lunch. Told her. She said: 'Oh, poor Antonia! You will be married to a writer over forty and past his best, of failing creativity.' I am too fond of Pat to make any comment, but Francis Wyndham pointed out later: she was manifestly talking about Vidia's friend Margaret, if he chose to leave Pat for *her*. I also thought privately what Harold would have said to the question of creativity: 'Fuck creativity.'

28 June

Managed to sit in the wrong pub waiting for Harold for nearly an hour. To me one pub is much like another, I have to say. Ever since Oxford, I have hated the smell of beer. Harold was somewhere in another pub – this was in Mayfair – but where? A sort of madness overtook me that we should never meet again, as at the end of *Majorie Morningstar*. In the end Sam Spiegel bowled up in a vast car, plus mistress and child, and rescued me. At that moment Harold appeared round the corner *running*. He's incredibly fit, I couldn't help noticing. I suppose it's all that cricket.

Vivien continued to alternate between rage and despair but Hugh, admirable as ever, said that he was becoming philosophical. Apparently Harold's son may come and live with us. More the merrier, says I. In the evening, Harold says: 'In spite of all the grievousness, and it may sound like a woman's magazine, but with you I have found happiness.' It is a lovely note to end the week on in spite of everything.

29 June

Worked a little on *Charles II:* therapy! Told Hugh about Harold's early life and he seemed rather interested in his detached way.

30 June

Took Harold to dinner with Peter Eyre. Peter said afterwards: 'He's very deep – but then I thought, that's not surprising, considering all the plays.'

3–6 July

Harold's son Daniel joined his father at Grosvenor House. I met him for the first time: slender, gangly, gym shoes and denim jacket brigade. But he courteously lent that jacket to me to protect me against the night air outside Morton's. Face dreamily handsome inside its curly hair. Very clever.

Harold and I sit in two deckchairs in Green Park. Later in the bar at the Washington, we found that Arthur Ashe had won Wimbledon: well, that was good news, and Harold told me that the smile had come back to my face.

Dinner with Penelope, Jonathan Aitken's ever-glamorous mother. Jonathan to me: 'Why are you here alone? Oh, I've worked it out. Sunday night. Cricket night.' He was of course quite right.

7–12 July

In Oxford at the Randolph Hotel, in a large Gothic room over the front porch. I pattered about various rooms in the dark small hours. Harold went to the theatre to see *Otherwise Engaged* in its pre-West End run and had supper with the cast. I felt very content after the alarums of the week before except one night when I waited for him until three, reading *Anna Karenina* and got in a stew – not perhaps the best choice of reading in my situation. I liked Simon Gray particularly and thought I would like to know him better, if it came about. Harold pleased me by saying he was looking forward to living with a writer, not an actress, because first nights had been such a strain, the play and the leading lady competing for attention. I had previously felt that by not being an actress, particularly not a famous one like Vivien, I was lacking something. I had not seen the other side of the coin. There was a party on the last night and I was proud to be on Harold's arm.

22 July

Harold is now living in Donald Pleasence's house in Strand-on-the-Green and we have rented a house in Launceston Place for the future.

26 & 27 July

These dog days, the dog days of the end of my marriage, are a most strange experience of heat and night and telephone calls and frenzy – and also words of love.

I didn't write my diary again (unusually) until 5 August when I arrived in Scotland to be with the children. *Otherwise Engaged* was now in preview in the West End. In the meantime Vivien filed her petition.

28 July

I returned home from a drink with Harold to find some young men in shirts fooling about, vaguely in front of Campden Hill Square. It was an incredibly hot night. Paid the taxi inside the cab, for some prescient reason. Noticed drawing-room curtains drawn. Odd. Got out. Young man turned revealing camera on his hip. Back into the taxi *fast* and away. Where? They banged on the back of the taxi, shouting to get me to look up. Got back into Campden Hill Square by the back way. Went for the night to Diana Phipps, a true friend, in Elgin Crescent. Harold joined me. It turned out that Vivien had talked and talked hard. Shattered.

30 July

The next morning was even worse. More from Vivien. But the gossip-writers, in revenge at missing the scoop given by Vivien to one of their number, gathered all their venom into one pen. I went totally white. Sat on the bed. Tried to keep it from Harold. He noticed 'the strange absence' of the most venomous paper and found it. Forced myself to write my weekly review for the *Evening Standard* (I had been chief non-fiction reviewer for several years). I sat in Diana's garden in my long flowered cotton 'writing-dress' and a red hat against the intense heat. For a moment I just wanted not to BE: not to take any action to that effect but perhaps 'to cease upon the midnight with no pain'. But as Beckett would have said at the end of Harold's favourite *Molloy*: 'It was not midnight . . .' Harold came out into the garden and took my hand.

———

It is interesting, rereading this many years later, to wonder what would have happened to us in today's very different climate regarding privacy. After all, we were not celebrities in the modern sense. At the time two things saved me from collapse. The first was a still-surviving robust common sense: 'This is absurd. We are not Héloïse and Abelard nor even members of the royal family paid by the state. We're not running for office and never have. We're not trying to lead people in a new religion. We're a couple of middle-aged writers who have gone of their own free will to live together.' The other, of course, was Harold's love for me coupled with my love for him.

But of course such an experience of public printed prurience could not fail to have a profound effect on me. For one thing, I took myself in hand and swore an oath never to read hostile gossip or satire about myself and Harold if I could avoid it; my logic was: 'I can't stop them writing it because this is a free country. But equally they can't force me to read it. It's my right to ignore it. I'll read any hostile review of my work, grit my teeth and bear it, because that's fair comment, however unpleasant. But not nasty gossip.' Over the years, I derived wry amusement from the sugary indignation of those who had read these things and were eager to sympathize: 'Oh, how awful! How could they? I mean really . . .' Me, with equal sweetness: 'I'm afraid I haven't read it. I never do. But do tell me about it, if it will make you feel better.'

Finally of course you realize, if you have any sense of proportion, such things are very small *sub specie aeternitatis* or indeed more immediately in the scale of world concerns.

A little while later I happened to read the autobiography of Agatha Christie where she wrote of her persecution after she mysteriously 'disappeared' to Harrogate. She described how she had been the fox and they were the hounds. Yes, I too knew that feeling. For years afterwards, I would involuntarily shiver at the sight of a crowd of reporters and photographers jostling round a door – any door. It never quite went away until thirty years later, there was a joyous crowd of press warmly greeted by Harold, jostling around our house. But that is to anticipate.

There was one immediate effect on our relationship. It was difficult to avoid the conclusion that it was Vivien in 'Medea' mood with her colourful denunciations who had touched off the frenzy and allowed the press free rein to print where they might otherwise have hesitated, given the laws of libel. But then, like many people who seek vengeance, she herself ended up by being the final sufferer. Harold sent her a letter of one sentence: 'Do not try to talk to me except through my lawyer.' She had achieved the total break which was the last thing she wanted. She had turned all his chivalry and pity away from herself towards me. Although formal relations were restored after a while, as they needed to be, I could see that he never felt the same way about her again.

11 August

Scotland. I visit my dear friends Gerald Ogilvy-Laing, the sculptor, and Galina at Kinkell and we fall into each other's arms. 'We were so concerned for you.' They worried I might have gone under. I told them I hadn't – quite. I add that there is one thing which is sardonically amusing. I, the woman, am always the target. Harold is treated with more circumspection because Harold the lover doesn't quite fit the public perception of the master of the pause, etc. (maybe they should have read one or two of his plays!). In fact, one careful reference to the 'allegedly passionate playwright' made me laugh. 'You should sue,' I told Harold. 'What's alleged about it?'

16 August

Harold in London begins to plan our new life. Me: 'I've got to learn to live with someone. Togetherness. I've never really had that.' True. Thought I would when I first married but Hugh didn't want that. I remember instituting Bible readings in bed – togetherness – but Hugh, horrified, went to sleep! Who can blame him?

17–22 August

On Sunday I flew down from Inverness to live with Harold here, at 33 Launceston Place, off the Gloucester Road. He met me at the airport. Then we entered Launceston Place. The first thing I saw was a mass of white flowers in the hall. I had time to think, 'Harold probably forgot to move them', then he took my hand and led me into the drawing room. Lo! A *vast* arrangement of flowers including foxy lilies and other glories in the window, and another on the mantelpiece, and in the back room, all luxuriant, then on up the stairs. A *huge* arrangement this time of yellow flowers in the pink boudoir, more, pink, on my dressing-table, and pink also in the bathroom. At the time I wanted to photograph them. But having lived with them for a week, there is no need. They are in my 'inner eye which is the bliss of solitude'. I shall never forget them. Or Harold's expression. A mixture of excitement, triumph and laughter. It transpired he asked the flower lady from Grosvenor House (whom he knew from his time with Sam Spiegel when he sent me daily flowers) and commissioned them. 'Is it for a party?' she asked. 'No, it's for Sunday night.'

Chapter Three

———◆———

READER, WE LIVED TOGETHER . . .

So we settled into our new lives. It was not all flowers and romance – probably the least romantic time of our lives, in retrospect.

I would like to be able to say in the immortal words of Jane Eyre: 'Reader, I Married Him . . .' Actually, it was a case of 'Reader, We Lived Together'. I counted Anthony Powell as my uncle (the writer I admired so much was married to my father's sister Violet). A stickler for these things, Tony asked me in advance of our arrival at his Somerset house, The Chantry, how I described my relationship with Harold officially. He was interested in the modern etiquette, he said. 'Companion,' I said, to tease. Tony pondered this. 'Like an old lady?' 'Exactly like an old lady.' Tony, who told me he had much admired the TV film of Harold's play *The Lover*, looked puzzled. On that subject, Harold insisted on describing our relationship in the next CV in a National Theatre programme. 'Harold Pinter has lived with Antonia Fraser since 1975.' He told me that he heard on the grapevine that this was considered 'unusual' and somebody asked: 'Don't people generally try to cover up such things?'

19 August

Lunch with my father at l'Epicure which began well but got progressively worse as he tucked down his lips in a familiar grimace, following a perfectly satisfactory talk about Christopher Sykes' biography of Evelyn Waugh, and started on at me.

Me: 'I don't ask you to approve, but to try to understand.' But it's no good and I see that Dada basically feels crossed at not having his own way. He never likes that.

21 *August*

Harold's oldest friend Henry Woolf came to supper. Afterwards he performed Harold's play *Monologue*. I thought it was brilliant. The night before Harold had read me his revue sketches and I fell asleep!! This time I did not fall asleep.

22 *August*

New TV show at the BBC, hosted by Melvyn Bragg, about paperback books. Original and admirable idea. Since we are dogged by the tabloids, including outside Launceston Place, Melvyn was gallant and arranged for me to be spirited away afterwards by a back door. There is an adrenalin rush in the getaway as I watched from my taxi a reporter sitting on the front steps of the BBC waiting for me in vain.

24 *August*

Strange and pleasing day at Iver with the Johnsons. Harold dropped me there on his way to cricket. I thought Paul might be very disapproving. He was on the contrary extremely warm to me, as one who had had a hard time. Marigold and I went to watch Harold at his cricket, first time for me, seeing Harold play. Luckily for me, my father was a cricket enthusiast, one who knew Wisden by heart as a boy, so I knew the rules. We minced towards the field, fearing to be discovered watching the wrong match. Harold came towards us, looking very dashing and jolly. Then we watched resolutely. One run and not out! Well, it could be a lot worse.

27 *August*

My forty-third birthday. I'm in the aeroplane returning from Scotland where I went on a freezing sea picnic at Rosemarkie with the children, and afterwards hosted some agreeable charades. Hugh and I talked about money – frankly, we're both broke.

28 August

The birthday ended arriving at Launceston Place and finding the flashes of press photographers. Harold drew me in and gave me a wonderful necklace of coloured stones. He hovered nervously as I opened it: 'You can change it.' We went defiantly out to dinner. Harold suddenly very angry to photographers: 'Why don't you fuck off?' I bowed my head and recited my mantra in such circumstances: 'Oh God our help in ages past / Our hope for years to come.' The next day the photographs were on the front page of a tabloid. The necklace looked pretty. But – when people are being maimed by bombs in pubs and the world teeters economically – does a dinner date really rate such a billing?

29 August

Went to *No Man's Land* . . . Supper with the two knights (Gielgud and Richardson). Both very courtly towards me. Richardson discussed Pepys and Gielgud discussed Shaw's *Good King Charles's Golden Day*, both with regard to my future biography of Charles II. Harold's son Daniel, who has chosen to live with us, is silent but pleasant company.

6 September

Maurice Jarre, composer for *The Last Tycoon*, came round and played a haunting tune to Harold's lyric. Even I could pick it up! Must be a hit. (To think he composed Lara's Song for *Dr Zhivago*.) Dinner at Donald Pleasence's. Last time I went to that house what tensions were in our lives. Sense of calm is overcoming us both. Looked at Harold in the garden and he did indeed look very calm. Then some American children started shrieking next door, closely followed by an electric saw the other side . . . Things changed.

8 September

Heinemann's lunch for Tony Powell's twelfth volume of *A Dance to the Music of Time*. Sat next to Tony who had Jilly Cooper, blonde and lissom, on his other side. As the star guest (Tony adored her), she had begun on his right, but he had switched us over. 'When the Revolution comes, let it come. But at my lunch things will be done properly.' Being an earl's daughter, like Violet, I had to be on the right. Tony made a brilliant short speech in honour of his editor Roland Gant, perfectly worked out and ending: 'how they brought the good news from Aix to GANT'. Harold couldn't come but I wondered what his placement would have been. Although Tony had this historian's love of social hierarchy, his real respect, I noted, was always reserved for artists.

15 September

Grace Dudley came to Launceston Place for tea. Made me laugh with a touch of her endearing grandeur: 'And of course we do over the house at once.' 'But, Grace, we have only rented it for six months.' She loved Harold, who is of course very much the same type as Bob Silvers.

Things got a little better with Hugh going away for several days on political business, so that life was able to continue more or less serenely on the domestic front.

19 September

Our dog Figaro arrived: he actually woke Harold with his friendly damp nose but Harold took it well. Joan Bakewell (with whom, Harold told me, he had had an affair some years before) came to dinner with her new long-haired, much younger husband Jack Emery: all very jolly.

23 September

Felt a little impatient with Pat Naipaul at lunch although I hope I didn't show it. Not quite strong enough for lame ducks at present. I suppose it's because I'm a bit of a lame duck. Then I felt ashamed of myself.

26 September

Lunch with Antonia Byatt. We discussed *The White Devil*, God and The Good. That's what she's like. I love her company. In the evening Harold and his son read Hemingway: the half of Harold which is not Beckett is Hemingway.

29 September

A most unpleasant experience. A flurry of calls to me at Launceston Place about a flat which was apparently for rent by one Mrs A. Fraser. Details were correct. Thought it must be a misprint and got on to Classified. But it wasn't. An enemy hath done this. The Editor Charles Wintour, sweet and sympathetic, had it taken out at once. But such Malice from Unknown Persons is upsetting.

30 September

Dinner with A.J.P. Taylor who had sent me a sweet letter congratulating me on 'capturing the foremost playwright of the age'. This was both funny and welcome at a time when nobody much was congratulating me on anything (I knew him originally from my childhood in Oxford where he was a don: he had always been kind about my historical efforts). The hostess turned out to be his first wife – he has gone back to her having been abandoned by his second. Filthy North Oxford food: Dutch gin to drink. Harold quite amazed by it all.

5 October

Visit to Natasha at my old school, St Mary's Ascot. Sister Bridget (my old teacher) hugs me. 'Don't do anything desperate. Remember everything passes away.' I've got the most ghastly cold: so I say, 'Actually I feel I shall pass away at this moment.' I should say that the reaction of the Catholic Church has been markedly charitable and concerned for the children in the right kind of way.

10 October

Harold's birthday: I gave him *Imperial Cricket* bound in white vellum for which I had advertised. '£95,' said Harold, looking inside. 'I hope it doesn't cost that nowadays.' Silence. It had actually.

11 October

Stayed in Brighton. Harold went over to Hove to see his parents. I fell asleep. He came back with charming photographs of his parents in youth, his mother with the same dark sloe-eyes and his father looking quite a card.

14 October

John and Miriam Gross came to dinner to watch a Simon Gray play on TV. They make a most agreeable pair: you can't actually say 'with his brains and her beauty' because Miriam is also very clever.

18–21 October

In Paris to discuss possible Proust film with the director Joseph Losey. Joe: heavy, silvered, ageing but still handsome. He had drunk a good deal of vodka, and addressed me in the light of his Communist past: 'I don't generally like your sort, but I like you.' He said it several times and was prone to repeat it whenever we met. In spite of – or perhaps because of – this, I felt enduring affection for him. Patricia, small-faced and very pretty in a little green hat, a very sympathetic character. A strike prevented us leaving. We couldn't get a further night in L'Hotel where we had been staying. We sat hopelessly like refugees while fashion figures and their vast dogs gambolled about the red velvet lounge. In the end we were put up in the private apartment of the owner of L'Hotel whose name we never knew. A young man in a white suit accompanied by a white Alsatian, also anonymous, took us there. Harold sat up talking, I went to sleep. Bizarre but friendly episode, including strangers and territory, rather Pinteresque.

23 October

I didn't sleep, very rare, and took a Mogadon. Made coffee at about 8.40 a.m., very late for me. At 9 a.m. the telephone rang. Jean, our au pair, who had dropped my youngest son Orlando at school, was crying: 'There's been a bomb at Campden Hill Square' (where she had gone to collect post). Celia Goodhart, our neighbour there, took over the telephone. 'Jean is all right. Terribly shaken, of course. She saw the bomber place the bomb under the car.' Harold rings Campden Hill Square on his line. He gets Caroline Kennedy (her mother Jackie being an old friend of Hugh's, she was staying in the house for a course at Sotheby's). She's clipped, admirable – the poor girl *must* have thought it was aimed at her: 'Yeah, I'm fine.'

I am desperate to track poor Jean who must be in need of succour. I finally find her at Kensington police station. With great gallantry considering her ordeal, she is describing the death of the bomber to the police so there is an air of discreet satisfaction. Not from me. With rising horror I realize from the description that it is in fact our neighbour Gordon Hamilton-Fairley, the cancer specialist, who, alerted by his white poodle, had been poking under the car. To compound things, the press have by now surrounded Launceston Place (as well as more legitimately Campden Hill Square).

Hugh is grey in the face with shock at what has happened; he was blown backwards in his chair while drinking coffee by the blast and has just heard of our neighbour's death. Later he makes a statement of great dignity about Hamilton-Fairley in the House of Commons, ashen but splendidly upright, chest flung out. I collected Orlando from school. All the other children were told by telephone. Flora, with her extraordinary intuition, rang up out of the blue from Florence where she was studying (she never rang up) and thus heard the news. Seeing Campden Hill Square on TV that night – it was the most beautiful autumn day – now looking wrecked and shattered, I felt the most terrible guilt for everything in the world.

———

There was nothing rational about the guilt. The IRA bomber was part of the so-called Balcombe Street gang who were subsequently convicted and imprisoned. The bomber had gone for Hugh, it was said later, as a hard-line Tory over Northern Ireland – which wasn't even true: as a Catholic himself, Hugh had a lot of sympathy for the plight of the Catholics over there. Hugh however was not a member of the government and his conspicuous car in an outlying area was unprotected. As a result a noble man had died. But when is guilt ever rational?

24 October

We visited Campden Hill Square. Small, deep, round, black hole outside. Also a policeman. All the windows boarded or cellophaned. Stepped in, went upstairs, collected some of my work (I used to go there most days and stored all my work there).

30 October

The hundredth performance of *Otherwise Engaged*. Party on a boat given by the producer Michael Codron, who wore boating costume himself. It is a beautiful starry night. We crowd into the open poop of the boat as it slides through the canal. The star Alan Bates looks ragged but very glamorous. I was hardly in a party mood but tried to disguise it.

3 November

Harold agrees to go to an Andy Warhol party at Emma Tennant's. Harold: 'I'm ready for anything.' Emma: 'And anything is just what he will get.' The party was fine – except we didn't get to meet Andy Warhol.

The autumn proceeded with a lot of turbulence, including threats of further press revelations from Vivien – Me: 'What is there left to tell?' – plus private happiness.

18 November

Lunch with my aunt Violet Powell. She told me of the early days of Tony Powell's reviews, especially *A Buyer's Market* when they were so terrible that a lesser man might have abandoned the project (the sequence *A Dance to the Music of Time*). Herself at Chester Gate, up early to go to church, looking at the papers first and finding the reviews ghastly. She thought: a more religious person would have gone to church first and read the reviews afterwards. Me: 'But at least that way you could pray for endurance.' (Which is what I pray for these days.)

A bomb at the Walton Street restaurant. Thought of all our friends who might be there and try in vain to get news on the radio.

21 November

My father gave me lunch at Beotys, where all went well till the fatal 3 p.m. when I know he felt we had got on *too* well, on topics like the Irish bombers. So he insisted on trying to give me a lecture. Heated.

Depressing. Pointless. Furious with Dada's morality. All right to be unfaithful to my 'saintly' husband. Not all right to be faithful to Harold. I thought of trying to explain to him about passion, but what's the point? He only likes people like the convicted Moors murderess Myra Hindley who are apparently repenting of passion.

23 November

I went for a walk in the bright park. On my return I heard a whistle in Victoria Grove. It was Harold in a black leather jacket. He kissed me passionately in Hollywood style. At that moment a passer-by stopped and engaged me in trivialities on some neighbourhood issue, regardless. She paid no attention to Harold. We agreed that our mood was restored from the torturing troubles of previous days. Told me he had been going to rip open dramatically the invitations to our Xmas party and show me the wording: *Harold and Antonia invite you ...* 'That's our declaration to the world,' he said.

Throughout all this time Vivien's divorce action was pending; we warned the teachers at the various schools. At the last minute she with-drew it, being too ill to appear in court. The press ran a story saying that Hugh and I were reconciled which would have been grimly funny – it was so very far from being true – if it hadn't been so painful for all concerned.

5 December

Dada's seventieth birthday party. Since Harold was specifically not invited, and we had been officially living together for nearly five months, I decided to send a present – a thriller which Dada likes – but not attend. Harold persuaded me that I would regret not attending. Actually he was wrong. I deeply regretted going because there was the most boring family row (nothing to do with me) at dinner with a glass of champagne being thrown by A over B. Longed to be back in Launceston Place with Harold. I did choose to wear a red dress for fun. Laurence Kelly got the point: 'Here comes the scarlet woman,' he said, boomingly.

9 December

Harold and I went to Nottingham to see Gemma Jones in *A Streetcar Named Desire*: Harold had booked the Byron suite at the Albany Hotel. Told Harold Byron's story, my version, including Augusta. Harold thought I would have liked Byron: and so I would, but not for the reason he thought: rather for his essential wildness. Inspired to go to Newstead Abbey. When we reached Byron's own room, the caretaker coughed and proceeded to quote from *Don Juan*: 'the lucid lake'. By the time we walked out, the lake was grey and misty with birds rising off it as we passed.

12 December

Dinner at which the Evening Standard Drama Awards were decided. Went, amply prepared with notes, feeling rather nervous because of 'personal connections'. But a most satisfactory evening. Although *The Fool* nearly won, *Otherwise Engaged* actually won in the end. *No Man's Land* also mentioned with respect by Bernard Levin, while Milton Shulman felt no hesitation in attacking it.

Back home, rang Simon Gray (who sweetly kept on about *No Man's Land* losing) and Michael Codron the producer of *Otherwise Engaged*.

17 December

Harold heard that his brilliant son had got a scholarship to Oxford. A really good piece of news. Before Harold and I met, when he was about sixteen, Daniel had chosen to change his surname from Pinter. Harold couldn't understand but I could: Pinter is such a distinctive name that he must have got tired of being asked, 'Any relation?'

19 December

Meeting with Bob Silvers, Editor of the *New York Review of Books*, and
Grace Dudley; Harold likes them both very much. Grace is the most
elegant woman I know: always has been. Bob looked marvellously
handsome, now that Grace has dressed him so well and his black head
is slightly greying. *Eheu fugaces*, the slouchy young man in a mac I first
met with Emma Tennant.

21 December

Our Xmas party. Harold could remember nothing the next day except
for a warm glow of feeling that everyone had enjoyed themselves –
which was true; I think. I wore my Yuki silk jersey dress; Harold after
a good deal of talk – 'I'm at home: I shall wear my black jersey' – did
wear a black suit and the red shirt I gave him in Paris. The first silences
of the first guests were broken by Sir John Gielgud, who bustled in
talking, and kept talking and really made the party and broke the ice.
Wonderful man! Someone: 'Of course Shakespeare was in love with
Hamlet.' J.G.: 'Oh, do you think Shakespeare would have been in love
with me?' The odd shock of our bedroom and indeed our bed full of
people eating supper. Rachel is pregnant, and was accosted by Dr
Miriam Stoppard: 'Since you are pregnant you must drink no alcohol.'
Rachel firmly: 'It's too late.'

My elder daughters Rebecca and Flora appeared looking marvellous,
their brown hair tousled, their blue eyes bright – plus two young men.
Previously I had said: 'Girls, you are not bringing anyone.' 'No,
Mummy, of course not,' they had replied virtuously.

I then went up to Scotland to spend Christmas with the children. I always
loved Scotland in winter: the bareness of the outline of the country,
like a Japanese watercolour, mountains, snow-caps, stark trees, and the
beauty of the short-lived light in the middle of the day when it is

treasured. I found all the children very happy there and decided I must concentrate my financial efforts on continuing to support it for the time being. Made a resolution to work at *King Charles II* every single day including Sundays.

1976

8 January

Harold and I celebrated the anniversary of our meeting by having dinner with the novelist Olivia Manning, for Harold to see her husband Reggie Smith, his old friend. Then on to a party given by Alan Bates. We both felt we didn't regret the fatal meeting: then, having celebrated, we could go back to being neurotic for the rest of the year.

23 January

Haven't been writing so regularly because I have really been getting down to reading Pepys. Enjoying it madly. Everyone all round is now calmer.

24 January

Last night of *No Man's Land*. Sir Ralph, with his exquisite courtesy, had remembered that I liked whitebait and insisted on ordering some for me: 'I woo you with whitebait,' he said roguishly.

25 January

Our Poetry Reading at Launceston Place. There were strict rules. One poet each, no duplication, ten minutes, or three poems. The decisive decided quickly. John Gross rang up all week with different choices. Harold read Eliot brilliantly. Daniel had enormous panache reading Sir Philip Sidney and looked rather like him. Francis Wyndham bagged

Hardy, whom everyone wanted. Miriam Gross chicly read Goethe in German. Simon Gray concentrated on Wallace Stevens. I read Browning at the end: the Ethel Merman spot, said Peter Eyre. More food. Then we each read one poem by another author, and then we all started reading more and more ...

31 January

Took Orlando and Figaro the spaniel down to the Harwoods in the Mercedes. Icy wastes – the weather is freezing – but the welcome very warm. Ronnie Harwood was wonderful! Clever, charming, high-spirited. Harold and Ronnie had been young actors together; now he was a successful writer. I liked the way he was so visibly happily married to his beautiful Russian Natasha.

4 February

Evening Standard Drama Awards. I started to tremble at the sight of the serried press ranks – the first time like this since October after the bomb went off – and could not even hold a tiny sherry glass. Dorothy Tutin commented on it. Had to lift it to my mouth like a two-handled Celtic cup. Pathetic. Harold very cool. Simon Gray looked incredibly young when he received his award with his wonderful thick floppy hair, and Sir John Gielgud had tears pouring down his face when he received his for Spooner in *No Man's Land*.

6 February

Not unfriendly talk with Hugh about finances.

Me: 'Out of two houses now, I'm not living in either of them, having taken care financially of Scotland always and a large proportion of Campden Hill Square, to say nothing of school fees. So we must sort things out.' Matters were complicated by the fact that I actually owned the house Eilean Aigas in Scotland, although it was in the heart of

Hugh's family estate, and he owned Campden Hill Square, the house I had always loved and insisted on buying.

9 February

Lunch here for Charles Wintour to meet Alison Lurie, the American novelist. Afterwards Alison did my horoscope: 'You may become a heroine for the wrong reasons, just as you were attacked for the wrong reasons. A heroine for preferring literature to Scottish castles.' (!!) I told her not to discourage this ridiculous if imaginative view of my situation which is, she says, devoutly believed in by Jonathan Miller and others in NW1.

Chapter Four

———

THEATRE OF THE WORLD

As we set off on our First Theatrical Tour (as my Diary calls it) I bore in mind Mary Queen of Scots' epic words on the eve of her execution: 'Remember that the theatre of the world is wider than the realm of England.' First in Hamburg, then in Berlin, and a little later in Yugoslavia, all in terms of productions of Harold's plays, it was difficult to envisage the hullabaloo which had occurred in England, since everywhere we were treated as a perfectly ordinary couple. I had always enjoyed going to the theatre since my childhood in Oxford where the carpentry master at the Dragon School took me regularly to the New Theatre and the Playhouse: we did joke in later years that I enjoyed going to the theatre rather more than Harold did. As a matter of fact, as a spectator not a participant, I had relished the political world (Labour) in which I was brought up and the political world (Tory) into which I married. Deep down my private world of history was the one that mattered to me, also since childhood; but that was mine alone.

One of my mother's dire predictions: 'You will never be accepted in theatrical circles,' always made me laugh and we often quoted it in later years. What were they exactly? In reality, whether it was Harold's obvious devotion to me or mine to him that moved the members of these famous circles, I had the warmest welcome. Rather more so, I reflected, than as the daughter of a Labour peer married to a Tory MP. At which point it struck me that neither of my two marriages had been remotely what my parents wanted; rather the reverse. Much later, after Hugh's death, my mother confided to me that although she had loved the man deeply, she had abhorred Hugh's 'right-wing politics'. Yet it is to her credit that you would never have known it. I think some of this 'abhorrence' was due to the fact that Hugh and I had married at the time of Suez when he was a prominent advocate of military action and my parents equally strongly opposed to it.

12 February

There was a last gasp of the English press at the airport. A huge predatory crowd of photographers. It made me shake with helplessness. I just looked at the ground and recited Wordsworth: 'Earth hath not anything to show more fair . . .' Harold frightfully angry and tried to swat them away on the grounds they were flies. He also gave the V-sign and said: 'They won't print that.' (He was wrong.) In Berlin we were met by Klaus Juncker, Harold's agent since 1959, on the strength of *The Birthday Party*. He presented me with red roses in cellophane and gave Harold regards from another of his writers, a Czech called Václav Havel. Snowing. Collapsed at the Kempinski Hotel. I had flu but managed nevertheless to get to *No Man's Land*.

13 February – a Friday

Nothing particularly unlucky except my persistent flu. Knew I still had a temperature. Nevertheless spirit kept me going to see the Wall: its tattiness, its dirtiness, the chief impression, plus a certain disgusting element in the thick pipe which now tops it. Connotation of the sewer now resting on top of the world.

All round the Wall: a real *Niemandsland*. Mounted a platform to look at the other (East German) side. Klaus Juncker's old mother can now visit him from that side one month a year and he visits her. Nevertheless you see by the river-wall the white crosses to those who perished trying to cross it: '*Ein Unbekannter*' – 'An Unknown'. One was dated as late as 1973. And the Brandenburger Tor, now cordoned off to protect the Russian monument to their war dead. There are 'two real live Russian soldiers' standing there, as Harold puts it. Guide (a West German) points out enormous losses of Russians compared to Germans. Russians stand impassively but guide says they have been known to wave.

Driven through Checkpoint Charlie by a 'non-German' because Germans go through another point of entry. Our non-German is half Bulgarian with a Turkish passport. Showing passports a long, chilly procedure, in and out of car. Form-filling, both sides. Cold level look given to me by passport man on the East side: I begin to wonder if I *am* a spy. Car prodded like a bull at a fair. East Berlin very depressing except for a spontaneous visit to the Theatre of the Berliner Ensemble (Brecht). Young man showed us round. Longed to say: '*Dies ist der fantastisches Englander Schreiber* (my pidgin German) Harold Pinter.' Didn't have the nerve. (In any case Harold not yet performed in East Germany: too bourgeois or something.) My visit did for me and I spent the rest of the evening in bed reading Turgenev's *Fathers and Sons* while Harold went to Beckett's own production of *Waiting for Godot*. Wept (over book not his absence). Harold returns, enormously impressed.

14 February

On to Hamburg, also to see *No Man's Land*. Harold said publicly that he had discovered new things about his own play. Afterwards back at the Atlantic Hotel I felt a bit sleepy what with one thing and another. Not so Harold who continued to sit against the window, a dark silhouette, discussing *No Man's Land* till long after I remember.

15 February

Said goodbye to Klaus Juncker with real regret. Harold thought his early-morning energy was a bit much but I said that was surely a good thing in an agent. Arrived at L'Hotel in Saint-Germain. Tiny exquisite Empire-ish furnishings. It was lovely to see Rebecca (aged eighteen, studying there) who stalked in looking very tall and beautiful, like a young Diana, in high green suede boots and black culottes to which she drew attention as being 'very French', although bought in Kensington High Street. 'I'm starving,' she said. 'Is there any

champagne?' Dinner with the Loseys and Harold's translator Eric
Kahane.

16 February

The girls (Rebecca's friends Chloe, Naomi and Beatrice) came to
inspect the suite, led by Rebecca as cheer-leader. Harold heard her
clear voice at the bottom of the stairwell: 'Mummy'. Gave them all
lunch: they ate like schoolboys. He took me for dinner at the restaurant
where in May last year we had a delicate conversation about rock pools
and waves sweeping us ever nearer the sea. Drinks at the British
Embassy with Nicko Henderson, the Ambassador: my father's old
friend. Both Nicko and Mary Henderson very warm. Nicko talked
with irritation about my father's behaviour to me. My father's worship
of success and publicity. When Nicko joined the Foreign Office, my
father said: 'Won't you mind never having any publicity?' I was very
touched by Nicko's loyalty. He showed Harold the ballroom where he
imagined me dancing long ago, also the dining room. Nicko: 'Can you
imagine you and Antonia at either end of this table?' Harold: 'Yes, and
no one else there!'

17 February

Harold bought me a ravishing outfit at Saint-Laurent Rive Gauche:
blue and white stripes, Tissot or maybe Renoir. 'We've seen a thing
or two,' Harold said as we left, referring to my zest for art galleries,
which I think came as a surprise, maybe not an entirely welcome
one.

22 February

Signs of a détente with my parents: Mummy proposes to visit tomorrow
'at drink time' when she must know Harold is here, 'to see the children'.
Meantime Dada makes a jolly telephone call over our visit to the Paris

Embassy (duly reported, I note, by Nicko): 'I am sure Nicko would make a character in Harold's next play.' Overture of sorts, I think.

———

This was the beginning of a real friendship between my mother and Harold; her natural warmth and her interest in his work meant that there would be fifteen happy years in which we took her on family holidays abroad until she pleaded old age – to our sadness. Mummy and I swam together vigorously in the sea, she in her seventies rather more vigorously than me, while Harold lurked inside reading poetry.

23 February

Orlando emerged laughing from the St Paul's exam – is that a good sign? While waiting for Orlando I read *Waiting for Godot*, which made me laugh too. Gore Vidal told me that Lesley Blanche thought I was like one of her heroines, running off with a sheikh. I don't think Harold is a sheikh exactly, but I see what she means.

25 February

Party at the *New Review*. I see a handsome man who comes and shakes my hand and Harold's vigorously. John Stonehouse, MP. 'I want to sympathize with two fellow sufferers from the press.' We grin back. But want to say: 'Thank you. But we haven't embezzled, faked death, and are not standing trial at the Old Bailey.'

2 March

Alison Lurie and the Billingtons came round for supper. Harold denounced Solzhenitsyn for his broadcast on *Panorama* which actually none of us had seen. 'I hate messiahs,' he said. And: 'Why can't he talk about Chile?' Me: 'Perhaps he doesn't know about Chile.' Harold is obsessed by Chile. Far into the night after the guests had left.

6–7 March

The weekend at Sissinghurst where Christopher Falkus, my editor at Weidenfeld & Nicolson, and Gila have taken the South Cottage, once Harold Nicolson's own. Christopher taught Harold bridge!! A great success, confirming my theory of Harold's naturally brilliant brain, seen for example in his editing of my work although he is hardly famous for that sort of thing. Slept in Vita's bedroom, cold but grand. No ghosts.

13 March

I asked Hugh about Jackie Kennedy, an old friend but with whom his name had been recently linked by the press. I knew he had always liked and admired her. Hugh: 'How *can* one have a romance with someone followed everywhere by forty-eight press photographers?'

15 March

Lunched with Graham Watson, my, agent. Agreed to do endless books: thrillers on a convent (my idea) and the Highlands (his).

19 March

Vidia and Pat Naipaul to lunch. It's a great success. I see how much Vidia and Harold have in common including strong will and anger. They discuss anger like one might discuss a taste for port.

25 March

Went in the evening to the new National Theatre – the Lyttelton. Expedition marred by the absolutely *appalling* nature of John Osborne's play *Watch It Come Down*. Indulgent, ranting, and from this great writer we both admired! Only Susan Fleetwood brought some kind of joy or at least plausibility to her role. When we first met, Harold told me: 'You understand that I can never leave a play by a living author halfway.' So I was dreading the second act. Fortunately at the interval, he said to me: 'You remember that decision? Well, I've rethought it . . .'

26 March

Very nice letter from Charles Wintour about me leaving the *Evening Standard* as non-fiction reviewer at my own request, which set the seal on all that.

1 April

We have just learned that we have to quit this house by 14 December. Harold, airily: 'Well, we'll be in New York then' – he was going to direct two plays there. Me, unspoken: 'But my *things* won't be in New York.'

Oh dear, insecurity. Can I really bear to be set up in another rented house and be 'content' as in *The Homecoming*? In the meantime Daniel returns to live with us.

8 April

Arrive in Zagreb for a performance of *No Man's Land in* Serbo-Croat. Interestingly, Briggs and Foster were played as policemen, which we're assured is realistic in the current situation in Yugoslavia.

In various fish restaurants in Dubrovnik, money worries are discussed. Also Harold mentions dinners in the past with Joan Bakewell and their respective spouses: and how different levels of knowledge among four people in a room might make a play. Or not. He spends most of his time in the hotel in what I call as a result the Beckett suite, studying for his recital of *The Unnameable* at the National next week.

15 April

Morning of reading – *Venice Preserved* (re Charles II) for me and Eric

Kahane's translation of *No Man's Land* for Harold. Then we set off on a 'Riviera Cruise', as it is advertised. At one stopping point we are urged to climb up to a mausoleum. Harold to the guide: 'I prefer life to death.' Guide baffled.

18 April – Easter Sunday

I swam in the sea. At noon all the Easter bells in Dubrovnik rang out. I had made such a fuss about Mass that I had to go. The sermon was twenty-five minutes in Serbo-Croat and reminded me why I don't (always) go to Mass: I just hate being preached at, even in Serbo-Croat when I don't understand.

19–23 April

At Eilean Aigas. I managed to swim in Yugoslavia and Scotland on the same day.

24 April

Harold's Beckett reading. His voice started to go. Michael Foot was a VIP guest and I asked him what he, as a politician, did for the voice. 'I ask for the actor's remedy,' he said. So Harold the actor took the MP's advice and gargled with port.

26 April

Harold flew to New York for four days to cast two plays he would direct in the autumn. Took Natasha back to St Mary's Ascot. Sister Bridget tackled me about the situation, so I told her: 'No question of marriage for the time being.' Sister Bridget: 'Well, that's honest. You were always honest.'

Taken by ourselves in a booth at the airport the first time we travelled abroad together.

LEFT: Gaieties C.C.

BELOW: Harold and To
Stoppard, as the wicket
keeper, with his celebra
red gloves.

LEFT: 29 July 1975. Taking refuge at Diana Phipps' barn at Taynton. Harold, George Weidenfeld, Diana.

BELOW: At the barn.

LEFT: Patricia Losey, Joe Losey in a 'Proustian' T-shirt Harold: they were working on a film of *À la Recherche du Temps Perdu* (which was never made).

BELOW: Harold and Anthony Powell in the woods at The Chantry, Somerset.

OPPOSITE PAGE: New York.
ABOVE: Visiting the Tall Ships 4 July 1976.
BELOW: With Paddy Chayevsky, winter 1976.

New York. Outside the Carlyle Hotel for the American production of *Betrayal*.

With the theatrical lawyer Arnold Weissberger, 1978.

New York, 1979.

Jerusalem, May 1978. With Mayor Teddy Kollek.

4 May

The filming of *The Collection* for TV in Manchester. Laurence Olivier, Alan Bates, Malcolm McDowell and Helen Mirren. 'Not a bad cast,' says Harold modestly. Indeed, not. The most striking thing about these great stars and their recording is the abominable way they are treated by the system or the technicians or both. These long, long takes and then the boom in the way, a flare, a tea break. All are extremely patient, including Olivier who is quite frail and having difficulty manipulating a bottle top of whisky which is never replaced properly; he remains admirably courteous with an occasional dramatic wince. He is even more courteous at the dinner after the recording given by the producer Derek Granger. Although Derek actually pays, Olivier behaves as the genial host, ordering lots and lots of expensive drink.

Olivier to Harold: 'Is it true that if I hadn't been ill, I would have played Hirst in *No Man's Land*?' Harold smiles enigmatically. Actually, it is not true. Oddly enough, Gielgud also believed another version of it, as he said to us once: 'I only got the part of Spooner because Larry was dead, I mean ill.' The personal spell cast by Olivier over his contemporaries! Helen Mirren wears a white voile skirt, tatty high-heeled shoes, a white cricket shirt, a black leather jacket and looks fabulous. She is a card. The contrast between her image as the svelte Stella of TV, stroking her white cat in an elegant royal blue evening dress, could hardly be greater.

6 May

Harold had a drink with Beckett at lunchtime, before we went to the first night of *Endgame*. They discussed Harold's situation; Harold told me it was the closest he had ever felt to Sam, whom he reveres. Later: to Jocelyn Herbert's for a supper party for Beckett. I was knocked sideways by Beckett's physical appearance, the elegant severity of his tall, spare figure; thick grey-white hair and aquamarine eyes. Later I dreamed about him leading us through streets of blossom – not quite what you expect after *Endgame*! That night, Beckett played the piano; Haydn, I think. Something so lively and vigorous there, that you could not detect in his personality the anguish of his play.

———

Somehow during that long, hot summer, I got back to working on *King Charles II* and even re-entered the British Library.

24 May

Harold continues to face a barrage of attacks from Vivien.

30 May

Dinner with Tom and Miriam Stoppard. The latter tackles Harold about the swearing in *No Man's Land*: 'This must be something in you, Harold, waiting to get out.' Harold: 'But I don't plan my characters' lives.' Then to Tom: 'Don't you find they take over sometimes?' Tom: 'No.'

My first proper expedition to watch cricket. As usual, triumph and tragedy, or just drama, attends Harold in all he does. I took along Alison Lurie and her friend Edward for company. Alison showed a few American tendencies like ringing up on a clear if grey day to know if we were venturing to go in view of the weather . . . Picnic at Roehampton. Harold posed with his bat as W.G. Grace for Alison's camera but laid it down hastily when his team came out from the tent. Instead of his usual eight, Harold had got to thirty-seven, and was apparently preparing to declare when he took a tremendous swipe at the ball. Not knowing he had hit a four, he started haring down the pitch. Then there was a scream. His leg gave way. Harold was born off by a ring of white-clad cricketers. 'I knew it would be eventful,' said Alison with satisfaction (I had warned her that cricket generally wasn't).

20 June

Drove Flora to her new tutor, a grand old lady in the great tradition of
female dons. 'I thought your Mary Stuart was charming,' she told me,
'But your Cromwell was very stiff. I couldn't get through it.' Me: 'It
was so stiff I could hardly write it.' Take a B minus, Miss Pakenham.

27 June

Enormous heat continues. Images: Harold, Daniel and Orlando playing
night cricket in the garden about 10 p.m. Sleeping out: Harold and me
on separate mattresses; Harold slept till 9 a.m.; I woke at dawn.

4 July

New York: the two hundredth anniversary. But the real news of the
day was the rescue of the Israeli hostages at Entebbe in a James Bond-
like operation. My first words to Harold were to recall our argument in
Dubrovnik where Harold maintained the militaristic spirit of Israel was
no longer necessary although it had been once, and I disagreed due to
the marauders surrounding Israel. Now Harold, I noticed, unqualifiedly
thrilled by the rescue.

5 July

Said to Harold on the morning: 'You know, I'd really like to go down
and see the Tall Ships.' Alas, Harold put up the minimum resistance to
this wild plan. So off we went. First an hour's ride in an uncooled taxi.
Then debouched and walking in intense heat – I didn't even have a hat.
Propelled by police of exceptional unpleasantness. All we could see
occasionally were the flags on the masts. Occasionally I began to laugh,
thinking what on earth were we doing there and looking at Harold's
face.

7 July

Had a ghastly experience at a musical called *A Chorus Line* which is the hit of New York. We walked out and the attendants couldn't believe it: 'Is she sick or something?' But Harold's casting of *Otherwise Engaged* is going well.

8 July

Harold reading children for Miles and Flora in Henry James's *The Turn of the Screw*, adapted for a stage play. A crowd of eager tots and chaperones inside the stage door. In the course of the morning I completely reversed my opinion of the children. My original candidate for Miles was too knowing altogether. A minute flaxen-haired doll called Sarah, so small she could hardly read the script, proved to be the most brilliant actress. (Years later I was amused to realize that the minute flaxen-haired doll had become famous as Sarah Jessica Parker.) Went to our one New York party. Jackie Kennedy was there. In her soft, wondering voice: 'Why, Antonia, are you here for the Democratic Convention?' Me: 'Not exactly.'

9 July

Dinner at the discreet upper west side Carlyle Hotel with Steve McQueen to discuss *Old Times* as a film. What an erotic play it is! I read scenes in the hotel. Steve McQueen started quoting the most suggestive bits. 'I'm fearfully decadent,' he said, pronouncing it 'decayed-ent'. 'I love decayed-ent things.' He was a strange sight, having grown a true lion's mane of hair to his shoulders plus beard in order to walk about unrecognized. Only when he takes off his tinted glasses do you see the amazing blue eyes. And when he walks across the restaurant to take one of his many phone calls. Then you see the inimitable McQueen walk.

17 July

Dinner with the producer Michael Codron and his partner David Sutton in Chester Terrace. Many ghosts because Jack and Valerie Profumo lived there, and this was the garden Jack tended when he could not go out for fear of verbal and even physical abuse. Opposite were the wide doors of Chester Gate where after a party as a teenager I used to stay with Tony and Violet Powell because nobody would take me to my parents' home in Hampstead Garden Suburb (it was too expensive: thus I considered my romantic prospects blighted). The lights were on and no curtains drawn on the summer night; squatters are living there. I saw into the room where I lay aged sixteen, often in Mummy's 'borrowed' Victorian gold necklace, spilling my scarlet nail polish on poor Violet's white cloth. In the dining room where Tony began writing *Dance to the Music of Time* I saw dingy bicycles. Tony used to ask me about my young men and I used to invent improbable associations to amuse him, so long as he could place their parents somewhere in his extensive imaginative galaxy of relationships.

Dorset in the high summer; the heat so great that the fields were white. We rented a cottage from the hospitable Warners at Laverstock, a magical valley in a countryside of narrow lanes, Mabey's Farm Kitchen, hills, and just over the hills, THE SEA. Picnics of wasps and sand by the sea. The children very happy being driven about in Harold's Mercedes and eating chicken'n'chips in pub gardens. Thrilled when Harold ate three helpings of cherry pie. Harold spent a lot of time in what he calls 'the creative activity of swatting flies'. Boys join in with enthusiasm, I suspect because they know it annoys me. Natasha re Harold on the beach at West Bay: 'He looks quite different from everyone else. He's obviously deep in thought.' Meanwhile the children buried each other in the sand and Figaro tried to keep the sea away by barking.

30 July

Harold gave a performance of *Old Times* in the Warner kitchen. Said he had always wanted to play Deeley, 'the man defeated by women'. Simone Warner sang the snatches of the songs (as Anna) just as Harold wanted them.

31 July

The proofs of *Love Letters*, my anthology, arrived. Gave Harold a copy. Pointed out: 'For Harold' in the dedication. Harold: 'My heart gave a great leap.'

5 August

Harold and I went on a pilgrimage to East Coker where Harold recited the speech from *Four Quartets* he loved, ending 'Now and in England' (which actually turned out to be from 'Little Gidding'). We were reverential towards the plaque inside the church commemorating Thomas Stearns Eliot.

17 August

The anniversary of the day I flew down from Scotland and joined Harold in Launceston Place to find it full of flowers. We tried to celebrate but things are really unhappy and unresolved (with Harold and Vivien, not me and Hugh, who is merrily grouse-shooting). Two of Harold's old friends who wish Vivien well, chose to tell me separately that Harold is not actually doing her any favours by enabling her to stay in vast and now apparently mouldering Hanover Terrace, nearly eighteen months after he has departed. Naturally, he will buy her any house she wants. Perhaps they are right. It is of course Harold's guilt. But I am obviously the last person who can or should comment on this.

Chapter Five

Our Newfoundland

21 August 1976

Eilean Aigas. Listening to Radio 3. Heard a man's voice saying very clearly, tenderly and firmly, as though directly to me: 'It is a beauteous evening, calm and free / The holy time is quiet as a nun.' (Wordsworth's sonnet.) *Quiet as a nun!* This is the title of my projected mystery story which I tinkered with in Dorset, when it was too hot to work on the state papers of Charles II. I am inspired to write and write and write. In the end it takes me about six weeks altogether: a first and a last where I was concerned.

27 August

My forty-fourth birthday. Flew back from Scotland to Launceston Place. Went to dinner at Walton's with Claire Bloom, who will star in *The Innocents* in the autumn. Her companion Philip Roth is a wry man: I really liked him.

31 August

Vivien now says her doctor has told her she is an alcoholic. It would of course explain a lot. Harold, beyond repeating her statement, doesn't discuss it further. I don't wish to.

Harold goes to New York. Hugh and I manage to have a good talk about school fees, money and all the rest of it. He is in a very cheerful mood. 'Although I can of course never be happy again,' he tells me with a laugh, 'I am in fact extremely content.'

18 September

Certainly writing *Nun* has brought me great happiness, and because of my birthday, I have always begun my year in September. Then, very worrying news from Harold in Boston, where he was directing Claire Bloom in *The Innocents* before the transfer to Broadway. He has a temperature of 102. He's alone in a hotel. I long to bathe his fevered brow.

22 September

Harold diagnosed as having both glandular fever and hepatitis. He must have felt so weak for so long.

26 September

Off to Boston. Harold very pale when I arrived, looked young and poetic. One can see his faintness rising in his face. Woke at dawn and began to write a new mystery set in the Highlands: *The Wild Island* (which became *Tartan Tragedy*). Gradually Harold's strength returns and his pink-olive complexion re-establishes itself. The Ritz-Carlton is immensely of another age: Claire Bloom ejected for wearing trousers!

28 September

Saw *The Innocents*. Music by Harrison Birtwistle appropriately spooky. Claire Bloom said she had an off night but I thought she was brilliant.

30 September for a few days

Provincetown, Cape Cod for Harold to recover. Harold writing –
I don't know what. He shouted at Steve McQueen down the long
distance, which must be a good sign as he has been totally wan. Steve
McQueen: 'Don't shout at me, Harold, I'm not your butler.' Harold:
'I don't shout at my butler.'

8 October – Full moon. Thought it might mean something

London. Saturday morning. Telephone rings at 8 a.m. (I am still on
American hours). Hugh: 'Come round at once. I think we should get
divorced as soon as possible.' Me, utterly gaga: 'Ugh, yes, yes. But
won't next week do?' Hugh: 'No, now.' So I go round, visiting Mummy
on the way at Chesil Court and preventing her having her hair done
before *Any Questions?*, saying cruelly: 'You look fine and anyway it's
radio.' She is a mine of good sense. Thinks it is a good thing. Says:
'Dada thinks you should live alone and be a *femme de lettres*.' Me:
'*Femmes de lettres* don't live alone. They have exciting love lives. Tell
Dada he knows nothing about the subject.' Really good talk with
Hugh. He is positively enthusiastic about the idea of the divorce.

We worked out a house swap: Hugh to get Eilean Aigas and me to
get Campden Hill Square. Although the greater presumed value of
Campden Hill Square meant that I had to hand over to Hugh my surviving capital, it still seemed the right thing to do. The gap in 1976 was
not all that great as London property prices had not risen dramatically,
especially in Notting Hill which was not yet fashionable, and our house
had twice been badly damaged by bombs, in the war and 1975. Eilean
Aigas, much as I had loved transforming it with the *Mary Queen of Scots*
money, and queening it myself there ever after, was morally Hugh's
because it was within his family estate. Campden Hill Square on the
other hand he had strongly resisted buying in 1959 – too far from the

House of Commons, halfway to Portsmouth, etc. etc., egged on by his powerful mother Laura, Lady Lovat who accused me of ruining her son. Whereas I had walked into the house, tipped off by the neighbour Billa Harrod that an old lady had died and there would be a sale. It was all dark brown, untouched for sixty years, one old bathroom, no French windows, thus no drawing-room access to garden. 'I have to have it,' I said. After a while Hugh reluctantly agreed.

10 October

As the I Ching said, after Stagnation, Progress. Good old I Ching. Harold's forty-sixth birthday. Poetry reading at Launceston Place to celebrate. I read Henry Vaughan. Simon Gray read Wordsworth's Lucy poems including my favourite lines about death and burial: 'Rolled around in earth's diurnal course / With rocks and stones and trees'.

An extremely exhausting time followed. But on the telephone Dada actually asked after Harold's health. Mummy: 'Of course Harold is exactly the sort of serious person Dada would like. Maybe we could all meet out of doors; like quarrelling dogs, it's better out of doors.' I think: 'Aha, cricket!'

20 October

I have a ridiculous anxiety dream in which the exquisite, slender Claire Bloom, playing the Governess, gets pregnant and has to play every scene in a shawl.

22 October

Well, I wouldn't have believed it! One moment Harold was nudging me to look at the lights as we entered W. 45th Street: 'Claire Bloom in

The Innocents. Directed by Harold Pinter.' 'You may not see it again,' he said jokingly, referring to the kind of speedy Broadway closing for which this town is notorious and which Simon Gray, for example, experienced with an earlier play. And now it seems it has happened. Will happen. And I never even noticed! Thought the reviews were really rather good, and the play, of course, marvellous.

28 October

Wonderful news. Harold has heard that he has got his liver back to normal after six weeks of not drinking. And what a six weeks: the New York failure, the nightmare of the first night. All drinkless.

4 November

Delighted that Jimmy Carter won the election. I like anyone who comes from nowhere, i.e. Cromwell (admittedly he is not much like Cromwell). I cannot see that his attention to God is any worse than other people's concentration on making money.

10 November

George Weidenfeld's party which has been designated Longford Reconciliation Night. I am standing chatting when Dada comes up pettishly and says: 'Where is Harold? I want to shake his hand.' Harold is in the Gents, but when Dada is determined on A Good Deed, there is no putting him off. Eventually poor Harold is winkled out of the Gents. His hand is solemnly shaken. Dada goes away, satisfied. Harold is then really happy at having a long talk with Mummy about poetry.

13 November

Suddenly wrote a jape in the hairdresser's called *No Man's Homecoming* in which all Harold's characters from various plays got together and started chatting. Harold loves it and wants to circulate it to 'those interested in his work'.

15 November

Back in New York at the Carlyle in 11B. Yellow freesias from charming maître d'hotel Mr Goldenberg, Dom Pérignon from Peter Sharp the owner. 'Welcome back,' say the lift man and even the telephone operator.

———

We loved staying at the Carlyle and did so for many years until the pound began to sag against the dollar and Harold said: 'Have you noticed we're the only people staying here who are not millionaires?' So we took ourselves off downtown to the Wyndham. But I treasure memories of our Carlyle life and still have a tiny dish with a butterfly on it which mysteriously fluttered into my luggage to remind me of those halcyon days.

15 November, cont.

Ghastly night at the charity première of *The Last Tycoon* which Sam Spiegel insisted Harold attend. Unbelievably an anarchist group in the balcony attempted to *laugh* this subtle and romantic film off the screen! I kept going to sleep (jet lag) while this evil laughter rose and fell. Kazan the director did not attend but almost equally upset at hearing about it afterwards in the Carlyle Bar.

16 November

Beginning of my life in the New York Public Library. Young man at the information desk seemed to find my feeble enquiries 'a pleasure'. (Very different from London.) Then I was ensconced like a princess in the Wertheim Study, financed by the great Barbara Tuchman in memory of her father because she twice had her purse stolen in the library. 'Barbara Tuchman could afford it,' said the official. 'But she felt not everyone could.' I admire the great historian B.T. more than ever.

———

So began a very happy time in our lives. I thought of Donne and his bridal poem: 'O my America! My new-found-land'. In this case, America really was our newfoundland. Although we had both visited the US many times in our previous lives, we had never quite enjoyed before this feeling of freedom and novelty, which I suppose came from the fact that neither families (or previous lives) had travelled with us. Harold was rehearsing Tom Courtenay in *Otherwise Engaged*. I would walk all the way downtown to the library. The weather was sparkling: New York in autumn. Everyone we saw in the evenings seemed interesting, hard-working, women and men. We had our own domesticity at the hotel, ordering in from the delicatessen on Madison Avenue in a way which was not yet familiar to Londoners in the 1970s.

17 November

In a theatrical pub on Broadway I encounter the playwright Trevor Griffiths. He criticizes me for going on TV book shows such as Melvyn Bragg's; I criticize him for rewriting *The Cherry Orchard* from his own point of view to show Mme Ranevskaya not a bourgeois woman, etc. etc. Griffiths to me: 'Well, what are you doing in the NYPL?' Me: 'Rewriting Gibbon from my own point of view to prove he was a devout Christian.' Well, Harold was pleased as he had felt very indignant about *The Cherry Orchard* since he reveres Chekhov.

18 November

Went to *No Man's Land*. The best performance I have seen. The new Foster, Michael Kitchen, brilliantly attractive and perky, making a great difference to the first act. The Knights had honed their work. We took Michael out to Joe Allen's with his girlfriend Joanna Lumley of *Avengers* fame. Highly intelligent as well as pretty.

23 November

Party at the top agent Milton Goldman's. Leonard Bernstein had a long talk with Tom Courtenay, over my live body, about music. His gestures were terrific and swooping, but the noises he made were more like Indian war cries than Schubert. Tom, very politely: 'The trouble is, you're a conductor. I think we express things differently.' Later I asked Harold whether I would ever meet his parents as, apart from my curiosity, they must feel curiosity. Harold said they would dread something new and strange. I don't realize till later that he is really the one dreading it because he's been through it once before.

———

The Pinters disapproved of the fact that Vivien was not Jewish in 1956, compounded by the fact that Harold by mistake – as he could never explain since it would just have made it worse – got married on Yom Kippur.

24 November

Delightful American manners: two examples. Brendan Gill of the *New Yorker* came over to our table at the Algonquin where I was having lunch with Ivan Morris. I congratulated him on something or other. Gill, with great courtesy: 'I could not listen to your charming remarks if I did not mention that I have given *The Last Tycoon* an excoriatingly bad review.' Then my purse is stolen, in the twinkling of an eye, in the New York Public Library. Black security guard, 6'5" at least: 'It is the custom, Mrs Fraser, in the United States, even if it is not appropriate to the present occasion, to wish you Happy Thanksgiving. So – Happy Thanksgiving.' And we solemnly shake hands.

25 November – Thanksgiving

Walked across the park to our friends the writer and economic historian
Alexander Cockburn and Emma Rothschild at 3 p.m. Huge feast. Then
we went for a walk round the reservoir, Alex sporting the black hat of
a mugger, also a thick stick of anti-mugger, under a sickle moon.
I suppose it was highly dangerous but somehow a Thanksgiving lunch,
lasting three hours, had stopped us noticing. 'This is your water, New
Yorkers, keep it clean' reads a sign on the high fence round the
reservoir. Would this really deter a potential suicide? A sense of civic
duty at the last moment?

1 December

Finished *The Wild Island*, as the Scottish mystery is now called. Harold
read it. All about my Scottish past, and Hugh's relations, but not close
ones. Meanwhile a visit to the Beinecke Library at Yale (with Emma
Rothschild) and the Pierpont Morgan Library has restored my taste
for Charles II. Loved reading the King's saucy notes to his pal Taaffe.
Also in the Pierpont Morgan, King Charles's hand-written, evidently
furious declaration that he had never been married to anyone except
Catherine of Braganza. Described the thrill to Harold, who says: 'Yes,
that's how I feel about old cricket scores.'

11 December

Last day in New York and with Harold – for three weeks. During
which I've got to face the divorce, also Christmas. At my own request
I give lunch to three playwrights, Simon, Paddy Chayefsky (who is all
I hoped from that wonderful play *The Latent Heterosexual*) and Harold.
Chayefsky never draws breath, but nor does Simon so they are a good
foil for each other. Chayefsky: 'Playwrights like each other. Novelists
don't.' Among other things, Chayefsky told us that dentists always
knew how to get you a blue movie (because they were so rich) and

also that they had the highest suicide rate in New York. The bill was fifty dollars: the best fifty dollars I spent in New York. Harold gave me an elephant's-hair bracelet chased with gold, for luck, and I gave him a dark brown cashmere jersey for warmth, from Yves Saint-Laurent. Harold is going to Boston and Washington with the play.

15 December

The day I got divorced I went on my own to *La Bohème* and sat in a black velvet cloak and cried my heart and eyes out in the last act. This was pure self-indulgence as almost anyone I knew would have taken me out to dinner, including Hugh. The day I got divorced I also spent an hour at Euston Station waiting for my middle son Damian's school train from York. I told Kevin and Rachel (whose own wedding anniversary began at midnight) that if I could attend the first night of *The Birthday Party* again, I would do so: 'I have never regretted it.'

18 December

Took the children to see Ted Heath sign copies of his book in Rye – my father had published it at Sidgwick & Jackson. Oh, the irony of this warm and jolly creature, chuckling as he wielded the pen like the tiller of a yacht. Ted signed books with joy for exactly those women he had scorned as Tory Party workers.

21 December

Visited the Naipauls, first time for ages together, taking them a bottle of champagne. Vidia thin ('my exercises – I can now carry a dustbin with one hand again'), charming and courteous. Pat so happy he is back.

Xmas Day – Scotland

Unlike Xmas Eve, which I have always loathed, I like Xmas Day.

Harold even manages to telephone from Canada, a great feat. It must be said that Xmas Eve lived up to its proverbial promise: all hot water went off, followed by all water. Daniel rings up from Launceston Place to which he has returned and says: 'The heating has broken down. What shall I do?'

1977

1 January

I am awoken by Harold: 'Happy New Year, darling, and I love you.' Me, very sleepy: 'I love you too and now I think I'll go back to sleep and dream about you.' Actually I had stayed up till 2.30 a.m., the girls' friends all charming; one of the men did a strip-tease which stopped just in time, and a cousin did a sword-dance with skis. We danced reels.

16 January

I am going to be strong this year. Vivien out of the Priory where she went for treatment and has resumed telephoning. I speak calmly: 'It's Antonia. How are you feeling?' She is nonplussed but answers after a pause. Afterwards, I find I am shaking, but am pleased with my polite attitude all the same.

23 January

Flew to Washington. Saw *Otherwise Engaged*, Simon's savage (at heart) and moving play. Tom Courtenay lacks Alan Bates' mordant humour but gives in the end more sense of how awful it is to be Simon Hench as well as pretty awful to live near him. Got lost walking from National Theatre to our hotel; Washington is like Berlin after the bombing although the buildings are new and the vast space planned.

26 January

There are Haitian refugees placarding the White House: 'Haiti, paradise for tourists, hell for the people.' Harold says we should learn more before going there as planned, on the advice of Harold's extremely left-wing editor Barney Rosset.

27 January

Lunch with the Harrimans; Bob Silvers described Averell Harriman as a Renaissance Prince and this quality impresses Harold. Pamela Harriman plump, charming and motherly to us all. She speaks about the problems of women in politics. Begins sentences: 'We, the women'. Pam!! She is wonderful. (As Pamela Churchill, she had been a friend of Hugh's and was godmother to our daughter Rebecca.)

28 January

Lunch at the British Embassy for 'theatrical personalities'. Elizabeth Taylor was there, in purple jersey dress and matronly turban: but the purple eyes incomparable. She lacked animation, as if the gaze of the curious had long ago drained it away from her. It was odd being at the Embassy where long ago Hugh and I gambolled with David and Sissy Harlech in Kennedy days after David was appointed Ambassador. Harold replied to the toast for the British theatre in an excellent, short, impromptu speech. That night at dinner at Evangeline Bruce's, Harold talks happily to Aidan Crawley, the politician who had formerly played for England, about cricket. We still seem to be going to Haiti, thank goodness. Later we went to a party at Carl Bernstein's (we were keen to go, having seen the film *All the President's Men*). Alexander Cockburn: 'The apartment is a young journalist's dream of what he would do if he got a million dollars.'

2 *February*

The opening of *Otherwise Engaged* in New York. A runner came with the first TV reviews: 'Britain has sent us a beaut.' 'That's me,' said Simon. An enthusiastic *New York Times* review is dictated down the phone to the producer and the 'Adman'. Nobody thinks of telling Simon, who is standing by.

3 *February*

A 'nervous hit' when we go to bed. A 'solid hit' when we get up. My financial situation not very good at home. I need a £60,000 loan. I'll simply have to work very hard. And not think about it, better still. It's only money.

6 *February*

We knew we were in Haiti when the Customs men gave us a real search, much worse than in Poland in 1969. It was books they were after: Harold's *The Collected Works of Louis MacNeice* looked extremely suspicious on the counter. We had been warned not to bring Graham Greene's *The Comedians*. We are in the Olafson Hotel, appropriately enough in the John Gielgud suite. We begin to relax. Harold even swims towards evening, thrashing round and round the pool with great attack, his eyes rolling fiercely. I am reminded of a dog thrown into a pool who wants to get out.

9 *February*

Lunched at the American Embassy, with an introduction from Arthur Schlesinger, to meet the writer Jean Dominique and wife. He has survived many regimes.

When an enormous coconut fell into Harold's glass, breaking it into smithereens, Dominique clearly thought it was a bomb. Talked of the father and the old man and the boy – Papa and Baby Doc – but never mentioned either Duvaliers' name out in the open.

15 February

Back at Heathrow. P.S. I had a short-lived reign as one of the world's best-dressed women. Journalist in Haiti, having read of my (temporary) inclusion on the newspaper list: '*Voilà une des femmes les plus soignées du monde*.' Wow! Harold very impressed. But was photographed getting out of the plane in check jacket and crumpled dress, old shoes. Haystack hair. End of reign.

24 February

Last night of *No Man's Land*. Sir Ralph absolutely superb; I would have hated to miss one savage glint of his eyeball.

26 February

A night with the Oliviers after a performance of *Stevie* in Brighton. I liked their home life, their happy home with a lovely Etty nude hanging on the wall. Sir L.: 'I have never got over a schoolboy taste for such things.' So I sent him a Haitian P C of a similarly pneumatic beautiful black lady as a thank you.

3 March

Francis Wyndham has given me a short story by Henry James about the man who wanted 'the uncontested possession of the long sweet stupid day'. It quickly becomes a catchphrase between Harold and me: 'I'd like the uncontested possession . . .'

10 March

Bad day at Black Rock. Our landlady Yvonne Finch in hysterics: it turns out she has illegally sublet to us although it had been done through an agency. She must have vacant possession in two weeks. You can imagine ...

17 March

Alan Ayckbourn's *Bedroom Farce* at the National: Harold laughed so much at Derek Newark's frustrated rage and impotence (seeing himself, he said) I thought he would explode.

21 March

A large kindly young man, our house lawyer, comes round to sort out this wretched mess about the house. Tells me that we cannot be expected to perjure ourselves as we rented in good faith. We shall not therefore be got out till we want to go in August.

30 March

Signed books – *Love Letters* – at the new Cartier boutique at Harvey Nichols. A dotty lady appeared who had sung in the choir at my wedding at Our Lady of the Assumption, Warwick Street: 'Those boys are all dead now' – as though they had died in the trenches.

31 March

Angus Wilson and Tony Garrett come to dinner. They argue about *Otherwise Engaged*. Angus: 'Simon Hench is part of the uncompassionate society of the strong turning on the weak, as represented by Mrs Thatcher.' Harold: 'No, it's not. It's about the demands the weak make on the strong.'

5 April

Laverstock life in Dorset where we stayed with the Warners. Jogging: even Harold appeared in his turquoise tracksuit, athletic glasses, and jogged away somewhere or other. Mine is blue and burgundy, Simone's black and white, Orlando's scarlet, Damian's bright blue.

29 April

Long but good meeting with Hugh at Campden Hill Square. A certain melancholy reality begins to creep in. Talk of going up to Eilean Aigas to collect 'my things' – like a housemaid! But the whole house is 'my things'.

Harold took a noble resolution under the circumstances that he would come and live with me in Campden Hill Square 'for my children's sake' and we would not buy another house; because they would like to remain in the house they knew (and where some of them had been born). It can't have been easy; and things were as usual very fraught in Hanover Terrace. But he told his son: 'I'm not going under.' It's been such a long time, of course. I had my doubts along the way about the going under. Again and again, Harold told me, he was saved by his feeling that I represented life, as opposed to the condition he was in when he wrote *No Man's Land*. He had after all expressed this in his poem to me of 1975: 'I Know the Place' which now ended without the original comma after 'me':

> Everything we do
> Connects the space
> Between death and me
> And you.

Chapter Six

———

OPEN-BOATING

28 May

Quiet as a Nun WAS published. The *Daily Mirror* saw 'echoes' of my affair with Harold . . . if you can see them in *Nun*, which is about a TV reporter obsessed with a married MP and a creepy Gothic convent, you can see them anywhere. A really nice, generous review from P.D. James, my heroine, in the *TLS*, made my day. Harold took me to watch the MCC against Australia at Lord's: 'I've never escorted a lady to cricket before.' When a really nasty review appeared in the *Sunday Times*, I didn't mind and I actually acquired the drawing of me as a nun by Mark Boxer.

5 June

Harold took Orlando to cricket (his club Gaieties CC) and after being on the TV show *Read All About It*, I went and found them. Orlando really loved it and the whole team sweet to him. Man among men is how Orlando sees himself.

16 June

We had a break in the South of France. The whole thing was overshadowed by me choosing to read Ellmann's life of Joyce. In the aeroplane on the way back I burst into tears. Me to Harold: 'What day is it?' Harold looks desperate, thinking it is one of our anniversaries he has missed. Me: 'It's Bloomsday!' More tears. While I cry, Harold: 'Don't be sad, darling, he knew he was a great writer.'

Earlier we found we were walking past the Villa Mauresque. Me, meaningfully to Harold: 'All this was earned by a writer' (meaning Somerset Maugham).

19 June

Hugh has read *The Wild Island* and begins by being very sulky: 'Is Colonel Henry meant to be me?' 'No, no' (actually it's his brother Shimi, if anyone). He gets crosser and crosser and I suddenly realize he wants it to be him. Once I say 'Of course it's you!' he's sunshine itself.

20 June

Harold observes that we are happy. 'When I saw you coming towards me in your blue dress, I was most happy to have made the choice.' Me: 'I suppose it's rather like when the bombing stopped in 1940: you only noticed gradually they weren't coming; you don't know at the time. You don't say, "that was the last Stuka".' But Harold had to go through those two years of intermittent colossal pain and unhappiness, which otherwise would not have given due weight to his eighteen years of marriage.

3 July

Went to Natasha's open day at St Mary's Ascot. I had a good time with the nuns commenting approvingly on *Quiet as a Nun*, all except Sister Oliver who said: 'Why are there no intelligent nuns? You had character nuns and Red nuns and mad nuns. But no intelligent nuns.' She made it clear to whom she was referring, as Sister Oliver is indeed very intelligent.

9 July

Dinner at L'Artiste Assoiffé as once we sat planning our new lives two years ago. Me: 'Leaving aside all the emotional side, I never knew I had it in me to break my marriage. Didn't know I had the guts.' Harold: 'Me too.' Me: 'You don't regret having met me that night?' (For we had been discussing all the tiny accidents which made the one meeting which changed so many lives so totally.) Harold: 'I'm the luckiest man in the world.' Later we sit in the Ladbroke Arms incongruously among off-duty police officers from across the way and think of our future in Campden Hill Square.

———

This is the first time Harold said these light words to me – 'I'm the luckiest man in the world' – which became a mantra he often repeated. Sometimes I tried responding by quoting Ophelia: about myself sucking 'the honey of his music vows' but as Harold was no Hamlet and I was certainly no Ophelia, in the end I took to merely nodding and agreeing. The words remain inscribed on many, many anniversary and birthday cards.

This particular Diary ended on a very happy note. Before we moved in, however, we took the three youngest children on a holiday to Ireland where we stayed with Thomas and Val Pakenham at Tullynally and Harold's friend Robert Shaw, new wife and numerous children in the west.

25 July

Tullynally Castle, Co. Westmeath. Damian on his first visit to Ireland, merely read *The Deep* by Peter Benchley and didn't look out of the window. Exactly the same atmosphere in the great hall, dark and lofty, as there was in the forties when Thomas and I used to come and stay with Uncle Edward and Aunt Christine (my father's elder brother, whom he succeeded in the Longford title in 1961, while Thomas inherited the property directly).

Otherwise a ballcock packs up somewhere, flooding the stairs, with Thomas and Val swearing at each other to mend it. Very funny. Oh,

Anglo-Ireland! But I do admire Val intensely for the way she copes with all this: huge house, small children, endless guests including hungry relatives and very little help. And Thomas.

30 July

Harold has been and gone and it has all been a great success. Except for the flies. It is impossible to exaggerate his hysterical hatred of flies: we nickname him the Moscophobe. Down at the lake: 'But Harold,' says Val, 'these are nice, clean Tullynally flies.' 'No, they are not. They're evil aggressive flies and what is more they are attacking me.' It was perfectly true; flies know their enemy. Finally he broke and ran like a horse, hooves stampeding, eyes rolling, back to the car, back to Tullynally and the flyless eighteenth-century library, the leather seats, the calm, which he loved.

But at breakfast the next day when Thomas suggested that Harold might like to count and list all the (mainly eighteenth-century) plays in the library for an article which he, Thomas, is writing, Harold looks politely blank as if Thomas must be talking to someone else.

5 August

There are – how many? ten, I think – of Robert Shaw's children in this house in Galway. Dark vital girls from his first marriage, paler children from his marriage to Mary Ure, and the baby boy with large blue eyes 'Miss J.' his present wife has given him, who is handed with love from girl to girl. The house is beautifully set. Water from Lough Mask on three sides. Robert looked magnetically handsome in a green tracksuit matching his green eyes. The trouble was that he had just returned from a fortnight's tour of Japan and Australia promoting *The Deep*; this meant that for him day was night and the strain of it all meant that he had a good deal of drink taken. I am beginning to hate drink – not of course to the point of refusing wine myself! although I'm not drinking at lunch. Yet how difficult it is to face the truth of what one drinks oneself while sharply noting it in others. Meanwhile the rain fell softly down. But there were very nice things: the charm of this family, so devoted to each other despite the oddities of parentage.

Harold went back and I took the children on further west, giving a history lesson about the Cromwellian settlement, the expulsion of the native Irish too late to plant their new crops (and installation of the East Anglian Pakenhams); they burn with generous indignation. On Sunday, heading for the boat to the Isle of Arran, we push through crowds outside churches. Me: 'What is this heathen rite?' (As I've made no attempt to take them to church, I pretend I don't recognize its existence. They giggle in a shocked way at my daring.)

13 August

52 Campden Hill Square. Here. Very happy. I've got a pink study again. And Harold is settling into his study with his own desk and chair, his cricket picture by Guy Vaesen, all he has been allowed from Hanover Terrace. He says it's enough. In my pink study, I find papers blowing about dated July 1975; a Sleeping Beauty-awakened element to the house.

27 August

A Saturday (and I was born on a Saturday). Thank goodness my horoscope in the *Evening Standard* promises: 'A Dull Year'. That's just what I want. Harold gives me an aquamarine necklace and Mummy promises a clematis for the garden I'm about to redo. Now I'm going to start on King Charles. Michael Holroyd, with whom I share a birthday, writes to say that he is going to start on George Bernard Shaw, according to our promise. The first sentence was buzzing in my head yesterday.

I wrote my Diary much less when I was concentrating on *King Charles II*, occasionally noting how happy I was, how handsome the children were becoming and so forth. Whatever the continuing difficulties of Harold's life, we were now secure together. The children went back to school. Two kittens, Rocky and Rowley, arrived, and were welcomed trustingly by Figaro who could not possibly believe they were cats: we would not do that to him. I note that Harold liked Simon Gray's new play very much and wanted to direct it.

5 October

Harold: 'While we are on the subject' – we were talking about tax, should we share an accountant, etc. – 'why don't we get married?' Me, in a dubious voice: 'This is your second proposal.' Harold, engagingly: 'No, in fact it's a return to my old proposal.' He talks briefly of his period of strain. 'I got through it because of you.' Me: 'What would we get married in?' Pause. 'You're going to say: a Dress.' We float the idea of New York where we find such contentment and have many friends but no family. In fact I do not imagine there will be any budging on the subject of divorce, so strongly demanded two years ago, now equally strongly denied, from Hanover Terrace.

19 October

We were lent Sam Spiegel's house in Saint-Tropez. Blasting heat. I was able to type outside in a cotton robe and swim three times daily. Also inadvertently went to a nudist beach due to my lack of understanding of taxi driver's French. I only cottoned on to his lewd jokes along the lines of 'so you like that kind of thing, madame?' too late when I got there. Stuck to my modest one-piece. Harold, dressed in black like Masha in *The Seagull*, read his book on the beach (a biography of Stanley, relevant to Simon's new play *The Rear Column*) and never noticed.

30 October

A Catholic priest told me: 'The Church used to take the line that divorced people living with other people were in a state of sin. There's been a shift. Now we think only God knows who is in a state of sin ... It is part of our pastoral care to help them.' Impressed by this sensible attitude.

5 November

Poetry reading of W.S. Graham's works in the Museum Tavern. Harold, Tony Astbury and Geoffrey Godbert. 'Sheer Spooner-land,' said Harold. The dirty upper room in the pub, unemptied ashtrays, wonderful verse. Hire: £3. Audience: two vast old poets, like antediluvian creatures waving their heads above the crowd, John Heath-Stubbs (blind) and David Wright (deaf). Both great poets. I see that people in the poetry world are animated by seriousness and love of the thing. Which makes these events so enjoyable.

27 November

Harold has begun to write a play: that's the great news. I think Benjie's friends crowding into the kitchen at half-term and making a fearful raucous noise, drove him upstairs. What happiness it brings him! He's quite different.

———

The play began with the image of Harold finding out from Michael Bakewell that he, Michael, had long known of Harold's affair with his wife Joan – from Joan herself. But Bakewell had not let on to Harold when he met him in the role of radio producer. Harold began by saying: 'I hope Joan won't mind.' At the time when I had not of course read the play, I thought she would be flattered. Joan and I got on well and we sometimes lunched together, when she was extremely helpful over my

TV presenter heroine Jemima Shore. Harold's seven-year affair with Joan, as described to me when we first met, was very much an on-off affair with prolonged gaps; it was also complicated by the fact that without Joan's knowledge (or Vivien's for that matter) Harold became obsessed with a woman in America whom he described as looking like Cleopatra, so there were many layers of deception. Harold and I, Joan and Jack Emery saw each other from time to time, always pleasant occasions. Harold told me that neither he nor Joan had ever contemplated breaking their marriages. In any case, Harold and I had, and needed to have, an unspoken amnesty where our respective pasts were concerned.

4 December

Harold has been reading the play, jokingly called *Unsolicited Manuscript*, to me. I see that it has completely taken off from the original image, as Harold tells me all his plays do wherever they start. It has become as much about the masculine non-homoerotic friendship, which means so much to Harold, witness his passion for cricket and his affection for cricketers. Harold says he was never particularly close to Michael Bakewell: certainly he's never mentioned his name in two and a half years, and yet he goes on a lot about his male friends, sees a lot of them, it's important to him. All the lines about playing squash: more Simon Gray I would guess. Without the twist of the wife. After all, Harold points out, wherever you start, finally a play is rooted in the imagination, is it not? Harold often returns to this theme about which he feel strongly. I notice he resents any effort to link his plays closely to a particular incident in his past, i.e. *The Homecoming*, sometimes claimed by this person or the other. (Who would want to claim *The Homecoming*??) I point out that it's human nature to make these links. He doesn't accept that.

The play is very funny, but there is also a lot of pain there. I wonder what its real title will be?

10 December

Verity Lambert and I agree on Maria Aitken for Jemima Shore in the
TV version to be made by Thames TV. I am thrilled. She comes
round for a drink: I know she'll be superb because she's naturally starry.

25 December Christmas Day

The first Christmas of my life in London. I love it. One's own home,
no journey. I think of my favourite Gerard Manley Hopkins poem,
'Heaven-Haven', except that is about a nun finding refuge and I'm
more of a Reverend Mother (as my mother used to call me, referring
to my organizational powers, not my piety). On that subject we went
to Midnight Mass at Westminster Cathedral: nearly three thousand
people and no seats by 11.15 p.m. I went to Communion for the first
time in three years. It was almost impossible not to because priests
rushed at you with wafers. Ah well, perhaps they are carrying out God's
secret will. Home at 1.30 a.m.: Harold still up and slightly inebriated
after a reunion with Mick Goldstein from Australia. Children opened
their stockings and so did Harold. He was extremely puzzled. 'Did you
give me all this?' he kept asking. 'No, Father Christmas did.' 'Did you
. . . ?' He was still examining his stocking with care and still looking
baffled the next morning when he was not at all inebriated.

27 December

Harold wrote for twelve hours the play he now calls *Betrayal*. He's very
excited.

31 December

Harold finished the first draft of *Torcello* as it's now become. I read it
and tentatively – very tentatively – suggested one scene was missing
(the penultimate scene of the actual play). Harold very cross and went

walking rapidly round Holland Park. Came back and wrote the scene. It was brilliant and not at all what I had asked for, of course.

1978

1–6 January

At the Grand Hotel, Eastbourne. I work flat out on *Charles II* and Harold sits about smoking his Black Sobranies and reading the *Guardian*. (We work in the same room, for the first and if I have anything to do with it, the last time.) At the end I have finished one chapter of *Charles II*. Harold has completely redrafted and polished off *Betrayal* – the name is back again. Names swirled about: now Patrick, Emma and Stephen having been Nick, Ned, Lucy, Jenny to name but a few. (In the end Robert, Emma and Jerry.) We talk endlessly about the play at meals. Harold is keen on Albert Finney for Stephen and I suggest Michael Gambon for Patrick: approved. Harold wonders whether Peter Hall would do it?

3 January

My first visit to Mr and Mrs Pinter in Hove. Me: 'Please warn them how tall I am. People don't realize who've only seen me on TV.' Mrs Pinter to Harold: 'Please warn her I haven't been able to have my hair done because of the New Year.' Mr Pinter is small and not nearly as fierce as Harold had indicated, in fact he's extremely jolly, winking at Harold, apparently, behind my back. The flat is extremely cosy, full of well-tended plants. Frances Pinter is quite tall, wonderful long legs, slender, very well turned-out; the hair of course looks beautiful, thick, iron grey; she looks amazingly young for mid seventies. They are perfectly sweet to me, producing the family album – from which I notice, with an interior giggle, all photographs of his marriage which might be thought to distress me or embarrass Harold have been hastily removed. Harold as a baby, round and laughing. But Mrs Pinter confirms that they never had another because Harold was so difficult. 'No peace for three years. We never went out,' says Mr Pinter. 'We tried to go out once, gradually relaxing my fingers from his, tip-toed out. By the time the wife and I reached the street, there was a reproachful little figure standing at the window, holding back the curtains . . .'

8 January

The third anniversary of our meeting. The Harwoods came to supper and Thomas dropped round, unexpectedly, talking about the Boer War when he came and talking about the Boer War when he left (he was writing a book on the subject). His concentration mesmerizes Harold, extending even to the moment when Damian exploded a can of Coke all over his shirt. Thomas talked on while others mopped him up.

I go forward with *Charles II*; Harold tinkers with *White Wedding* (as *Betrayal* has become) and rehearsals for *The Rear Column*. Harold also occupies himself refusing to let a single expletive be deleted from *No Man's Land* which is being filmed by Granada. As a result, no one knows whether it will go ahead or not.

27 January

What a happy morning! Harold brings me proofs of his *Poems and Prose*. 'One little thing to show you.' It is dedicated 'To Antonia'. Harold is thrilled by the appearance of this book. One should never forget that Harold wanted to be a poet and in many ways sees himself as a poet. He would agree with the order on Shakespeare's grave which we visited last year: 'Poet and Playwright', i.e. poet first.

Peter Hall rang up and will do the new play at the National. Harold had been oddly nervous about this but perhaps people always are. Peter says it's a bleak play but I think it's about the affirmation of love, hence the ending on love, even if it begins with bleakness *after* the ending of love. This probably says something about Peter's and my respective situations at the moment.

31 January

Harold read that jolly Larkin piece 'Aubade' to Tom and Miriam Stoppard and Henry Woolf. (He rushed in and read it to me with great excitement on Xmas Eve when I was in the bath. I thought: 'So this is what Xmas with Harold Pinter is all about: I have to hear about "unresting death, a whole day nearer now".')

1 February

Harold told Joan about *Betrayal* in the Ladbroke Arms. She is 'in a state of shock'. He always knew this was going to be quite a meeting. Me, idiotically: 'Apart from that, did she like the play?' Harold: 'That would be like asking Mrs Lincoln the same question.' I am a fool. Actually I feel extremely sympathetic to Joan over all this while Harold is torn between two desperate emotions, sympathy and the ruthlessness – I suppose that is the word – of the artist. The fact that it has always been so, doesn't make it any better for Joan now.

5 February

Joan now feels better about *Betrayal* but concentrates her attack on the title. Alison Lurie: 'You have to have something to betray.' She means love.

—

I wrote Joan a letter giving her my honest opinion that Emma is by far the most honourable character in the play ('both the men are shits,' I tell Harold cheerfully) because she at least is prepared to follow through the consequences of her behaviour. Robert and Jerry can't or won't.

But for me, the unique quality of *Betrayal* was best captured by Samuel Beckett in his note to Harold after he had read the script. He referred to the power of the last scene which is in fact the first scene chronologically, the dawn of the love affair: 'that first last look in the shadows, after all those in the light to come, a curtain of curtains'. It is that sense of foreknowledge which clutches me with pain every time I see the play.

23 February

The Rear Column has opened. Ghastly day. The reviews are terrible (except *The Times*). Completely unexpected. Simon in despair. Actors numbed. Simon tells actors: 'All the same, last night was the proudest night of my life.'

26 February

Sunday reviews even worse and there isn't even one dissenter. Harold feels very much for Simon: 'I'm looking forward to my turn in the autumn.' I beg him not to read the papers on his way to Hove and urge contact with a great mind, giving him Tolstoy's story *Master and Man*. Joan writes an absolutely lovely review for *The Wild Island*, my new Jemima Shore, in the *Mail*: generous and funny.

The Rear Column came off in a few weeks.

12 March

Garrick Club dinner given by Melvyn Bragg for Harold to meet John Le Carré (David Cornwell). Harold to Cornwell: 'How much are spies paid?' Cornwell explains that these days computers generate so much material and are so expensive to analyse that 'you are far better off bribing a secretary who knows what was really important'. Harold thrilled by the thought of this secretary. Harold's continual obsession with spies (i.e. Philby, and he loved John Le Carré's novel *The Honourable Schoolboy*) is one for the PhD students.

16 March

I quote a phrase taught me years ago by Ushy Adam about a man we knew: *Hausteufel, engelstrasse:* it describes a domestic tyrant, much loved by the outside world. Tell Harold he is the opposite: 'House angel, street devil'. It is perfectly true: Harold has the lowest domestic expectations, which is perhaps just as well under the circumstances, never makes angry fusses like 'Where's my shirt?', 'Where's my early-morning tea?', 'Polish my shoes!' etc. (Harold polishes his own shoes); but he sure can explode publicly! Harold loves the phrase.

18 April

Took all the children to see Alan Ayckbourn's *Ten Times Table*. Harold: 'What a good-natured man! He loves his characters. No one is totally derided.' He admires Ayckbourn enormously and will always go to a play by him.

22 April

Harold's long programme with Melvyn Bragg. I was pleased by the humour as well as the seriousness. Millions of people now realize that the brooding, menacing fellow actually tells a joke or two. Nice that he refers to the respect for learning in his parents' home. Harold reveals that his mother is absolutely fed up with the references to 'East End boy'. 'We lived in North London,' she says firmly. 'But Mum . . .' begins Harold.

7 May

Bernard Levin in the *Sunday Times* is predictably foul about *The Homecoming* (a new production by Kevin Billington); he calls it 'unendurable' and gets in a side-swipe at Simon into the bargain. Harold: 'I've been through it too often to care. I care much more about Simon.'

———

From 8 May to 22 May we were in Israel, coinciding with the thirtieth anniversary celebrations. Neither of us had ever been before. I had missed going with Hugh (a strong supporter of the state) several times, for trivial reasons of illness, children, etc. Harold was also a supporter; I didn't know why he had never visited it: his parents for example went at least once. I kept an elaborate Diary, typed daily while Harold had his bath, which, reread another thirty years later, gives me a mixture of pleasure and sorrow, even more than most Diary entries.

8–22 May

We are staying at the so-called artists' colony, Mishkenot Sha'anim. There are many labels in the kitchenette saying 'Meat' and 'Dairy'. I resolve not to let the side down by getting things wrong; Harold quite indifferent to this subject, I noted. Later however his religious past comes to our rescue when we get completely lost trying to return to our pad after dinner and the numbers are in Hebrew. Harold suddenly recalls his Bar Mitzvah lessons (he gave up the practice of religion thereafter) and saves the day by locating our apartment.

There was a magic moment in the early morning when I woke to the sound of Radio 3, and it was Rostropovich playing Bach, the Sarabande in G. To my surprise when I came to, I was in Israel . . . and the noise coming through the wall was Rostropovich himself practising for his concert in the evening. We later discovered, puzzled by the absence of this item on the programme, that he was practising for his third encore, for which he returned with great reluctance owing to the tumultuous demands of the audience. Quite right too.

Security is intense, beginning at the airport – nothing which we had remotely experienced, but travellers to Israel had been blown up at Orly Airport shortly before we departed. It was summed up by Harold looking up in a crowded shopping street and seeing a soldier with a gun sitting just above us: 'Looking for a familiar face in the crowd.' The security provided one amusing moment when the very young female soldier-interrogator asked, looking at our passports: 'Pinter. Fraser. Why are you here together?' 'We are lovers,' declared Harold, opening his arms wide. This tough heroine looked deeply embarrassed.

———

We both believed strongly in the right of Israel to exist, a point of view from which Harold never deviated, despite his criticisms, publicly expressed – which he thought to be his duty as a Jew – of the state in later years in its treatment of the Palestinians. I note from my Diary that we never met any Arabs, although we met many 'liberal' Israelis, admired Shimon Peres and the Mayor Teddy Kollek. We both read Moshe Dayan's autobiography while we were there and pondered the problem represented by the dreadful yo-yo of Israel's existence. Without military strength, it would surely have been extinguished in 1978. Yet Begin (the new PM) seems far from the democratic and secular values on which the state was founded.

A cousin of Harold's who lives in Israel and was a pioneer says: 'I'm sorry you come here when we have a Fascist regime.' He's rather disagreeable and out to annoy because he clearly resents Harold's arrival. He is a strong Socialist and explains the Kibbutz principle to us: 'The man who negotiates a million-dollar deal and the man who picks a tomato are paid the same.' I see from my Diary that I continue to ponder the question of settlements – Americans and Indians all over again, who is right? Is there any right in history? – without of course reaching any conclusion. All the same ... Instead we concentrate on the thirtieth anniversary concert held in the great valley below Mishkenot, in Jerusalem.

Ten thousand people. Real cannons beneath us roar in Tchaikovsky's 1812 symphony, the only firing, although several people mutter: 'an opportunity for Arafat'. At the end Harold reveals the real reason he didn't come before, not covered by the terse reply he generally gives to that question: 'Well, I'm here now.' He says he privately feared to dislike the place, the people. But he doesn't. On the contrary he is very happy with both. Above all he likes the intelligence and seriousness of everyone we meet.

Of our expeditions, there was one successful one: for my sake we went to the Dead Sea so that I could add wallowing there to my swimming experiences. Harold's own strain at the journey and the heat was alleviated by the imaginative sympathy of Lois Sieff, wife of the chairman of Marks & Spencer, here on a visit. 'He needs a cold beer,' she said — and promptly went and got one. Masada on the other hand was a disaster. Arriving at the cable car at an early hour (the energetic Peter Halban made us rise early to avoid the tourists), Harold starts like a nervous horse at the sight of the stable door. Claustrophobia, fear of heights, you name it . . . In the end he puts his head down and endures the journey upwards. I busy myself having a historical experience, having done much reading on the subject: the gallant stand of the Jews in their mighty fortress, which cannot be stormed from the front but having to watch the encroaching rampart which the Romans are building at the back growing ever nearer and nearer . . . with no possibility of escape.

But Harold is totally shaken by the vertiginous rise, and at the prospect of returning on the narrow footpath to get to the cable car — on the outside this time, above the vast abyss which he has glimpsed while I am sight-seeing — simply says he can't go down. He looks terribly white. I mean, will he live up here? Like the Zealots? Till the Romans come again? Peter Halban is wonderful. He simply forces the upcoming tourists to travel on the outside, keeping the inside for Harold. Then Harold brilliantly takes off his spectacles which means he can see nothing and I guide him down, with much trepidation, thinking of the two Jewish women who survived the mass suicide of the inhabitants of Masada by hiding in the gullies. Is there a gully for me? Josephus reveals to me later that one of the surviving women is 'intelligent beyond the run of women'. I can't help thinking that someone intelligent beyond the run of women might not have insisted on taking Harold up Masada, and resolve not to be so foolish again.

For all my good resolutions I never did quite cure myself of this tendency to suggest we went out in open boats in storms, up the Leaning Tower of Pisa at sunset and so forth and so on. I like to think that Harold really loved me for it. Perhaps all it really showed was that Darwinian law by which two open-boaters must not be linked to each other, otherwise human endeavour would get altogether too reckless.

Chapter Seven

A Super Study

31 May 1978

Harold took me out to dinner and asked me to be his Literary Executor (he was forty-seven so the possibility of death seemed mercifully remote). I was enormously flattered and promised to be sterner than any Literary Executor has ever been before: 'Not a comma will be changed, not a pause unpaused.'

2 June

Harold had an upset fit (three years later, things very bad in Hanover Terrace) and said we had to go and live in Ireland for tax reasons. Had vision of Harold, cross and lonely in a bog, drinking a great deal, and me soon to equal him. Luckily the fit passed.

24 June

Read Tom Stoppard's new play *Night and Day*, admirable. Like *Professional Foul*. Feel privileged to be his friend. At a buffet in their house, Miriam is in curvaceous beige, black black hair and eyelashes flowing, the highest heels you ever saw. She's fantastic.

1 July

Our friend Diana Phipps gave a fancy-dress ball in the country. Harold went in a dinner jacket and red bow tie. He said he was an out-of-work violinist. I wore a wreath of bay leaves and my usual golden kaftan and said I was a muse. Told an Austrian princeling – one of Diana's relations – that the essence of a fancy-dress party was to spend no money (I picked the bay leaves in the garden, although I must admit they were wilting badly). I suddenly notice he is wearing a vast jewelled turban, two foot high, which he had clearly had specially constructed. 'I carried it across Europe. Everyone thought it was a bomb,' he told me proudly. George Weidenfeld went as Scarpia and Lord Goodman as Friar Lawrence in *Romeo and Juliet*.

29 July

The Guardian match (Harold's own team v. the *Guardian*'s at Gunnersbury). Damian aged thirteen saved the match as eleventh man by refusing to run when John Hurt opposite tried to score a single and might have been run out. He put up a magisterial hand and stayed him. So it was a draw. Ronnie Harwood ebullient and rather good; Simon a great bat after having grumbled about his low position in the batting order last year; Tom as ever highly professional as wicket keeper in huge bright red gloves. Harold scored a duck, was mistakenly clapped heartily by us (Natasha Harwood and me) as he walked back to the pavilion because we were chatting and hadn't noticed, thus he got in a wax. Furious with *Guardian* for putting on a fast bowler in a bad light, having taken off his own; etc. etc. All good fun. Many cheerful drinks afterwards at a pub in Strand-on-the-Green.

—

We took the children to Italy for two weeks. Marina di Pietrasanta turned out to be North Oxford-by-the-Sea. Totally flat. Much bicycling: we all bicycled, including Harold, in stately fashion. Children adored eating Italian food in very cheap family restaurants every night. I swam in the sea. Children only cross when I said that everybody but everybody had to have a siesta as I wanted to read my book. I learned afterwards that they went secretly bicycling about the town, every afternoon. Best expedition – beyond the obligatory one when I urged Harold to drive us up some vertiginous mountain – was to Puccini's villa at Torre del Lago to see *Madama Butterfly*. As the light of the Italian summer faded across the lake, you saw her still white form, waiting for his return.

I paid for it all. I was after all the one who wanted to go, the holiday being in the nature of an experiment (although Harold paid for all the dinners). As a result we flew out in very economical fashion, thanks to an offer I'd seen in a small advertisement in a newspaper. Harold said later that he'd enjoyed it all very much, the novelty, having never spent two weeks in a house with eight people in his life before. But in future he would pay for everything and thus make the appropriate travel arrangements. Thirty years of so-called FamHols followed, abroad and latterly in England: all a great deal more luxurious.

28 August

Harold very shaken by the death of Robert Shaw. First, the friend: 'I'd looked forward to all our conversations when we were old.' Then the dread: he died, in effect, of drink. Harold has promised me he won't.

31 August

Argument with John Gross on the subject of James Joyce's love letters. I haven't read them out of deference to Harold's strong views about Joyce's privacy being invaded. Francis Wyndham said rather sweetly: 'I felt it was all right for me to read them, but no one else.' John said Joyce the writer was a public person. Definitely not Harold's view.

6 September

Harold and I have a row before I fly to Edinburgh to give a talk, it's my fault not his. Harold, percipiently: 'Isn't this about the length of time you have been working on *Charles II*? Not about us at all.' He's right.

After that I really buckled down to it and it was finished early the following year, published in early September. I hadn't had a full-length non-fiction book out for six years (although I'd written a short book on King James VI and I, and two mysteries). The book went well in the UK, owing much both to the editing and the commercial promotion of my publisher at Weidenfeld & Nicolson, Christopher Falkus, who was a genius at making book club deals. It went much less well in the States, where my friend and editor Bob Gottlieb of Knopf said gloomily: 'Here in the US we don't know the difference between Charles I and Charles II.' Strong implication: 'and we don't care'. The book is dubbed *Royal Charles* in the hope, it seems, that some sucker will think it is about today's Prince Charles. Either there are no suckers or suckers do not care about Princes Charles either. But this is to anticipate.

17 September Sunday

Go with Harold and John Gross to the East End – or North London, as Frances Pinter would say – in the hot autumn sunshine. I get over excited, have the impression of something very green and garden-like, sun on the waters at Clapton Pond. It needs Harold at lunch at Bloom's later to say: 'You don't understand. It was a terribly depressing place.' John's grandmother lived in Thistlethwaite Road opposite Harold's parents. I photographed Harold and John outside the synagogue where Harold made his Bar Mitzvah. But I do see the force of Frances' observation: this areas with its little gardens was not a place of first refuge: it was the next step on the ladder.

Preparations for *Betrayal:* the cast was now Dan Massey, Penelope Wilton and Michael Gambon, directed by Peter Hall. Also Harold had begun to work with the director Karel Reisz on the screenplay for *The French Lieutenant's Woman*, something he had long wanted to do. The Reiszes – she is the film star Betsy Blair – come to dinner and play bridge. (This was the beginning of a lifelong friendship between the four of us.) In October Harold and Karel went down to Lyme Regis to inspect the Cobb, John Fowles, and other Dorset sights.

27 October

Rehearsals are not going well at the National. Perhaps this is always the case at this stage? Dan strikes his breast frequently and says he doesn't feel it here, the humanity of the character. Answer in a chorus: how about acting it then? Penelope (who's his wife in reality): 'For that matter, I haven't had a seven-year affair.' Then *sotto voce* to Harold: 'But if he goes on like this, I may soon.'

30 October

Betrayal is now wonderful, Harold says, and he is in love with Penelope Wilton. But there is a threat of wild-cat strikes at the National Theatre which may ruin everything.

The strikes continued to threaten, causing much anguish all round except to Peter Hall, apparently, who either had nerves of steel or gallantly pretended to have them. On the first night, no one knew for sure until the curtain went up whether the play would take place. The uncertainty did not necessarily affect the critics' reaction but they were certainly lukewarm. Read over his shoulder at breakfast in *The Times:* 'Pinter master of ambiguity, is blankly obvious.' Billington of the *Guardian*, normally so intelligent, read us a lecture about bourgeois-affluent culture patterns ... 'Just what I expected,' says Harold philosophically. He has after all been here before.

18 November

Sunday critics re *Betrayal* are even worse than the dailies. I read the ghastly self-important Bernard Levin; not sure whether Harold does.

24 November

Harold rings from the station (on his way to see his parents). Rave review from Benedict Nightingale in the *New Statesman* who also reviewed the reviewers: 'glassy-eyed and furry-eared oafs'.

In December a house was bought for Vivien in Blackheath and Harold looked like getting back his books which, unlike the rest of the contents of palatial Hanover Terrace, he had pined for since 1975. (When we first lived together, he brought his desk, his chair and a picture of a cricket match.)

24/25 December

Midnight Mass at Farm Street. Haydn's St Nicholas Mass which I had just been playing to Harold. Midnight Mass was over in fifty-five minutes, unlike the horror at Westminster Cathedral last year. Fr Peter Knott's sermon began: 'I don't believe in long sermons for Midnight Mass.' The Jesuits really know how to run things. Flora and I went thumbs-up. Harold's stocking this year was a flighty long black nylon with a seam. I gave everyone an appropriate mug. His mug said: 'You are a Genius.' The mug vanished, the stocking hung around.

1979

New Year resolutions: 1) Be calm, have a calm centre, turn towards the calm centre and inspect it, contemplate my soul, if any. 2) Take joy in what Wordsworth called 'the meanest flower that blows'; especially the mean flowers of Campden Hill Square (whose refurbished garden was once more my delight).

Despite these good resolutions, the spring of 1979 was not particularly calm. The strike situation at the National Theatre rumbled on, and bedevilled a production once again; this time Simon Gray's *Close of Play* which Harold directed. 'Union selfishness and violent behaviour at the National' was what convinced Harold to vote Tory in May. I too voted Tory but that was quite unashamedly in order to see a woman walk into No. 10. Neither of us knew much about Mrs Thatcher's politics: on a trip to the Booksellers' Conference in Guernsey, I took the trouble to break away and watch the new Prime Minister making this historic entry. Mrs Thatcher, a small, broad, light blue figure, paused and read aloud from St Francis. A journalist got bored and indicated she should now stop. Mrs T. put up her hand and stayed him. Implacably she read on. So they were warned.

Subsequently Harold, by his own account, regretted his vote. I didn't: it was just this kind of defiance of what had hitherto been the masculine establishment which appealed to me (although I never voted for her again). My mother hated Mrs Thatcher and told me she hit my father – an unprecedented event – when he said something nice about her reading of St Francis. Mummy, gloomily: 'Of course taxation will change and we'll all be much better off.' Me, to tease: 'But, Mummy, won't you give it all to charity?' Mummy: 'Yes, a charity called the Bernhurst carpet.'

Although the children flourished, one of my cats – Rocky the rover – disappeared at the age of eighteen months. I thought of what it must be like for the parents of 'disappeared' children, as I listened for the sound of the cat-flap which did not come, and glimpsed the wrong cat at street corners. (His brother Rowley, after King Charles II's popular nickname, clung close to me and lived for another sixteen years.)

4 April

Excitement! Harold will buy the little house in Aubrey Road! I wanted to buy it myself in September in Monopoly fashion, since it abutted my garden, but my bank politely suggested that since I could not afford the house I was in, it was not on. Harold desperately needs something for his books. Also as he says about Campden Hill Square, which was becoming a cheerful maelstrom of activity: 'Although I adore all your children and their numerous friends . . .' Me: 'I know. They're not exactly shrinking, are they?' Harold talks about the 'reclusive' side of his nature. I say that my idea of happiness is to be alone in a room in a house full of people.

So Harold's wonderful Super-Study, as it was called (actually his study and his secretary's office) was born, joined to the big house by the garden, with a new door. Harold walked to work, as he put it. Before he could change his mind, I hastily moved into his previous study and for the first time in my life did not work in a little hole off my bedroom.

9 April

Harold has signed the deed of separation with Vivien.

14 May

Evening with Beckett and Pinter. Beckett is exhausted from directing Billie Whitelaw in *Happy Days* at the Royal Court. 'We are discovering a woman, whereas I believe Peggy Ashcroft arrived with a preconception.' (But he also heard she was very good.) Harold is moved to enact most of *Close of Play* for him, as Beckett seems never to go to the theatre and was quite alarmed at the notion that he should actually visit this. His eyes shine at Harold's depiction. Barbara Bray behaves quite well until the end when she starts declaiming that everything in art is political: she is rehearsing for doing *The Critics* on radio and I suspect that *Close of Play* will not fare well. Harold, vehemently: 'Nothing I have written, Barbara, nothing ever, is political.' Sam: 'This very absence of politics is in itself a political statement.' But Barbara couldn't leave it at that. She went on and on. Finally, Beckett, lighting one of his little black cheroots: 'Oh, why do you talk so much . . . ?' After that, we all got on better. Barbara still talked but she stopped lecturing Harold on his own work.

3 June

Went on *Read All About It*, now chaired by Ronnie Harwood. We interviewed Vidia Naipaul in connection with *India – A Wounded Civilization*. I asked him about writing fiction and non-fiction. 'I know it's a corny question,' I said, 'but you are famously tolerant.' Afterwards one of the people on the programme said she was glad to hear this because she had thought him 'a wee bit intolerant' (!) Vidia reveals that he writes fiction and non-fiction quite differently – typewriter v. hand-writing. I love hearing details of writers' craft, as cannibals eat the brains of clever men to get cleverer.

6 June

Visit to Venice. We have to visit Torcello because of the mention of Robert's visit in *Betrayal*. We also do a spirited rendering of the play itself, the two of us. I am a particularly fine Jerry, the lover, I feel, and Harold a feisty Emma as well as the husband Robert. The latter is actually his favourite part in the play – he says it's the best part. (He subsequently acted it on radio.)

We have a long conversation about occupation beginning with what would have happened if England had been occupied by the Germans. Harold: 'I would have taken to the Welsh Hills and joined the resistance.' Me: 'No, you would have been killed before you got there, as a prominent Jewish intellectual, but would have taken one or two

Germans with you.' We then turn to the agonizing subject of the 'occupation' by Israel of Arab lands v. the Jewish right to a national home. I remind him of the disquiet of our friends in Israel that Jews should in any way be an occupying power. In this endless discussion, we tend to reverse positions according to what the other person says, I notice.

More happily, Harold works hard on the screenplay of *The French Lieutenant's Woman*. A sinister experience crossing back to the Cipriani in the hotel motorboat with other revellers, staid but elegant couples, mainly American. Suddenly Harold gives a shout. The lights of the island have all vanished. I look up and see a small strongboat with lights on the mast fore and aft which has just passed us. But right on top of us, totally black and enormous, is a vast menacing ocean liner which is in fact being towed out to sea by the little boat. Like a monster, rearing up out of the deep, quite silently, it has blocked out all the light.

At lunch on Torcello, the *gatti* prowl about, one all too like poor vanished Rocky, the rest like Rowley, but their eyes are fierce and pessimistic as they prowl among the tables, not like the confident, more innocent eyes of English cats. I buy a tablecloth from the traders outside, in imitation of Emma in *Betrayal*. I get a call from London saying that income tax is being cut drastically. All round us, wealthy English guests are rejoicing and of course it's wonderful for us, most welcome at just this juncture, to put it mildly. But, I think: who gets poorer? As usual with my Diary cogitations, there is no answer.

3 July

We stayed with Clarissa Avon at Alfrediston. This is a perfect country house arranged with all the harmony I remember. I passionately appreciate Clarissa's sense of order, huge pots of regale lilies, a *jardinière* of pink and white geraniums; two pots of fuchsia – Ballerina? Harold says in awe of his own dressing room: 'My old black jersey has been neatly folded.' David and Rachel Cecil come to dinner, bringing Iris Murdoch and John Bayley. David rings up to say they won't be

changing, 'since the Bayleys don't seem to have brought any luggage'.
Later, when they've gone, Clarissa asks: 'How can you bear to hear
about it, Harold's old girlfriends, Isobel, Dilys and the rest?' (Harold
had been talking about his past). Me: 'It's the memorable path which
led to wonderful me!' Clarissa comments that she hates competition
(she is so beautiful, so well-read, that I don't think she can face much
of it). 'The only sport I like is swimming, which is not competitive.'
Cecil Beaton came to lunch, every conceivable inch of him immaculate
in white tussore. He is an advertisement for the stroke from which he
has recovered, full of chat and malice.

14 July

John Fowles has written Harold a charming letter approving the
screenplay: 'I had doubts about the interweaving of past and present
(the present was all invented by Harold, at Karel Reisz's suggestion)
but found myself really looking forward to your bits, the bits typed in
red.'

---

52 Campden Hill Square – that Haven – was becoming more and more
of a tip, with the influx of quantities of teenage children and their friends
who never got up and if they did get up, never washed up. Harold, an
only child, a fastidious only child, was in despair with which I totally
sympathized.

23 July

The Reign of Terror has started. Decide to wake both Benjie and
Damian, my elder sons. 'You can't talk to him. He's still asleep,' says
an unwise voice from upstairs. 'GET HIM UP! IT'S HIS MOTHER
SPEAKING!' 'Why?' said the unwise voice still more unwisely.
'BECAUSE I SAY SO.' Stormed about the house ranting and
shrieking, having read a learned medical article in the *Guardian* that

morning saying that people who suppress their anger fall dangerously ill. An hour later I shout: 'Damian!' '*Jawohl*, Stalin,' he replies. 'It's the Cheka come to get us,' wail the unhappy teenagers. Soon the house is clean and tidy. Victory.

27 *August*

My forty-seventh birthday. Day haunted by Mountbatten murders. Later I continue to be haunted by the subject, not the death of the grand old boy, dying a hero's death full of years and honours, to merit a Ceremonial Funeral, but those children, those bright young faces on TV including an Irish boat-boy.

8 *September*

Frances Pinter is reading *Charles II* with evident enjoyment. She has also written one of the most charming letters I have ever received in my life, saying in effect, how happy I have made Harold. It's odd. Laura Lady Lovat didn't want me to marry Hugh, wearing black at our wedding which shocked my mother (I still have the black hat labelled 'the hat I wore at poor Hugh's wedding' which I found after her death), yet I was young, Catholic and willing. My crime was that I had no money, as she made clear from time to time. Harold's parents might justifiably shrink from the Catholic, divorced mother of six, yet they are displaying great warmth now they have got over the shock.

18 *September*

We revisit the Hotel Lancaster in Paris for the French production of *No Man's Land*. I recall to Harold his remark four years ago that he might find it difficult to live with children. Me: 'You were quite right. Who can?' (It has become one of our jokes.) Harold to me, last thing: 'You may not agree but I am actually very calm these days.' In the meantime I have floated the idea of writing a study of women in the seventeenth century: both George Weidenfeld and Bob Gottlieb seem keen.

This became *The Weaker Vessel:* enormously successful in the US in 1984, largely due to the energetic promotion of Bob Gottlieb who made it into a bestseller; in the UK in contrast it was perhaps ahead of its time as women's history – America much more advanced in that respect – although it did win a Wolfson History Award, to my eternal joy. It remains the book of which I am proudest, because it was so difficult to write: 'Fifty-one per cent of the population for a hundred years, no narrative structure, no nice neat birth, life and death,' as I groaned to Harold on the first day I sat down to write.

29 September

Poets at the Purcell Room for a TV programme directed by Harold. (It never came to anything but a good time was had by all, since the poets included those famous *bon viveurs* George Barker and W.S. Graham.) The most touching moment came when Judy Gascoyne, wife of David Gascoyne, got up and recited her life story as if it was a poem. Which it was really, and I laid it out as such in my Diary.

> I was married to a vet
> For thirty years
> He left me for another woman
> But it's essential, isn't it?
> To keep cheerful
> Anyway, that is what I did
> I went to the asylum
> I read to the insane
> For them I read poetry
> My favourite poetry
> So one day in an asylum

I said: 'This is a poem
A poem by David Gascoyne'
And one of the inmates
The sad and desperate inmates
Said: 'I am David Gascoyne'

8 October

Flew to Dublin for the production of *Close of Play* which has been a bone of contention with the actors of the National Theatre (an official British institution), because of the security risk following the Mountbatten death and surrounding carnage. Despite heroic work by the Pope recently touring round Phoenix Park in his popemobile, urging 'Thou shalt not kill.' One of the actors discovered that there was no legal necessity to tour in a foreign country – Ireland – as not contracted to do so. Some of the stauncher actors, including Michael Gambon, metaphorically shrugged their shoulders like troops going over the top and said: 'Oh well, count me in, I suppose.' Other parts had to be re-recruited. We stayed at the brand-new Bloom's Hotel, every modern luxury, the smart European Ireland that is evolving, Anna Livia Plurabelle Restaurant, Boylan's Brasserie, etc. Harold: 'What would Joyce have thought of all this? Blind and poor.' Me, reminding him: 'But when I cried on Bloomsday, finishing Ellmann's life, you said, "He knew he was a great artist and nothing else matters."'

In fact security at the Olympia Theatre is negligible, and no one is searched, although my brother Thomas is carrying an enormous, obviously weighty bag. In *Close of Play* Dubliners love the readily identifiable character of Benedict – an alcoholic but a witty one, played by the superb, urbane John Standing.

10 October

Dublin. Harold's forty-ninth birthday. I brought over an edition of
East Coker specially designed by Julian Rothenstein. Harold loved it.

15 November

In New York for rehearsals of *Betrayal*, once again directed by Peter
Hall, this time with Blythe Danner, Roy Scheider and Raul Julia, who
tells me he has been over to London and patrolled Westminster Abbey
to acquire the correct English accent. Don't dare tell him that he is
more likely to have acquired an Australian or even a Japanese accent in
the Abbey . . . Harold tells me afterwards that at dinner with Peter Hall
he looked across to me and thought: 'You have given me a sense of the
present, the happiness of the present. I've never had that before.'

I give an interview focused on the re-named *Royal Charles* to the
Washington Post. Man, hopefully, at the end: 'Just one more question,
what is Harold Pinter like about the house, all those pauses and
enigmatic statements, I've always wondered.' Me, briskly: 'Keep
wondering.'

17 November

Harold outraged about the Anthony Blunt affair. (Blunt, despite his
background as a spy for Russia, had been deliberately left in position
as Keeper of the Queen's Pictures.) I think he has the sense of a cover-
up by the Establishment, which is the more acute because he has never
remotely belonged to it – or wished to. I am fascinated by other things
such as how did the poor Queen conduct her conversations with Blunt?

1 December

Back in London. Day of winter gardening (planting bulbs, my favourite
activity). Diana Phipps has created a fantastic world for Harold in his

new Super-Study out of the really poor material of the original house. I love the way there is now a great deal of purposeful movement between the two houses, all of it through my garden.

2 December

Society of West End Theatre Managers' Awards (later the Oliviers). Had to arrive by 6 p.m. Interminable. Harold mellow however and got mellower as the drink flowed down the hours. There was really nothing else to do until 1 a.m. when 'Carriages' were to be called. He was stunned when Sir Ralph Richardson went on to the platform, waved the envelope and said, sonorously: 'A prize for an old friend of mine!' It was for *Betrayal* as Best New Play. Harold wove his way with difficulty to the platform and said: 'I'm very surprised, but not as surprised, I'm sure, as Michael Billington.' (Evidently not forgiven for his stinking review of *Betrayal*.) Nobody could understand what he meant. Billington looked completely bewildered. 'Why me? What did I do?' Harold meanwhile, minus specs and beaming is making another speech to anybody who will listen. 'I love women. I'm resolutely heterosexual. Listen, a woman's waist is the most beautiful thing in the world.' He puts his arm round the nearest waist which happens by pure coincidence to be that of a woman, and by a further happy coincidence, mine.

Chapter Eight

IT IS HERE

1980

1 January

I know the eighties are going to be good in so many ways. The seventies were violent, as the newspapers were saying; it spread everywhere. I decide to 'know thyself' as the Bible tells us to do. I know that I am hard-working, affectionate and kind. I also know that I am lazy, nagging and neurotic. God – if She exists – knows how that works out.

5 January

First night of *Betrayal* in New York. Bar full of rich Philistines. It was thus amusing when I heard one say to the other in the interval: 'Yeah, I like it, but it won't have broad appeal. You see, we're a very special audience.' One turns to me and says kindly: 'This will interest you. We're going to play squash.' (A subject Robert and Jerry discuss aggressively in the play.)

6 January: Twelfth Night

And the three kings did come bearing gifts – or two of them. There was a rumour via somebody's children's nanny (New York!) that Mrs Kerr, wife of the great Walter Kerr of the *New York Times*, on whose word we depend for the survival of *Betrayal*, rather thought that Walter ... And it was true. Harold, putting down the paper. 'Well,

I can only call this a rave.' I have never heard him use such language before. The telephone rings off the hook and so we shall go back to England in a haze and a blaze of glory. Before we went home, Harold proposed to Sam Spiegel that he should make a film of *Betrayal*.

On 8 January 1980 we had known each other for five years and Harold was coming up for the fifth anniversary of his departure from the former marital home. He would thus shortly be entitled to seek a divorce unilaterally on these grounds.

7 February

Harold very exercised over Chile: the Foreign Office now apparently denying that Dr Sheila Cassidy was tortured. I feel exercised over the whole world – not that there's much point in that.

23 February

After the most horrific delays, *The French Lieutenant's Woman* the movie is at last on as of Thursday night. Hear Harold's voice about midnight. 'Oh, my God' very loud. Thought it was off. But it's on. Meryl Streep and Jeremy Irons. Delighted to think that the wonderful Meryl will be in my life if only a tiny bit: I fell in love with her in the TV series *Holocaust*, affection continued when I met her in person at Karel Reisz's: she was so extraordinarily jolly and sensible, despite the porcelain beauty. As for Jeremy Irons, Betsy Reisz and I had constantly pointed out to Karel that he was deeply attractive to women: take it from us.

Flora aged twenty-one and Robert Powell-Jones, a Chancery barrister, got engaged on 29 February and married almost immediately afterwards – for the good old-fashioned reason of being deeply in love; this, despite the fact that Flora was still at Oxford. Although the marriage did not last, and Robert died sadly young, I shall always treasure the memory of that happy time including the years when they came on the FamHol with us, Robert, the polymath, learning local languages with engaging facility and stunning us with the erudition he took for granted.

12 March

In Barbados. At night we discuss biography (prompted by Charles Osborne's life of Auden) and the question of Harold's biography, if any. 'What a morbid subject,' he says. I don't find it so. On the one hand, I never believe anyone I know will die; on the other hand, to me biography (of the dead) is a professional subject, not an emotive one, something to do well if done at all. After much talk it is established that Harold would want a reference to Joan and the off-and-on Seven Years, but his alluring American friend who overlapped should be mentioned under the name of Cleopatra. (I have since met 'Cleopatra' and found her fascinating.) Harold: 'I've had girlfriends since I was thirteen. What about all the others? What about Pauline Flanagan, the Catholic girl I nearly married in Ireland when I was twenty-one?' We agree that if Harold chokes on his local fish tonight, Ronnie Harwood would be the person, because he really understands both the theatre and biography.

Every time I swim out from the villa where the water is deep and turquoise, I think of Eliot's lines: 'I should have been a pair of ragged claws / Scuttling across the floors of silent seas.' Harold in horror: 'You don't mean you saw a pair of claws?' He doesn't think it much better to want to be a pair of claws, despite his love of Eliot.

6 April

First meeting of the Pinters and the Longfords; they come over from Hove to Bernhurst. Jack was in splendid form: 'All politicians are villains, Lord Longford,' he said. 'Take it from me.' And he made his jokes; Harold looked black and everyone else loved them. Frances in her usual sweet way was absolutely out to enjoy herself.

Went to a lecture given by the great Barbara Tuchman, my role model, at the Guildhall. At dinner thereafter, a handsome blond American businessman tries to pick me up then desists, at the sight of my place card. ('I thought you were the sort of girl I could ask to lunch at Bray and now I see you're Lady Antonia Fraser.') Surely a non sequitur?

20 May

Seckford Hall, Suffolk. We are here having one of our breakaways, what Damian calls a PinHol (which is extremely luxurious and *à deux*) as opposed to a FamHol. Damian says that one day when he receives one of my traditional postcards of some idyllic spot with the message 'Wish you were here!' he will just leave school and turn up to gratify my wish. There was something strange and dream-like about our journeyings in East Anglia, in between reading Flaubert's letters, recommended by everyone I know.

26 May

Now it's work – for Harold. We're in Dorset and visiting the sets of *The French Lieutenant's Woman*. The Reiszes are staying in the Dairy House where John Fowles actually wrote the book plus Jeremy Irons plus Master Sam Irons aged eighteen months. The next day is the first day of shooting and later we have dinner with John Fowles. He and I discuss fans' letters which ask for advice. His is, briefly: 'Those who need to ask how to be a writer will never make it.' Mine, to married women wanting to be 'a writer like you': 'You need to be a very, very selfish person.' No doubt households, hitherto peaceful, are being widely disrupted where the wife has taken my advice.

30 May

The film of *Betrayal* is going ahead with Mike Nichols as director. The divorce also really seems to be going ahead; although Vivien once again changes her mind at the last moment and says *she* must be the one to divorce Harold; it must not after all be of his petition as has been arranged – 'Not fair.' 'That's reasonable,' I say to Harold, thinking his dark mutterings on the subject for once unjustified. In a hot week in London – most meals in our garden – I fall platonically in love with Mike Nichols and so, I think, does Harold. We feel in his company that we have become not only more intelligent and even witty (no one is funnier than Mike) but somehow more glamorous.

The marvellous friendship lasted although Mike did not in the end direct *Betrayal*. Other projects fell through but Harold did at least act in a cameo role in *Wit*, directed by Mike Nichols, as the father of the star, his civil rights campaigning friend Emma Thompson. We once stayed with Mike and Diane Sawyer at their house on the Hudson River, where a freshly baked loaf of bread was delivered to our door every morning: although neither Harold nor I ate bread, we agreed it was the acme of luxury.

9 June

Harold criticizes Jonathan Pryce's delivery of 'To Be or Not To Be' at the Royal Court. He spoke the immortal lines directly and burningly to Ophelia, although she is supposed to be off stage, according to Shakespeare's text, in order for Hamlet to greet her entry at the end of the speech: 'Soft you now! The fair Ophelia . . .' Harold: 'When Ophelia says to Hamlet at the end: "Good my Lord, how does your honour?", this Hamlet should have exclaimed: "But I've just been *telling* you in one of the most famous speeches in history."' In short, he admires Jonathan enormously as an actor but not this production: anti-textual interpretations always get his goat. (Later Jonathan did a brilliant Mick

in *The Caretaker* at the National Theatre in which there were absolutely
no anti-textual interpretations.)

11 June

Dame Peggy Ashcroft came to lunch, having indicated that she would
like to do so. So I am FORGIVEN! (She had feared that my arrival as
the first person in Harold's life would disrupt the *amitié amoureuse* both
treasured: which of course it didn't.) She discusses the question of her
biographer. Me: 'Why not have a treat and choose someone really
young?' Peggy, little laugh: 'But one might prefer, you know, someone
who had seen one in one's prime.' That's the trouble. Of all the people
I know Peggy is the only one who treats old age with absolute
astonishment and outrage. It's because she really is so young inside that
she cannot be reconciled to it.

12 June

Dinner with Teresa Gatacre and John Wells who praise us as an
example of domestic bliss because we don't quarrel. Well, not in public!
Me: 'The thing is, we all have to learn how to quarrel, without
quarrelling about it.'

14 June

Official announcement that Hugh is to be knighted: the Wild Knight
we call him. General delight throughout family and friends. 'I hope
they don't think they can muzzle me,' he harrumphs, referring to his
eternally and admirably independent political views. Everyone assures
him this is impossible.

3 July

Harold played in the fathers' match at Colet Court (where Orlando was
just concluding his time). He was evidently chuffed to do so.

6 July

With Isaiah Berlin at Jacob Rothschild's London palace in Maida Vale, after a Brahms concert in the Festival Hall. Me: 'Did Ann Fleming sleep with Hugh Gaitskell?' Isaiah: 'That is a factual question to which there must be an answer: Yes or No.' But we never, in the course of a long and very enjoyable conversation, actually get to it.

9 July

Ann Fleming's party for Angus Wilson's knighthood. A.W. is delighted despite squalid behaviour of newspapers, one daring to call his magnificent, loyal partner Tony Garrett, 'Lady Wilson'. Angus: 'At last I understand what you and Harold went through.' Long talk with Stuart Hampshire about his wife's death: 'I concentrated totally on one individual.' At the end he presses my hand and tells me: 'You mention Harold's name in every sentence. That moves me and cheers me.'

1 August

Harold's divorce actually went through. No fuss, not withdrawn at the last minute, etc. etc. (Vivien believed to be in a caravan in Scotland with her carpenter admirer – good move as it removed her from the clutches of the press). Harold, lying in bed with bronchitis and croaking: 'I'm divorced.' He takes me to the Belvedere Restaurant where he originally proposed. And proposed again. Silence. I thought it over. Then I said yes. Harold: 'My God, I thought you were going to say No.'

14 August

FamHol in the Algarve. Bridge continues to be a feature as we are by now a four and we change partners every rubber. Damian aged fifteen is undoubtedly the best player (plays for Ampleforth), but he feels the necessity for a critical analysis of his partner's play in a way that does not go down well with Harold – or me. It's especially annoying for Damian that a) we are not very responsive to the opportunities he gives us for self-improvement, and b) he's getting lousy cards. So Orlando on points, is consistently the overall winner. Later we go to a Fado-on-the-shore, an exceptionally noisy dance party, since our guidebook says of Fado, 'if you can't beat it join it', and we've already endured one sleepless night. The high point is a sexy Dutchwoman lugging an apparently reluctant Harold on to the floor. She soon regrets her predatory approach when Harold flings himself about, giving it all he's got in true Hackney style (he says), the Baryshnikov of East London now living again in Praia de Luz.

21 September

Harold wrote a radio play *Family Voices* while we were in Praia, and Dame Peg received it with rapture. She will play in it, Peter Hall will direct, also as a Platform at the National. I found a lot of my wistful middle-of-the-night thoughts about Benjie (who spent nine months away as a jackeroo in Australia) mysteriously echoed; yet I had never discussed the subject with Harold.

We had a merry time planning our wedding party at Campden Hill Square: it was to take place on the eve of Harold's fiftieth birthday on 10 October.

26 September

Went to Jean Muir's salon in Bruton Street and had a fitting for my 'wedding dress' – actually a swirling white crepe number, high neck, scattered crystal new moons and stars, which I will wear at the party. I shall feel like Titania.

At 52 Campden Hill Square celebrating the wedding which actually took place six weeks later.

BELOW: In my white Jean Muir 'Titania' dress.

PREVIOUS PAGE: 27 November 1980. The Pinters: leaving Kensington Registry Office.

The Pinters meet the Longfords: Bernhurst, East Sussex, 1980. Jack Pinter, Elizabeth Longford, Frances Pinter, Antonia, Frank Longford, Harold.

At 52 Campden Hill Square. © *Ivan Kyncl*

hn Fowles and Harold during the filming of *The French Lieutenant's Woman.*

Harold and Karel Reisz, the director.

ith Oliver Sacks, City Island, NY, after Harold was inspired by his *Awakenings* to write *A Kind of Alaska.*

Harold showing me Caerhays Castle, Cornwall, where he was evacuated at the beginning of World War II.

Harold at the grave of Tennessee Williams, St Louis, having directed *Sweet Bird of Youth* with Lauren Bacall.

Roger Lloyd Pack, Alan Bates and Harold: cast party at Campden Hill Square after the first production of *One for the Road* which Harold directed at the Lyric Studio, Hammersmith.

The Playwrights' Express comes to Paxos: Simon Gray, Harold, Ronnie Harwood.

LEFT: Doing 'optical research' for my book *The Warrior Queens: Boadicea's Chariot*; Grime's Graves ne
Ixworth.

RIGHT: Harold in the 'cow shed' in Corfu, painted by Elizabeth Longford as he wrote the screenplay f
Kafka's *The Trial*.

It was just as well we planned both the wedding and Harold's birthday together because in the event, there was a final flick of the serpent's tail from Vivien, who refused to sign the decree absolute at the last minute. Even her lawyer was appalled, Harold told me. The cat-and-mouse game was very wearing on all our nerves. But we were able to have a good party all the same, at which most people thought we had actually got married. It was especially pleasing that both sets of parents came: Jack and Frances sat with the latter's brother, Uncle Lou, who assiduously wrote down the names of the guests 'in case I forget'.

Although we did not manage to get married, we went on a not-the-honeymoon to Venice and Palermo where there was a conference about Haroldo Pinter. On the eve of the conference there was an awkward moment when Harold announced he would not attend the discussion about his works due the next morning: 'I can't just sit there, listening to "And you, Harold Pinter ... "' Seeing crestfallen faces, I volunteered cheerfully to attend: after all I hadn't written all the plays ... All went well, except for an annoying English don based in Palermo who insisted on translating for me what I could perfectly well understand, such was the perfection of the academic diction, the rotund flourishes. I asked him to stop translating. That is to say, all went well until the professor reached his peroration. He referred to Pinter's modesty at not being present, and then something I couldn't quite catch. But I was the foremost to clap at the end, clapping ever longer and stronger despite TV camera zooming about (they did seem to be getting very close as I clapped). 'I don't think you quite realize,' hissed my companion, 'that you are clapping yourself. The professor's last words were to say that although we don't have Pinter, we have *sua moglie* – his wife.' Hence the cameras. Of course the irony was that I wasn't actually his *moglie* at this point, but we had drawn a discreet veil over that, due to the general confusion in the newspapers about what did or did not happen on 19 October.

While we were away Harold talked interestingly about Vivien in a way that he had never done before. The resentment that developed in her at his success as early as 1963 onwards. How she scarcely spoke to him for two months because he accepted to act in *Huis Clos* (acting was her thing and in any case that particular director had treated her badly). And then when he himself came to direct! Horrors! Much trouble when he wrote *Landscape* in 1967 and asked Peggy Ashcroft to star instead of her – she thought it was her right. Once again she withdrew into a prolonged enigmatic silence 'which played better on the stage than at home'. Harold spoke of her now – after five years, five very turbulent years – without guilt but with pity. Then he added honestly: 'But she was a great actress, also a wonderful comic talent which people forgot when she was creating the mysterious, sexy Pinter Woman so unforgettably, the way no one could do better.'

27 November – The Diary of Lady Antonia Pinter

That is how I began the entry for our wedding day. Even the surname had a surprise element: I had not really intended to change my name. After twenty-four years Fraser remained of course my professional name despite being that of my first husband; at the time I took comfort from the fact that the great Agatha Christie found herself in exactly the same situation after Colonel Christie vanished and she married Max Mallowan. Later, owing to my great affection for Scotland and Scottish history – to say nothing of the name itself – I tacitly allowed it to be assumed, anyway in the US, that it was in some mysterious way an extra maiden name. On my passport, to avoid confusion over professional journeys and tickets in an age of security, I finally made it one of my forenames. But my witness Emma Tennant gave me a fountain pen with the name Antonia Pinter engraved on it. I took rather a fancy to it, and Harold even more so; quite touchingly, when I realized that both his wife and son had abandoned the name Pinter. So we became – at long last – the Pinters.

The use of 'Lady' in the Diary entry refers to an amusing moment outside the Registry Office. The world's press was in excited attendance, hoping for a dramatic last-minute cancellation as had happened in October. As we left, one optimistic journalist called out: 'How does it feel to be plain Mrs Pinter?' 'She's not,' snapped Harold. The next day the *Daily Mirror* of all people explained the rules of the British peerage to its readers: how 'Lady' came from my father, an earl, not my previous husband, and being purely a 'courtesy' not a real title, I could carry it with me however many times I married. 'Besides,' added the *Mirror* sweetly, 'Lady Antonia is not plain.'

We had already had our honeymoon, which turned out to be not-the-honeymoon. Now we went down to the Bear at Woodstock; the snow had begun to fall all over England (to adapt the passage about Ireland at the end of Joyce's story *The Dead* which Harold loved and was fond of quoting). In the morning, in piercing cold and bright sun, we strode out through Blenheim Park. Peasants, as they seemed to us to be, were gathering wood in the snow round the dark palace in a scene out of Brueghel, or come to think of it, *Dr Zhivago*. That night, I see that we talked about this Diary. I showed the long entry about our wedding to Harold; he applauded it.

28 November

My Diary: it's not about great writing. It's my friend, my record, and sometimes my consolation as in the bad years of 1975/6; while in the last few weeks it has recorded my celebration. Harold: 'Well, it's a great record of – us.'

29 November

Went to lunch with Isaiah and Aline Berlin in Headington. Aline greeted us with champagne: 'We're very much in favour of marriage. We too changed our lives in mid life.' They had been forty-one and forty-seven, she told us; we were roughly the same, forty-two and forty-four when we met.

2 December

Dinner with Claire Bloom and Philip Roth. They presented us with a handsome jar of pot-pourri although Philip disapproves of marriage as he frequently lets the world know. Philip: 'I was married once in 1959. Let me tell you about it. In fact I've written about it.' Typical Roth humour: always very funny (he's marvellous company) but never very far from the works of Roth.

———

At the end of *Long Day's Journey into Night* Mary says: 'I fell in love with James Tyrone and was so happy for a time', a line that has always wrenched me. That was not true of us: we were extremely happy to have achieved at last what we had wanted for so long. And got happier. This is borne out by the stream of cards accompanying flowers, late-night messages, little Valentine boxes, the occasional letter (we were seldom apart) and above all the poems which I treasured. After Harold's death, I found in his desk almost every note or message I had written him over twenty-eight years of married life. My favourite of all the poems he wrote me, 'It Is Here', written a few years later, sums it up:

> What sound was that?
> I turn away, into the shaking room.
> What was that sound that came in on the dark?
> What is this maze of light it leaves us in?
> What is this stance we take,
> To turn away and then turn back?
> What did we hear?
> It was the breath we took when we first met.
> Listen. It is here.

PART TWO

Chapter Nine

Writing Images

Living with Harold the writer was a rewarding experience since he behaved exactly like artists behave in books but seldom do in real life. He never wrote unless he had a sudden inspiration, an image, as he often used to explain. The image might come to him at any time and anywhere – in a taxi, in a bar, late at night at his desk looking out of his window into the street lamps punctuating the darkness. Once or twice I was commissioned to write down a sentence or a phrase. At the same time he worked on his work, as it were, extremely hard. Poems or plays might be dashed off in the first instance but then a process of grind, revision began. One poem took a year to perfect.

He also felt strongly that his characters took on a life of their own which had to be respected. I was reminded of this years later when I read an anecdote about Pushkin during the writing of *Eugene Onegin*: 'Imagine what happened to my Tatiana!' he told a certain princess at dinner. 'She upped and rejected Onegin . . . I never expected it of her.' Harold too believed in the autonomy of Emma and Ruth, Hirst and Spooner, and so forth.

Harold's total seriousness in anything he undertook extended, I began to notice, to his reading. It was not exactly that he never read for relaxation (although he personally might not have recognized reading cricket magazines under that description), more that since he gave every book his close attention, he had no appetite for the delightful genres such as crime and mystery with which I beguiled my leisure hours. He did not understand the mentality of one who was keenly awaiting the publication of the next Lee Child thriller. On one occasion we had dinner *à trois* with Bob Gottlieb in New York: Bob and I spent the whole meal expatiating on the merits of the novelist Joanna Trollope while Harold sat completely bemused (although he admired Joanna Trollope the person for her magnetism).

In other ways, say, directing or writing screenplays, he was extremely diligent as well as serious, in observing a schedule (his own however). He was generous with reading his stuff aloud in the first instance to me, then to anyone who happened to visit the house. Bridge games in which he rejoiced might well end with a reading, as when Joe Brearley, his old English teacher at Hackney Downs died. Harold, who felt he owed much to Joe's encouragement, both as an actor and a reader of literature, immediately wrote a poem when he got the news. I remember the emotion that very night when he subsequently read it aloud to Christopher and Gila Falkus.

JOSEPH BREARLEY 1909–1977
(TEACHER OF ENGLISH)

Dear Joe, I'd like to walk with you
From Clapton Pond to Stamford Hill
And on,
Through Manor House to Finsbury Park,
And back,
On the dead 653 trolleybus,
To Clapton Pond,
And walk across the shadows on to Hackney Downs,
And stop by the old bandstand,
And the quickness in which it all happened,
And the quick shadow in which it persists.
You're gone. I'm at your side,
Walking with you from Clapton Pond to Finsbury Park,
And on, and on.

1981

1 March

We had been married three months. Our visit to Caerhays Castle, Cornwall where Harold had been evacuated 1939–40 (but Harold is imprecise about dates, his mind is not linear). Most unusually Harold then wrote three pages about his experience of evacuation and his impressions of Cornwall in my Diary:-

> The image from childhood is dark green, bottle green, black trunks, vast flowering bushes, along the drive, a prison of green, sudden curtains drawn on the sky, far more sky than had ever been imagined, shut out again by black and green and stone, shut inside the castle, shut inside the castle, long black nights, crash of the sea, misery, strangeness, separation, happiness – rowing across the lake, fish running, seeing live fish for the first time. Not fishing for tiddlers, as in the River Lea in London.
>
> It is still dark green, the hedges, the narrow roads through woods, on the way to the castle. But the sky lighter, flashing, bursts of rain and sunshine.
>
> Something enclosed about the place, private. When I was an inhabitant I couldn't get out. Now I can't really get in.
>
> Somewhere there was a glade. We couldn't find it. Perhaps it was never there.
>
> The whole experience is well lost. It was desolate. But I was scarred by its beauty.
>
> Felt a thousand times happier to be accompanied by my most charming and lovely companion, my wife. If only she had been there then!
>
> (Signed) Harold Pinter

12 March

At the PEN Writers' Day I sat next to Mario Vargas Llosa whose handsome horse-like features and flashing smile made a most favourable impression on me. As a result when he said that he admired Harold's work intensely 'especially *Who's Afraid of Virginia Woolf?*' – which just happens to be by Edward Albee – I merely replied 'Mmm' where a less attractive man might have got a curt correction.

18 March

Harold went to the House of Lords and had lunch with Dada, about the only person not in trouble – so far as we know – to be invited. (Dada's guests tended to be down on their luck for any number of reasons.) He adored it and gave a wonderful description of Dada taking him round the dining room, and introducing him as 'my son-in-law the playwright', mainly to dukes, it seems: he then interrogated them about the amount of Harold's plays they had seen. It was the ladies, or rather the duchesses, who came up trumps, said Harold. Apparently dukes don't do plays. Then a wonderful thing happened. Harold was drinking a glass of port. 'Do you know what that is?' asked Jack Donaldson. 'Dow 1963,' replied Harold with élan. They called for the waiter. 'It's Dow '63,' he replied. General astonishment of all lords and dukes present, even the waiter. Actually Dow '63 is the only port Harold had heard of. But Dada tremendously impressed: he likes the traditional things of his youth. 'My son-in-law, you know, he may be a playwright, but he's a fine judge of port . . .'

27 April

Harold has gone to America for two days (naturally he travels on the day of a Civil Service disruption) about the film of *Betrayal*. Harold remembers it is the five months' anniversary of our wedding and sends me white stocks, roses and freesias with the message, pace *Betrayal*:

'Five months!!!' Robert exclaims to Emma over her affair: 'Two *years*!' I thought as I got into my bed alone that if my marriage only lasts five months, I will have known what it is to be *really* happy.

12 May

Tony Powell came to dinner. It was lovely to see his handsome silver head here again. Tony talked about how good writers should be friends with other good writers, as pretty girls should live together to make them seem prettier. He loved the story of Dada and the port: it is evident that he finds Dada as ridiculous as ever – they were at Eton together – and showed gloomy interest at hearing that Dada now drinks a lot of white wine.

———

I spent a great deal of time that summer preparing my commentary for the Royal Wedding of Prince Charles and Lady Diana Spencer – all very enjoyable and profitable as well – while Harold directed Simon Gray's new play *Quartermaine's Terms*, first of all on tour and then in the West End. We met at the end of the Wedding Day, which began at 5 a.m. for me, at a restaurant. Harold had been having a technical rehearsal of *Quartermaine* which had had its first night postponed from the actual day of the wedding, to his surprise and annoyance: he simply couldn't understand why. When we met, Harold listened to my royal travellers' tales and then asked: 'What is the bride's name?' This – sincere – question illustrated to me Harold's complete indifference to the subject of royalty, beyond a general admiration for the Queen, which meant conversely he was not remotely interested in republicanism. He thought there were other more important topics of dissent to be discussed.

At some point in the ensuing FamHol in Ischia, Harold asked me to write down the words 'Something is happening . . .' because I had a typewriter and he didn't.

13 November

Harold is reading *Awakenings* by Oliver Sacks. Apparently that line which he dictated was an 'awakening' of his own; an idea; one of his images; a woman speaking. But he hadn't read the book, only heard talk about it. Now he's reading the book.

20 December

Harold has written a play, a one-acter, based on the idea of Oliver Sacks' book. I found it very moving, very complete. He read it to me as I lay in my bath. There's always such an exciting feeling in this house when Harold writes. And he's so happy.

25 December

Christmas lunch. Peter Hall and Maria Ewing came. Harold told Peter about the new play and that it would last an hour. Peter smiled in a pasha-like way and said, 'That could be encompassed.'

28 December

The play is now called *A Kind of Alaska*, having had a short period as *A White Tent*. My parents came to dinner and afterwards Harold read the play to them. I was touched by the immense concentration with which Mummy listened, her face getting closer and closer to the script as she leaned forward. She takes an acute interest in Harold's work with occasionally unexpected results. For example, when she watched a video of *The Lover* she was endlessly intrigued by the sexual fantasies played out by the husband and wife. Mummy: 'Did Harold study the subject? Did he read medical books?' Me: '*Mummy*!!!' She adds hastily: 'Perhaps he had a friend with these problems, so that was how he knew.'

1982

5 January

Harold read his new sketch *Victoria Station* to Natasha and me; we howled with laughter. It's based on something that happened to him in a minicab going to see his parents, and drove him to a frenzy. It's twenty minutes so the composite evening is adding up.

12 January

Harold waiting anxiously for Peter Hall's call re *Alaska* and is quite thrilled when Peter announces: 'the first play I've read for ages that has excited me'.

20 January

Every day is Christmas. Peter does like *Victoria Station*: his silence which put Harold in a state of early-to-bed depression was due to his being in Scarborough.

27 February

PEN protest in favour of Solidarity outside the Polish Embassy was one of those things which oddly worked well. Protests in my experience are not always successful as such, although the causes are always good. However in this case Andrew Graham-Yooll got us such good press coverage that maybe our protest will be like the mustard seed in the Bible. News of it went out in Polish on the BBC external service. The weather was freezing. 'Colder in Poland,' says I loyally into one of the many mikes. I have to say that there are more mikes than writers: news reports talk about 100 writers but there were actually 100 journalists performing an excellent service by swelling our ranks.

We congregate on a traffic island outside the Polish Embassy in

Portland Place, on the walls of which I notice a plaque to Field-Marshal Lord Roberts. I point it out to Angus Wilson. 'Little Bobs! Oh, he'd turn in his grave,' says Angus, roaring with laughter. Only three of our number, led by V.S. Pritchett, stalwart figure in his eighties, are allowed inside. Harold and I shiver outside, feeling like the excluded boy on the hillside in the Pied Piper of Hamelin: will we ever see them again? Finally they emerge after a confrontation with a security guard who tries to fob them off with a cultural attaché: 'But this is a political matter,' says Francis King. Finally we go to the pub to warm up, accompanied by someone who I hope will be our new friend: Salman Rushdie. I take an instant fancy to him, helped by my enormous admiration for *Midnight's Children* of course, but fuelled by his warmth and general liveliness. (Always delightful when you like both artist and work, although it doesn't always happen with such perfect synchronicity as it did in Salman's case.) On the way we see a huge bus full of policemen looking menacing. Salman and Harold imagine them getting ready for action: 'Some of these writers can be awful toughs,' Salman pictures them saying. The policemen must have been disappointed by our sober behaviour.

13 March

Worrying moment when Harold is told by a third person that Oliver Sacks objects to his use of 'copyright material'. It was actually the image which inspired Harold not the book (he only read the book when he had roughed out the play). Next day Jonathan Miller acts most helpfully as a go-between and establishes that Oliver Sacks loves the play: calls it 'a work of art'. Life given again to these poor creatures who have mainly by this time lost it. Has written an enthusiastic letter but Harold just hasn't received it. Harold tells me that his heart leaps up when he gets this call.

23 March

Salman and Clarissa Rushdie come to dinner: she has romantic Celtic looks. Towards the end of the evening I nod off. Harold hastens to explain by telling the oft-related story of me sleeping during his sketch-reading, our first night in Launceston Place. Clarissa, brightly: 'Yes, if I ever can't get to sleep, I ask Salman to read to me.'

3 April

Invasion of the Falkland Islands brings political unity to the family lunch table. We listen to the House of Commons debate with approval, Harold's patriotic feelings to the fore. Hateful Fascist Argentina is imposing its evil rule on the poor little Falkland Islanders: 'we should fight.'

10–12 April

Staying at Oare with Henry Keswick and Tessa (born Fraser, Hugh's niece). I've always been deeply fond of Henry, memories of the boy in Scotland, now transformed into the great Taipan of Hong Kong and a noble host. And then Tessa is utterly beguiling, I've always thought, her cat's face, soft cat's purr – and sharp intelligence beneath.

Harold likes them both very much, despite Tessa's very different political views. And how could he *not* be transported by the beauty of Oare, the gardens, the fairyland of magnolias in front of the house, the hillside opening behind and the beauty of the life it provides? Plus every known modern comfort that a returned Taipan can provide. The only trouble is what I call Post-Oare Syndrome when we have to return home at the end of the weekend to a good deal less luxury.

17 April

Damian (aged seventeen and a half) and I went to Paris, representing

Harold at the French opening of *Betrayal*, since Harold is much involved in *Betrayal* the English film. Staying at Harold's expense at the Meurice, taken everywhere by his genial translator Eric Kahane, we decide we can get used to this life.

18 June

To Rome where Harold has been nominated for an Italian Oscar, called a Donatello, for *The French Lieutenant's Woman*. Wherever we go with other nominees, the press push us aside in order to photograph Warren Beatty. I would like to photograph him too as he is absolutely delightful. He has a perfect boy-angel's face, about seven foot of him in a crumpled white suit. Standing in line for the President of Italy's handshake, he murmurs to me: 'If you hadn't met Harold, you would have had a lot of trouble with me.' He adds: 'Do you have a sister? How would she feel about a thirty-eight-year-old Hollywood degenerate?' The man deserves his reputation! Later I watch him working the gold salon, evidently saying something along the same lines to every woman in the room, regardless of age, as a result of which a lot of women are very, very happy. Harold, neurotically later: 'Warren *knew*.' 'Knew what?' 'He knew we walked out of *Reds*.' (As this had been in some obscure English cinema, I thought it unlikely.) Me, firmly: 'We *saw Reds*, Harold, and we loved it.' Harold, with relief: 'Quite right. It all comes back to me. All three hours of it.'

29 July

Off to the US for a FamHol, fixed up in the spring when Harold had a play on in Rhode Island and I took the opportunity to rent a house. Harold, sleepily, the morning of our departure: 'East, West, home's best. Won't it be wonderful when we get back from America and you say that?'

This more or less represented Harold's view on travel, especially since it always seemed that dreadful unexpected things that did not happen to other travellers, happened to him. Nevertheless a good time was had by all, the boys in their casual breakfast wear – shorts and that's it – transfixing the visiting Mrs Gandhi's security guards at the Carlyle Hotel on the way, and the house by the sea, with its old books and faded flowered covers reminding me of Eilean Aigas in Scotland. The sea in which I persistently swam, to the bafflement of the courteous local inhabitants, was so cold that the boys screamed with pain and wished, they said, for the Pacific.

5 August

Incident at dinner left me shaken. An extremely gracious dinner at which only Harold is not wearing a tie. Many tables. Harold and I are separated. Suddenly I notice Harold's black face and think someone has raised the subject of El Salvador. Later I learn that an old, rather drunken man has made a series of remarks described as 'Fascist' but actually blaming the Jews for starting both world wars. Harold, very wearily as he said later, feels he cannot let this pass. Hostess naturally very upset (at the drunken man, who was described as 'a bit of a lunatic', not Harold). Harold tells me the worst moment is overhearing someone explaining to the 'Fascist' that he, Harold, is Jewish, as if that was in any way the point. Having recorded this, I should also record that the next day at Bailey's Beach Harold was the centre of polite and sincere attention, and every single person who had been at the dinner came and apologized formally and sweetly. One Senator's wife said she spoke 'on behalf of Rhode Island'.

27 August 1982

My fiftieth birthday. Harold has brought us all to the North British Hotel, Edinburgh. I'm probably one of the luckiest women to be fifty.

To be happily married, no, very happily married to someone who is the centre of my life, to have six of the best in the way of children. Harold of course tells me that I look twenty-seven, and when I say, 'Oh, come on,' and he replies, 'Well, thirty-seven then,' I'm affronted and find I prefer twenty-seven after all.

Picnic on King Arthur's Seat. I see Benjie after a long gap because he has been working in Scotland and going to a restaurant without my glasses, cry out: 'My son, my son!' A total stranger rises from his seat and says, 'I've always wanted to have a mother.' Benjie looks incredibly well and handsome when I do manage to find the right person: how could I have been mistaken?

9 October

World premiere of *Other Places* at the NT, the overall title for *A Kind of Alaska*, *Victoria Station* and *Family Voices*. I suppose I will see *Alaska* many, many times in my life with many, many actresses but I shall never see the experience of Deborah more simply, perfectly and painfully created than by Judi Dench. Those first movements after twenty-nine years asleep: the little broad child-woman, stubby legged, strong as an animal, balancing, unbalancing, falling. And at the end, after the regression (totally convincing, it was happening to *her*) those last, sad words of a woman going back into the void: 'I think I have the matter in proportion.' Pause. 'Thank you.'

14 October

Press night. I began to sob, silently I hope, during Judi's last agonizing, heart-rending speech, and as we got into the little manager's office afterwards, collapsed in floods. Peter and Jenny Hall backed out hastily, thinking they had walked in on some personal tragedy: 'The play, the play–' I wept.

Dr Oliver Sacks came from the US and this was the beginning of the privilege of his friendship. Later Harold gave him dinner, together with his close friends Jonathan and Rachel Miller. Harold asked Ollie: 'May I ask what it is you *do*?' He meant: 'Do you plan to cure people, do good, alleviate, or make medical discoveries?' Ollie responded with a long letter. I get a helpful book on migraine from him which helps me to understand this wretched condition from which I am a mild and my mother a serious sufferer.

1983

I record in my Diary in 1983 that 'our bridge is strangely brilliant these days'. We win and win, defeating far better players like Peter Jay and Hugh Stephenson and the Waldegraves. I write a poem for our wedding anniversary which expresses my romantic feelings about our union in that respect (as Susanna Gross says much later: bridge, because it's about partnership, is a romantic game).

FOR MY PARTNER

You're my two-hearts-as-one
Doubled into game
You're my Blackwood
You're my Gerber
You're my Grand Slam, vulnerable
Doubled and redoubled
Making all other contracts
Tame.

27 November 1983

24 January

Went for a walk with Harold in Kew Gardens in winter sunshine. A notice runs: 'The wildlife may attack you at certain seasons of the year.' Harold points to it: 'But I am in a mellow mood.' A placid meander: vivid yellow witch hazel, and the huge lovely new temperate plant house.

3 February

In Jamaica where Harold's old school friend (co-evacuee to Caerhays) Maurice Stoppi now lives with his wife, Tiny Henriques – and she is tiny, also exquisite with speedwell blue eyes behind her Christian Dior sunglasses. Maurice vividly remembers Harold as a little boy of ten with a shiny black cash notebook, scribbling stories in it with the stub of a pencil: 'Cars screeched down the streets of Chicago and there was the rat-a-tat of cross machine-gun fire', etc. Taxed Harold with this later: 'Your first work?' 'I do remember the notebook. My father gave it to me. He nicked a bundle of those notebooks from the ARP station where he was a warden in the Blitz. So I must have wanted to write something.'

Harold now writes the first of many little poems about my habit of swimming which intrigues him (he himself rarely swims; when he does it's with a great splashing like a dog retrieving a ball). It includes the lines: 'How you swim / Like a flower / Unfolding forever'. Then he reads me 'Dover Beach', and he proceeds to make it his task to learn it by heart. Later he talks about his current inability to write since the death of Vivien six months earlier. All he can do is write a private poem about his happiness with me but: 'Happiness is not dramatic,' he says sternly. Harold: 'While she was alive, if you think about it, so much of my work was about unhappy frozen married relationships.' He gives the example of *Landscape* and the wife's retreat at the end into memories of a happy marriage-that-never-was. Harold: 'I could never write the Strindberg thing. It's not my way. Not the way of my art anyway. Too cruel.'

17 February

New York on the way back. Poor Harold arrives with a serious chest infection which does not help him to face the ceremonies arranged by Sam Spiegel for the launch of the film *Betrayal* with equanimity. The best thing that happens to us is having dinner in Soho with Oliver Sacks. This is the place where he comes and sits in a booth and just scribbles and scribbles: 'I always have a notebook and pen with me. The pen must be green.' For me, meeting Ollie is like having bumped into a prophet by chance. Harold *very* ill, almost floating with it but groans: 'I'm sorry you're not having a nice time.' As though *he* was. Actually meeting Ollie is as nice a time as anyone could possibly have.

——

The next year we went to City Island to see him. He was standing bear-like as ever, in the porch of his little dark-red clapboard house, smiling in the sunshine. Harold swears his first words were: 'And so . . .' The house was extremely close to the sea and Ollie told us that he swims in and out of the moored boats like a seal.

18 February

Sam Spiegel arranges a two-hour press conference. Harold cuts and runs, to find me just finishing lunch with the distinguished scholar Elaine Pagels. We are discussing the asceticism of the Jewish–Christian tradition, and how St Augustine thought that in Paradise there would have been no desire, thus no pleasure in sex; thus pleasure in sex is wrong. Despite the sheer fascination of this conversation, Harold went upstairs and collapsed. I learned later that the questioning went like this: Man: 'The first performance of *The Caretaker* was at the Royal Court, wasn't it?' Harold: 'No.' Man: 'What is interesting is that my father had a pub just round the corner from the Royal Court.' Harold: 'Oh.' He flees and meets second interviewer in the lift. Second interviewer: 'Ho, ho, now you can't escape me.' Harold: 'Oh, yes I can,' and so on. And so he did.

15 March

Rebecca West dies. I felt oddly sad, despite her great age – no feelings like 'She had a good life.' More: 'Why couldn't it go on?' She was always very nice to me. Unlike the rest of the world, I think she liked our 'scandal' and identified with it! I always remember her in a taxi after we judged the Booker Prize together. She asked me about *Mary Queen of Scots*, newly published: 'Are you making lots of lovely money?' Me: 'Well, certainly more than I've ever had.' Rebecca: 'Then *spend* it' – said triumphantly – 'while you are young and pretty.' Nothing Puritan about her.

19 May

Harold's anvil is beginning to strike sparks. At Le Caprice, he starts to talk about a play about imprisonment and torture: 'These people would be very aware of their condition ... wryly so. Nothing explicit. No blood, no torture scene.' Me: 'Quick, quick, there must be a paper and pencil here. This is Le Caprice, Jeffrey Archer's favourite restaurant.' Harold then cites the end of Jacobo Timerman's book about being a political prisoner in the Argentine. He describes a woman taken down from her cell for the morning session. The guard is heard saying: 'Hurry up, you stupid bitch.' She's never seen again.

This was the first sighting of the play that became *One for the Road* but the image vanished until the following January.

9 June

General Election. Harold and I toddled up the hill to Fox Primary

School to vote. He finally decided to vote SDP as a protest against the Tories, and also against Labour's dishonesty over nuclear weapons (Healey and co. not telling the truth whichever way you look at it).

23 July

The Guardian Match (Harold's own XI against the newspaper's team). As Simon Gray, ever to the point, said: 'The Guardian Match is like Christmas, all that anticipation, dread, drama, regret, disappointment, pleasure – and then it's over.' It's true. Like Christmas, the Guardian Match, in my mother's favourite rhyme, 'comes but once a year but when it comes it brings good cheer'. Buffet here first in garden, including Ossie Gooding, the prized West Indian bowler, and Benjie, specially here from Scotland. At the match all three boys play. As Hugh specifically broke away from Ascot and 'the Big Race' in order to see his three sons performing, it was written in the stars that all three (normally accomplished players) should get ducks. But Hugh in genial mood nonetheless. His appearance was much appreciated by all and he marched about pouring tea for the cricketers out of the huge teapot with much vigour as though this was a constituency event; he particularly liked Ossie Gooding with whom he was able to discuss the West Indies, where he had gone many times as Under-Secretary at the Colonial Office.

26 July

In Chichester to see Patricia Hodge, heroine of both the film *Betrayal* and the TV series *Jemima Shore Investigates*, as Rosalind, a ravishing girl by Watteau come to life. I dashed into Chichester Cathedral at 9 a.m. while Harold bought some shoes nearby, in his eternal quest for a good pair of shoes (shades of Davies in *The Caretaker*). A strange mystical experience. For I saw for the first time the Earl and Countess of Arundel lying in stone. Larkin's poem to their joint tomb was pinned to a nearby pillar. Their hands were touching. 'All that remains of us is love.' Deeply moved. Flew to the shoe shop and extricated Harold who clearly thought it was a little early in the morning for all this. Other thoughts were running through his head, to do with plastic bags of shoes and American Express, while I meditated soppily on our 'stone fidelity'. Finally he did put down the shoes and he did recite the poem and all was well. So in a way, the faint absurdity, it was quite a Larkinesque scene, if not quite in the touching romantic way I had originally imagined.

27 November

Gave a party for our third wedding anniversary. Everyone commented on the congenial atmosphere. Rachel pointed out that everyone we asked (the first fifty people who came into my mind) was creative. True when I looked: whether Jean Muir or Alan Bates.

1984

6 January

Harold has a row with two Turkish girls on the subject of torture at a family birthday party; ('little monsters'). I fell asleep afterwards and awoke to hear Harold saying 'I'm writing.'

7 January

Late at night Harold comes back from the Super-Study: 'I'd like to read it to you.' And oh my God! It's all there – power and powerlessness. I dreamed about it in agonies all night. My personal nightmare: powerlessness to protect those you love. Harold will call it *One for the Road*: he used Anglo-Saxon names to make it universal 'although such things don't usually happen here'. Goes through names of cricketers. I stop him when he starts choosing a name for the child. The child is not seen (thank heaven). But Harold changes his mind: 'No, I'll have the child there.' And writes a new scene there and then, producing the most chilling line of all: 'My soldiers don't like you either, my little darling.' Harold: 'It feels so good to write. I'd forgotten.' Me, feelingly: 'Well, you haven't lost your touch, to put it mildly.'

15 February

Paris. Pinter to Beckett (in the Coupole) after talking for some time about politics: 'I'm sorry, Sam, if I sound very gloomy.' Beckett to Pinter: 'Oh, you couldn't be more gloomy than I am, Harold.' It's exactly the sort of dialogue people would imagine the two masters having when alone. Beckett shows extraordinarily good manners in waiting for me and Damian, late in arrival, and then talking knowledgeably to Damian about rugger.

13 March

First public preview directed by the author of *One for the Road*. I understood why Andrew Graham-Yooll's wife had to leave: 'She felt we might so easily have been the parents of Nicky.' During rehearsals I had watched the two little boys who shared the part of Nicky (according to regulations) playing tag all round the theatre. I wanted to cry out: 'Oh, run away, run away, you don't know what is going to happen to you.' Alan Bates as Nicolas: I suppose it's the most terrifying performance I have ever seen. Harold has written two plays within two years, the most moving part for a woman, the 'frozen' Deborah in *A Kind of Alaska*, and the most terrifying part for a man, that of Nicolas. The actors refused even to take a bow. They felt it would be wrong. Harold says: 'I'm letting them off today. I'll put it back tomorrow.' The play was actually performed at lunchtime, which added in a strange way to the emotion of it all. Emerging after such a powerful experience into the daylight of King Street, a Hammersmith shopping street, was in itself weirdly dislocating. 'There's Marks and Spencer's, people look unmoved and busy, don't they know ... ?'

As to the character of Nicolas, Simon Gray who had played a conclusive part in persuading his great friend Alan Bates to take the role, had described it to him, after reading the play, as a 'Dickensian role . . . school of Fagin'. All I can say is that in performance, the grotesque and thus humorous Faginesque element which one had read in the text seemed to vanish in view of what happened to the man, the woman and above all the child: the ruined family.

15 March

Shattering press night – or rather press lunch – of *One for the Road*. It's worse when you know what's coming, the boy's fate, the poor wrecked woman – as I suppose torture is worse when you wait for it. This morning Michael Billington in the *Guardian* asks for a precise political location – wants to know exactly what these people have done – and then complains that Harold has lost the mystery. Surely the whole point is that everything horrific is performed off stage and thus resides in our imagination, all the more haunting for that.

14 April

We gave a lunch, which turned out to take place in the garden at Campden Hill Square, to mark the end of the run of *One for the Road*. For once Nature was not out to thwart us, so we were able to give a party when the garden was flourishing and not 'between seasons' as generally happens: there were masses of very dark blue hyacinths, daffodils, tall ones, all kinds of pink camellia including the ravishing 'Countess Lavinia'. The actors brought their children who gambolled about, Roger Lloyd Pack's son Spencer, Jenny Quayle's Jack and Alan's handsome tall dark-haired twin sons Ben and Tristram. I felt that the presence of these children defused the grim experience we had all been through.

Chapter Ten

Unreasonable but Right?

Politics began to feature increasingly in Harold's life now that he had become, in his oft-repeated words, 'the luckiest man in the world'. I sometimes speculated whether this interest would have arisen earlier, if he had not been occupied with his own demons, wrestling with them in his work. It has to be said that this was not a popular move in the general estimation. Critics who had not previously regarded his plays particularly highly, asked him to go back to writing them in the old way. One might adapt the saying 'Nobody liked it but the public' as follows: 'Nobody liked Harold's frequent stands on human rights – except the people he was defending.'

Nevertheless Harold strongly rebutted the idea that the artist was honour-bound to stick to his art and had no duties as a citizen. He believed the artist had in fact special duties just because he was at the same time a citizen: it was a concept he would stress with increasing conviction as time passed. On the other hand there would always be people, not necessarily critics, who believed Harold represented his public stances best by simply writing plays and otherwise shutting up: in short, leave politics to the politicians. (This was my father's view, for he believed innately that the House of Lords was the correct forum for any political debate and could never understand Harold's total lack of any desire to belong to it) He was even accused of 'taking advantage' of his position as a playwright of world-wide renown, for it was possible to argue like many other artists in the past and Arthur Miller in his own day, that Harold was more popular abroad than in his own country. Harold accepted the charge with joy.

I should point out that there was nothing superficial about this interest. Harold spent a large proportion of his day, it seemed to me, studying these things; the Super-Study in Aubrey Road gradually became a kind of emporium of Human Rights literature and books. This was the substance, the backing, behind the speeches, demonstrations and appearances on TV calling attention to a wide number of issues.

However, not everyone who found themselves having a political discussion with Harold in the eighties and nineties, believed that he or she was the luckiest person in the world. I note from my Diary that Harold had a row with Joan Didion in New York as early as January 1981 about US policy towards El Salvador. She countered: 'What about the Malvinas?' (the Falkland Islands: Britain's attitude to them). Joan told him, or he told her, or both, that the other was 'unreasonable' but of course they embraced warmly on departure.

Unreasonable, but was he right? Harold countered this by asking: 'Why don't they concentrate on what I'm angry about?' Certainly the accusation of being 'unreasonable' or 'irrational' was often flung at Harold in political discussions, even, it has to be said, by myself: 'How can you ignore the fate of writers in Cuba ...' (After Harold died, among the little souvenirs he had kept in his desk I found a place card for some long-forgotten dinner party marked 'Antonia' in an italic hand. There had clearly been some row on the opposite side of the table. On the back I have scribbled: 'Darling – You are right. So SHUT UP.' This certainly represented my own attitude upon occasion: I felt both honoured and touched to find that Harold had treasured the card.)

In fact Harold's efforts in the world of international protest concentrated on three main areas. First, there was Latin and South America, with a special interest in Nicaragua. Then there was Eastern Europe and the fate of the dissidents, with a special interest in Czechoslovakia. Lastly there was Turkey. Although these campaigns brought him different allies (Eastern Europe was viewed far more sympathetically by our English friends than Latin America), I could see, when I was in a detached frame of mind, that it was not a question of reason or the lack of it with Harold. He felt profoundly about justice world-wide, and equally detested authoritarianism wherever he perceived it, as he had done since his East End youth: his Conscientious Objection to National Service when he was eighteen being probably the earliest public manifestation of that. Much later I told an interviewer that Harold questioned all rules except the rules of cricket – which just about summed it up.

In the spring of 1985 Harold visited Turkey with Arthur Miller on behalf of PEN International, to protest against the imprisonment and torture of intellectuals. Their guide incidentally was a young writer called Orhan Pamuk.

22 March

Ulysses is back with his Penelope. Gives me the details of the trip. The wives of imprisoned writers and journalists come hundreds of miles once a month to queue all day for three to five minutes' talk; during this day's wait, they are harassed by Doberman Pinschers (several bitten) to give sport to the soldiers. As always, it's the small details – if a dog bite is a small detail – which are so appalling.

Harold: 'And at every meeting, dinner, lunch, you encounter the ruined lives.' He means the people who have been imprisoned and tortured, some by now just in a trance. Harold admired Arthur more and more throughout the trip: his complete integrity and cheerful independence. Even when the American Ambassador in effect threw Harold out of the Embassy over his 'offensive' remarks on the subject of torture, Arthur insisted on leaving too. On quite a different level, Harold gained an understanding of what Arthur goes through.

The woman journalist (on a right-wing paper) who concluded the interview in her office by producing a half-clothed photograph of Marilyn Monroe. 'Mr Miller, may I be photographed with you, holding this?' Answer: NO!

24 March

Harold has just heard from Mehmet Dikerdem, the son of the former Ambassador who had been a victim of a show trial in Turkey, that he and Arthur have been proscribed by military decree in Turkey, following their press conference. (Arthur came back here and gave a stirring speech about Turkey at PEN's Writers' Day: How America is pumping millions of dollars of arms into it.)

———

The next play that Harold wrote, *Mountain Language*, arose directly out of his feeling for the oppressed Kurds: he learnt that the Kurdish language was forbidden, even among Kurds themselves, and Harold saw in this a bleak symbol of oppression which was always so tightly connected in his mind to language. He began it immediately after his return to England and then put it away until 1986.

3 April 1986

Harold has resurrected *Mountain Language*, taken it out of its drawer and rewritten it. It's short, powerful, terrible. He had called it 'a cartoon' when he first wrote it. Now he has explicitly withdrawn that.

15 April

Harold's cheerfulness is delightful. 'I've written a play!' Also to be at the National, so good actors guaranteed and perhaps even the great Miranda Richardson so long coveted by Harold for one of his plays. So what was apparently a few pages, in 1985, then a quiver of the Muse at the Battersea Arts Centre during a Marguerite Duras play, is now a jewel. (Pretty upsetting jewel too.) Simon Gray compares it to a poem by Browning: very apt. So I am learning 'Porphyria's Lover' as a tribute, my latest attempt to combat insomnia with Positive Thinking above lying awake.

18 October

'Please say thank you to your husband.' These words, said by a middle-aged woman, foreign, German Jewish at a guess, seem to sum up what Harold has done with *Mountain Language*. Of course there will be other very different reactions and I gather from Richard Eyre (Director of the National Theatre) there have been already. But what I saw that first Monday at 6.15 spoke for all women outside all prisons. The performances were of a strength which even given Harold's committed direction – committed to perfection – took me by surprise. Eileen Atkins, with only two lines to speak but an infinity of expressions, was the star. About the same period Harold gives an interview to *Omnibus*. Afterwards he gets a stack of letters: 'At last someone has spoken out . . . I have been feeling voiceless, but now you . . .' His political stance is widely described as 'courageous'. But Harold didn't have to be courageous to take a stance, he just had to be Harold! He loves speaking out against the established order; it comes naturally to him.

An extraordinary incident eight years later brought the relevance of *Mountain Language* – even in England – sharply into focus.

22 June 1996

Some unfortunate Kurds, in exile in North London, performed *Mountain Language*, having hired stage guns from the National Theatre. They were all arrested by thirty to forty armed police. Who refused to read the National Theatre weapon-certificate of harmlessness. And what is more – this is the unbelievable fact – refused to allow them to speak Kurdish to one another. Talk of life imitating art . . .

5 July

We went to see this *Mountain Language* in Hoxton. A ramshackle hall and rooms in a little street, guarded by a very young soldier in camouflage uniform and with a machine gun. Many Kurdish women and children: an impression of very pale faces, heart-shaped, big dark eyes, strongly marked eyebrows, not very tall but well made. Rana Kabbani told me once that the famous Circassians, from whom the most beautiful members of the harem were taken, were actually Kurds. The performance began with the terrifying enactment of what had happened to them the other night, which also acted all too neatly as a Prologue to Harold's play. During the play itself, however, they actually showed the torture, which, as ever with Harold, according to the text, was supposed to take place off stage. Afterwards I congratulated the actor via an interpreter and told him he was 'very convincing'. Actor: 'It was easy for me to be convincing because I myself was tortured just like that.'

———

In general, however, taking part in marches and demonstrating outside embassies, whether to protest the imprisonment of poets such as the Russian Irina Ratushinskaya and the Malawian Jack Mpanje or the fate of the people of the East Timor, filled one with a proper sense of gratitude at living in England with the privilege of speaking up. As to the efficacy of such things, it was well put by Christopher Hampton when, along with other members of English PEN, we were getting together a fund-raising evening known as *The Night of the Day of the Imprisoned Writer*: 'If one guard kicks one prisoner less hard, it will have been worth it,' he said.

And there were the lighter moments as when I found myself marching with Ian McEwan, Caroline Blackwood and other writers, carrying white flowers for peace, in the general direction of 10 Downing Street. (Having chosen to parade with a long white lily, I felt like the Angel Gabriel in a pre-Raphaelite picture about to annunciate something or other.) The policeman who was walking alongside us asked me: 'What's the name of that gentleman ahead? I know his face awfully well from this kind of thing.' Me: 'E.P. Thompson, author of *The Making of the English Working Class*.' Policeman: 'Of course it is. He's a very nice gentleman. Never any trouble.'

11 September 1986

Marched with Harold and members of the Solidarity Committee to mark the thirteenth anniversary of the Chilean anti-Allende coup. Sunlit day. Me to fellow marcher: 'I like the architectural view of London you get walking slowly down the middle of a main road.' Fellow member: 'It makes a change from shouting "Maggie out! Maggie out!"' We are led by Chilean girls, black scarves over thick tumbling black hair: they are in mourning. We carry banners with photographs of the Disappeared on them. Policemen escort us from Portman Square to Devonshire Street and guard us from the traffic. I think what it must be like to march and know you will be *attacked* by the same policemen who are courteously guarding us.

Less satisfying – in that it is difficult in retrospect to see that it achieved anything at all except some hot-air balloons rising – was our experience with the so-called June 20 Group.

19 March 1988

Dinner at Kensington Place restaurant on the night of the Budget given by John and Penny Mortimer. A lot of discussion about the fall in the top rate of tax: John Mortimer as always speaks out where others don't have his frankness. How he'll benefit. I mutter that Nigel Lawson should have helped the Health Service as well, which is a sort of cop-out.

Out of this dinner came the idea of an Arts/Politics discussion group. I told John Mortimer, whose idea it was, that there has been just such a group, but High Tory, held at Campden Hill Square by Hugh. John Casey, who attended it, and adored Mrs Thatcher, told me of how she sat on the sofa (now my sofa again): 'To think her hips sat on that sofa–' Me: 'And did those hips in ancient time?' Our group became known as the June 20 Group after the date of the first meeting. In a move I subsequently came to regret, I offered our house for the first exploratory meeting – the regret was due to the fact that the group became inevitably identified with us, rather than the body of other writers it included, led by John Mortimer.

Monday 20 June

The dinner. We have decided to meet again in September. So that's what came out of it. On the subject of censorship, personally I would have liked us to have made ourselves more of a philosophy group – for that's what's lacking – whereas pressure against censorship is almost universal and most of us present spend a great deal of time signing letters, etc. on the subject. But I noticed there was a division between those who wanted it to be a purely writers' discussion group and those – particularly those who were not writers themselves – who thought we would be affiliated in some way to the Labour Party. Nevertheless the evening was very jolly: twenty-one people. Tony Howard addressed us for forty minutes – a bit long – and made one provocative statement: 'How can any of you write for the Murdoch press?' John Mortimer, leading reviewer for the *Sunday Times*, merely smiled. Germaine Greer, *sotto voce*, well, just about: 'How can anyone employed by Tiny Rowland (i.e. the *Observer*) protest to us about writing for the *TLS*?' Later when they had all gone, Harold read Shakespeare's sonnets to me with the perfume of my regale lilies, especially strong this year, filling the drawing room. That was really the best part of the evening.

Later I record the last meeting in our house. I am convinced that pro- portionately we now have far too many journalists and political com- mentators, and too few real writers. After all, those commentators have plenty of outlets. The best intervention came from David Hare about the meaning of political action as he saw it, to help the working class to escape from restrictions. But that's the end of it for us. Future meetings will be elsewhere. At least we 'were the first that ever burst into that sunless sea; a Labour philosophy group as opposed to a Tory one. Even though it's been a failure, I'm proud of that.

Looking back on it (and reading the Diary entries) I can see the fact that it was much mocked by the press was really the most sociologically interesting thing about the whole enterprise: in the summer of 1988, there was considered to be something absurd about any kind of theoretical talk which was not Tory.

In 1989 we gave a party at Campden Hill Square for Daniel Ortega on his visit to London, as President of Nicaragua. Harold had visited the country the year before and was active in its defence.

Sunday 7 May

Blessed by golden weather – *Viva Nicaragua!* Graham Greene was the big thrill for everyone, green-eyed, red eye-balled, a *hero* since he had cracked his rib in his hotel but insisted on coming despite his age – mid eighties. Melvyn Bragg, Peter Stanford, young editor of the *Catholic Herald*, Bianca Jagger plus surprise guest of her daughter Jade, aged fourteen, the famous Jagger mouth, very nice manners; Rosanna Arquette, tiny, blonde, exquisite mouse, and at least twelve more Nicaraguans than we had bargained for. Then Harold had pleaded for no more than five Special Branch but they filled the hall, the house, everywhere, quite apart from the Nicaraguans, who had broad shoulders, short, very handsome broad faces. Indeed Nicaraguans in general are a very good-looking race viz. Bianca and Daniel Ortega himself. We stood at the drawing-room window and witnessed the motorcade: flashing lights, men on motorbikes, sirens, then dozens of people hustled out of two huge super-limos, all in dark suits except for Daniel Ortega, in khaki, red flash on shoulder, very neat, the famous big sunglasses. Apparently he gets all of this from the British government as a head of state – even a revolutionary state! Rosario

Murillo (his lady) short very curly hair, mini skirt, enormous eyes, even larger earrings.

Daniel makes a very long, very serious speech. All agree: 'A really straight man.' I asked a question about the Arts: after all this was supposed to be an Arts for Nicaragua occasion. He looked rather surprised: 'The revolution is the real cultural contribution of Nicaragua' was his instinctive reaction before going on to emphasize the general freedom of the arts in Nicaragua. Rosario, who is Minister of Culture, tried to add to this but was shut up by Harold under the impression she was Bianca Jagger. President Ortega was overheard having a discussion with Nathalia (our housekeeper) about the recipe for her Portuguese pancakes. It was only the next day that I listened to two of our neighbours talking on their roof – the weather remained intensely hot and still. One said to the other, indicating our garden: 'You see, I could have taken out Daniel Ortega.'

Where protest was concerned, both Harold and I were absolutely straightforward in our reaction to the *fatwa* against our friend, Salman Rushdie.

We were actually in Venice in January 1989 when we got the first inkling that something extraordinary – and horrible – might be happening. We were there for Harold to imbibe local atmosphere as he wrote the screenplay for Ian McEwan's *The Comfort of Strangers*. In the mornings Harold sat around in his black silk dressing-gown at the Hotel Danieli 'thinking of ways to kill Colin' as he put it, referring to the unfortunate doomed young man in Ian's novel. It was extremely foggy and you could not see across the lagoon, which seemed appropriate enough for this sinister, compelling tale of the backwaters of Venice.

In the afternoon, I became pathfinder and led us through the murk towards the Zattere. We were rewarded by the dazzling, sparkling sun which suddenly found us there and we emerged on the side of the water blinking like the prisoners in *Fidelio*. Harold was moved to quote Yeats saying that you had to choose between life and art, but he didn't see the

necessity provided he could sit on the Zattere with me in th
winter sun, look across to the Palladian churches on the Giudecca . . .
and drink Corvo Bianco. This elegiac mood was splintered when we
watched Salman's book *The Satanic Verses* being publicly burned in
Bradford to the accompaniment of raucous shouts. We gazed uncom-
prehendingly. Was this really happening in England? We were both old
enough to have been told that people had quoted Heine in the 1930s
about Germany and the rise of Nazism: 'Wherever books are burnt,
men, also, in the end are burned.'

We were leaving Bruce Chatwin's memorial service in the Moscow
Road, Bayswater on 14 February when the actual news of the *fatwa* was
published. A member of the press approached Harold as he was leaving
the Greek Orthodox Church and surprised him by asking him if he was
Salman Rushdie. 'No look behind you,' I said, jokingly, pointing to
Tom Maschler. We were told the hideous truth at the wake for Bruce.
Thereafter, in my desperate wish to do something, it was at least con-
soling to be the current president of English PEN, the international
writers' organization. At least I was able to lead deputations to two
successive foreign secretaries on the subject. On one occasion the
Foreign Secretary said to me as we all gathered in the extremely gracious
official drawing room: 'I believe Mr Rushdie is not *too* uncomfortable.'
He spoke in a patrician tone which somehow implied that Salman, a man
of substance both by upbringing and by his own achievements, was
enjoying running water for the first time in his life.

Naturally Harold's concern for all the issues involved – justice to the
individual against an authoritarian decree and the whole question of free
speech – made him vehement in public defence of Salman. It was an
unequivocal issue for him. It wasn't a question of any political party.
I tried explaining this to Tony Powell when I had lunch with him. 'These
days I only come up to London for the dentist and Mrs Thatcher,' he
told me. 'I'm madly keen on her,' he says. 'It's like being eighteen again,
as I desperately try and think of things to interest her.' He went on: 'Of
course I hear that your and Harold's politics these days are practically
Militant Tendency.' Me: 'Oh, far to the left of that.' Then he asked

how Harold fitted his admiration for Larkin with the latter's politics. I explained that Harold's views on literature were quite unaffected, so far as I could see, by his views on social justice, in fact justice in general. He maintained them quite independently without being troubled by the fact that, for example, Eliot's views on many things would have been very different from his own.

26 February

Tough week. I can't relate in detail the many, many meetings, calls and manoeuvres. Harold constantly on TV to the extent that worried people rang me up. Highlights: good row with Dada (Mummy on my side) who is in favour of a *strong* anti-blasphemy law. Much international action: Harold spent all Friday getting Beckett's signature. Right-wing press, predictably, manages to condemn a) Islam b) Salman c) anyone, i.e. us, who supports him d) the feebleness of the intellectuals' response in *not* supporting him.

28 February

Moving moment at 12.30 when telephone rang: 'Antonia, it's Salman . . .' His distress that in England only, people have found it *de rigueur* to rubbish the book, while defending his right to publish it. It's all right to say this to me because he knows that Harold and I liked his work even before we liked *him*. Then he adds he has been taken down from Danger One to Danger Two. Me: 'Congratulations! I suppose.'

4 March

Writers' Day (PEN). Sweet, cosy, humorous speech by P.D. James and a fine one from Chinua Achebe. Though some members wanted 'a survey of African literature', I preferred his discussion of the roots of imaginative literature. The questions included one referring to Salman about the artist's *responsibility* as well as the artist's freedom. In reply Harold made a fine speech about Salman being in the Joycean tradition.

6 March

No one talks about anything else except the Rushdie affair, but rather like Suez in 1956, you can't immediately predict exactly what the reaction will be. A Muslim woman friend said she had been surprised both ways by Bernard Lewis who she thought would be favourable to Salman and Edward Said who she thought would not. I tell her that beneath most people's attitudes, if you know them, you can discern other very deep-seated convictions they have always had. An example: Harold's rejection of the dominance of the Jewish religion in his youth, is there somewhere; as well as his feeling for the plight of the artist.

7 March

Salman rings up. 'Antonia I have a favour to ask you.' He wants to come and spend the night to see his son and meet his own family.

12–13 March

The visit. We arranged for the entire equipage to be downstairs in the more or less self-contained basement, in order to have some privacy, not quite realizing that there is not and should not be, any such thing as privacy from Special Branch. Although they were – and are, I'm writing this with them still in the house – amazingly tactful.

At 12.15 p.m. a ring on the front door bell, an hour early. Rushed to it. I see an enormous, handsome, burly black man with a broad smile: 'Lenny . . . Special Branch.' He showed me his card, adding: 'You've got visitors.' He went over the garden to the Super-Study, where Salman in a red beret and scarf with his wife Marianne were let in the back way. Much drawing of our curtains, so as to obscure visitors but not so as to draw attention to our house on a bright Sunday morning.

Two more Special Branch, all in thick jerseys and all wearing lovely reassuring smiles. In the middle of it all Orlando arrived from Cambridge since I had forgotten to tell him to keep away. It's complicated by the fact that he has brought his guns with him in the boot of his car, being about to shoot for the University at Bisley. Special Branch rose however magnificently to this challenge and gave him excellent advice. (They were rather disappointed later when, after all this, he didn't win.)

The Rushdie family: Mrs Rushdie sad and dignified in a sari; sister Samin very fine-looking, aquiline features with Salman's heavy-lidded eyes, in flowing trousers and loose tunic holding enchanting baby Maia. Zoffeir, a sweet, gentle little boy looked more like his mother in type. Salman tells us: 'This is nothing to do with Islam. This is a monster which has come out of a bottle as sometimes happens in history.'

17 March

We presented our word-wide petition to the UN offices here. Received by a Dr Jensen in a grey suit, grey hair, little eyes, very polite. Though he told us 'privately' that he sympathized with our point of view, he burbled on about the Secretary-General's need to balance 'freedom of speech' with 'religious freedom'. Which actually means nothing at all if you think about it, since the Muslims are free, as they should be. It's Salman who isn't. And nobody should be free to make death threats with impunity.

———

A year later when the danger had only intensified, Salman invited Harold to read his lecture at the ICA, in Pall Mall, in his place. There was no way, under the present circumstances, Salman could appear in person. Harold of course immediately accepted.

6 February 1990

How brave, everyone kept saying when it was announced. I kept a straight bat: 'But of course there's no real danger.' It was only in the afternoon that it hit me. Up till then I had been buoyed up by Salman's pleasure a few nights ago, at being able to answer back in his own words at last. Me to Harold: 'Are you apprehensive?' Harold: 'A bit, naturally. But mostly about getting my tongue round the words, not getting dry, doing justice to his language which is not my own.' Me, anxiously: 'This ghastly situation is spiralling.' I referred to the deaths of innocent people such as Salman's Japanese translator: 'You could withdraw.' By way of reply, Harold quoted Horatio nagging Hamlet and Hamlet's reply. Horatio: 'I will say you are not fit.' Hamlet: 'If it be now, 'tis not to come . . . the readiness is all.'

The security was extraordinary, two sets of guards and masses of police outside – all a few hundred yards from Buckingham Palace. But the event at the I C A had of course been publicly announced. So who knew what might happen . . . ? As for the lecture, tears had come into my eyes when I first read it a week ago: under such dire circumstances, Salman had managed to produce something so *good*, and Harold of course reads brilliantly. Lately he talks to Salman on the telephone. 'Next time we'll do it the other way,' says Salman cheerfully. 'You'll write the piece and I'll deliver it.'

Chapter Eleven

MOON OVER PRAGUE

It was all very well attending protests in London and writing letters to imprisoned writers: but what about an actual visit behind the Iron Curtain? I had in fact visited Poland in 1969 but Harold had never been beyond Germany. In spite of several invitations to Russia, he said he had felt inhibited about accepting any kind of official invitation given the position of the Soviet Jews, although he had been part of initiatives to help people like Anatole Sharansky. June 1989 saw our first visit to Czechoslovakia, a country for which we both formed an enormous affection.

It was our close friend Diana Phipps, Czech by birth, who had first suggested the actual visit, and then arranged it, guided by her cousin Kari Schwarzenberg. But Harold had long been an admirer of the dissident Czech playwright Václav Havel and had corresponded with him (they were linked by their German agent Klaus Juncker). He had also acted in Havel's plays in England in order to draw attention to them and persistently advocated his freedom from arrest. We were also frequently told about the value of Western protest to dissidents in the East.

8 June

We are driven through Moravia by Kari Schwarzenberg, a great handsome force of a man, to meet Mrs Jirous, wife of a prominent dissident. The border post was like a dreary English bus station, plus machine guns, but absolutely no feeling of menace. Masses of poppies decorate the fields on either side, also iris, lupines and peonies in front of the village houses, plenty of little chapels and shrines for this is a very

Catholic part of the country. Mrs Jirous has taken refuge with her parents while her husband is in prison and we sit with her outside in the garden, possibly because it's already very hot, more likely because you must expect every room indoors to be bugged. She tells us that her husband has been moved to a new prison, which is comparatively pleasant. And he has only one man with him in the cell – this is a prison where some cells house as many as twenty-five men. He is even allowed to play ping-pong! Mrs Jirous attributes this welcome change to the tremendous fuss made in the West at the time of his trial in March. Kari Schwarzenberg went to this trial as President of Helsinki Watch. If the West keeps up the fuss, the sentence may even be reduced.

Later in Prague, Kari introduces us to a select band of intellectuals: a low, rather airless room but tremendously friendly atmosphere. My most interesting discussion was with Jaroslav Koran and Zdenek Urbánek, translators of Frayn, Stoppard and Shakespeare, about the future of Czech PEN. Apparently it was currently dormant at its own request, and (as President of English PEN) I had been asked to find out whether there was a move to revive it. They reveal that there is a considerable potential split here between those who 'will not sit down with the collaborators' and those who think it must be possible to work out some kind of compromise of the 'good' with the 'bad'. These problems eternally beset International PEN, by the very nature of its structure, as restrictive regimes come and go (not only in Eastern Europe but all over the world). Yet somehow it always manages to keep going, and keep supporting the vital principle of free expression. Harold makes a good, grave speech and drinks a lot of beer which has to be specially brought in. Naturally he pays for it, but then the Czechs insist on *us* taking the un-drunk bottles away; they are impressively dignified in their desire to seem like dissidents against the state regime, not like spongers.

9 June

Set out to stay with Václav Havel in convoy with Zdenek Urbánek and

Rita Klimova. We drive and drive and drive and drive, me feeling fairly sick in the back of masterful Kari's car (he is a very good but *swaying* driver). At 5 p.m. we reach Havel's house at Hradecek, near Trutnov. A Union Jack is pinned to the outbuilding. Olga and Václav come out smiling and welcoming but worried because we are so late: had expected us at one, but we stopped off to eat lunch at a merry 'Cinska' restaurant i.e. Chinese restaurant run by Czechs. Olga is very thin, in black trousers, with white hair that frames a noble face, strong nose, lovely blue-grey eyes, altogether a beautiful woman. Havel is small, really small, very energetic, bustling about, grinning, sandy hair thinning but a good deal of it still around his attractive rather cherubic face, sensual big mouth. I can easily see the attraction for women (as with Harold, it's the magnetism of energy). Klaus Juncker has told Harold on the telephone: 'Václav is a charming man but look out for Lady Antonia.' Harold to me: 'Was he serious?' Me: 'I hope so!' We are installed in the living room where among the CDs is the same Jessye Norman I am currently playing at home. Bottles of Czech champagne are opened.

——

Havel himself was only just out of prison and the dreadful news of the deaths of the young at Tiananmen Square were filtering through to us: altogether it seemed a perilous time for civil liberties world-wide. If some seer had gazed into the future and told me that we were camping out with the future President of Czechoslovakia – in only six months' time – I would not have believed him (or her).

9 June cont.

Eggs and black caviar provided. We all toast Václav. He gets out a piece of paper and in a rather manic way (he says later 'I am a pedant') reads out a schedule which has already been destroyed by our late arrival. Nevertheless he reads it all out. It includes, I note, an hour and a half interview with Harold on the state of the theatre . . . *Je verrai* as Louis XIV was fond of saying.

Then we are shown our rooms. Some embarrassment when Diana and Kari (in fact cousins and friends) are jointly given Olga's room. Kari, gallantly: 'Alas, she never liked me.' In fact he sleeps as a kind of janitor on a mattress in the upper half of this barn-like structure. Václav and Olga will climb a red ladder and sleep in the loft: they're used to people sleeping over, it's the dissident way of life. Harold and I are greatly honoured to be ushered into Václav's workroom, which used to be the woodshed, now adapted into a pleasant light ground-floor room, glass doors on to the great outdoors. Table with large pink notice on it: HERE WILL BE MY NEW COMPUTER CALLED HAROLD. (A lot of us had contributed financially to this computer after the police took the first one.) Havel says Harold is the first contributor he has met. Large photo of Graham Greene on the landing, with a note from him pinned to it; also Beckett (Harold's own heroes); plus Jack Kennedy. A favourite poster in various forms is 'All You Need Is Love' including one with a picture of two rhinos mating. Václav points on the landing to a samizdat collection of books worth '100,000 kroners. They didn't take it at the last search because they didn't have a lorry; the time before they took everything.'

Dinner, pork and beef, salad, strawberries and whipped cream followed by the interview – and it does last for almost exactly an hour and a half, nor does Harold protest, thanks to his being under Havel's spell. At dinner, the charming Urbánek, an ebullient silver-haired seventy-year-old, and Harold agree that in effect anything good is 'left wing' and if 'left wing' people do bad things, then they become 'right wing'. How convenient! Everyone argues. Kari says he could argue equally that left wing still has a meaning and that it doesn't. Urbánek remains romantic about the notion of 'left wing' as does Harold. (In this at least Harold agrees with the English fogies of the right who denounce him.) Myself I distrust all these labels; by their fruits, ye shall know them, says I. It's something Harold and I argue about: even if you can get away with Stalin being 'right wing', you just can't with Pol

Pot if language has any meaning at all. Harold tries to deal with him by just saying 'He's a monster.' Urbánek hisses at Václav: 'I told you you shouldn't have talked to the *Salisbury Review*' (a right-wing periodical).

Harold ends the interview by reading *Mountain Language* and then Havel rounds it off by reading from his new play, which like *Mountain Language* has a scene of prison-visiting. Bed at 2 a.m. Harold insisted, still in his left-wing mode, that the critics of Nick Ward's excellent play about the homeless in London disliked it because of its subject: 'They don't want to know.' He adds: '*The Caretaker* is not about a man looking for his identity; it's about a man looking for a home.' Václav, with great dignity: 'We don't have the problems of homelessness here. So may we connect your play to our own problems?'

Václav tells us that, unlike Harold, he is getting more and more interested in the mystery – I think he means the mystery of existence (see his *Letters to Olga*). That is what he likes about Harold's plays. We are amazed to find that no one appears to have heard of David Hare, our most successful playwright with *Pravda* and *The Secret Rapture* packing them in, even when I spell out the name. I point out that critics love him, he's also at the National Theatre – as for that matter is *Mountain Language*. But it's getting a little late for all this. At one point Harold clutches Václav's hand: 'If I had been in your circumstances, I like to think that I would have behaved as you have.' Pause. 'I think I would.' Olga took photographs for their album, which the police never confiscate: 'They like to know what's going on.'

Of Havel, my main impression is of gentleness combined with authority: a humanity and humanitarianism, due to what he has gone through, which may not have been there before in this jolly extravert fellow. The comparison to Albie Sachs, seen at PEN the night before we left, the South African who had also been in prison, and his declaration of abandoning violence, is strong in my mind. Both men have been persecuted: the result is to concentrate them on 'the mystery' as Václav calls it. Harold, who mercifully has not, can talk spiritedly about the behaviour of the CIA in Chile – as he did. Looking at Václav's expression, which was benign but detached, I could see him thinking: 'We know all that, alas both ways, because if you know it one way, you know it the other.'

In the dawn I pull up the blind to see the landscape: and am confronted by a little wooden house, really near, which is full of policemen, watching us.

10 June

Václav chucked us out of his workroom: 'I have to type out a manifesto before I go to Bratislava.' Me to Harold: 'It's just the writer regretting his generous impulse and getting interlopers out of his workroom as soon as possible.' I remind Harold of our wedding night in his Super-Study when he asked me next morning, 'Are you planning to stay long?' as he eyed his desk. 'A lifetime,' I should have said. Before we go, we sign postcards to Tom Stoppard and others. Havel with a laugh: 'I always sign in green, the colour of hope.'

We learn later that Václav reached Bratislava – no mean distance – and was acclaimed by Joan Baez and the crowd, then the police tried to stop him partying with her afterwards. Also a banned singer Ivan Hoffman started to perform: police cut off the sound, crowd roared with fury. Subsequently, the amazing Havel did manage to party, then drove to Prague, picked up Klaus Juncker here in Czechoslovakia for the first time in thirteen years, drove back to Hradecek, further partying, except it's really more political plotting. Everyone is worried about his health (coughing, for example, ghastly). It's tension that keeps this heroic man going.

11 June

Party of about fourteen for dissident writers; Harold allowed at last to pay as they took American Express; he was also able to donate to Helsinki Watch. Sat with the novelist Ivan Klíma, also Miroslav Holub, a poet whose work Harold much admires, a grave man of great presence, a bio-chemist by profession. Klíma is anxious to revive PEN by including all three grades of writers: 1) dissident 2) 'greyzone' 3) state okayed. Klíma emphasizes 'our willingness to solve it all positively'. The younger writers, I note, think that change really is in the wind; the older, including Holub, fear a repetition of 1968, the news of arrests in China not exactly allaying these deep anxieties.

12 June

Harold went to see Urbánek to do an interview for a video. He loved his book-lined study, for he felt he was looking at a typical Central European intellectual's room. I taxied to the Castle and walked all the way back on the cobbles (ouch, wrong shoes! In agony this morning). In a bookshop I saw the first signs of the Soviet Union: Russian newspapers, plenty of them, including *Pravda*, nothing else foreign even in German. In the bookshop, dusty Russian books and books in Czech about Russia: the only foreign author I can make out is Balzac. No catering for tourists in this most beautiful of cities, which makes it a heady relief from Venice. Big effort to find a postcard and only on the Karl Bridge a few leather knick-knacks.

While we were at Prague Airport on our way home, we wrapped up kroners and posted them, according to instructions by Diana, to a young fifth-year student about whom Harold was concerned. You wrap the money up in paper, put it in a hotel envelope, but take care to post it from the airport.

Our next visit to Czechoslovakia was in February 1990. By this time Václav Havel had become president of the country – a post he would occupy for fourteen years in the course of which Czechoslovakia was transformed into the Czech Republic. Harold had kept up contacts in the intervening months and was tremendously pleased when Havel gave an interview to the *Observer* in which he referred to the 'brotherhood' he immediately felt with Harold on their first meeting. We had both watched the events of the Velvet Revolution, transfixed, in late

November 1989. I thought of Pepys writing about the Restoration of King Charles II in 1660: how it was not to be imagined, 'the suddenness and the glory of it all'.

7 February

General jollity at the airport including from a large body of handsome youths whose luggage establishes them as having come from Cuba. 'Football?' I ask hopefully but get nowhere. The answer turns out to be 'Wrestling'. I bring presents of bath oil, perfume and body lotion for my Czech women friends. (Rita Klimova told Diana she still had the bath oil I bought for her in June – which was not supposed to be the point, she was supposed to *wallow*.) Vlasta Gallerova, theatre manager, tells us that this is a bad time for the theatre, which used to be the centre of opposition: but nowadays 'we sit at home watching television' where such exciting things are happening. Frantisek Fröhlich (Harold's translator) confirms this: 'We never even had a television. Now we watch it all the time.' 'Dramas?' 'No, news programmes, documentaries.' We realize that *Mountain Language* will no longer have the same resonance. Frantisek is a very sympathetic man. Tells me that when he hears certain loud noises, he thinks 'Here they come again.' For example a helicopter overhead – ironically it turns out to have contained Havel himself. 'You see, as a little boy' – he's born in 1934 – 'I remember the Germans coming in 1939, then the Russians in 1945 which seemed good, then the Russians in 1948, not good, then again in 1968. Always this noise haunts me: "Here they come again."' He is Jewish and spent the war in Theresienstadt miraculously surviving, along with his mother, though his father and the rest of his family vanished.

8 February

Went to Wenceslas Square. People hurrying. Mild weather. Walked the whole way with anticipation, but all the same was taken by surprise by the simple, round memorial to Jan Palach, the student who burned himself to death as a political protest, inset on to the pavement. His face in a photograph, handsome, forever young, looking out of the mass of flowers, mostly made up of quite small bunches, carnations, freesias, daffodils. Then I read the New Year tribute of 'Pan President Havel 1 January 1990' when he had been in office all of three days. Marked by its red ribbons, most moving of all the deep – two foot at least – mass of melded and melted wax of many colours from thousands of candles lighted over the years. The statue of St Wenceslas himself is flanked by posters: IT'S OVER: CZECHS ARE FREE! is the one I like best.

That night at the theatre, Olga, more beautiful than ever, but looking less pained than in June, greets us instantly: 'What things have happened!' You couldn't have put it better or more simply. Olga and Rita described the hideous state of the apartments at the Castle. 'The Bolshevik had no taste' is the local saying. She tells us that the police in the little wooden house outside the farm at Hradecek have in theory been replaced by another kind of security 'because people come to stare'. But sometimes, says Olga, they recognize the same police faces. Rita Klimova is to be Ambassador in Washington: she tells me she felt like giggling when Václav handed her the insignia. She is tremendously excited although the Foreign Office have taken 20 per cent off her salary 'because I don't have a wife'. Then we met Havel himself, equally jolly, looking much healthier, in an open-necked check shirt. He's longing to have his new play put on: not since 1968 . . . He was finally dragged away, very late, by Olga. 'You see, I am still a prisoner. Now I am a prisoner to my wife.'

9 February

We had a moving experience of what Václav means to the young Czechs. It was now about 10.30 p.m. after a long cheerful dinner which Harold gave. Suddenly Václav made one of his swift moves: 'Come on, come on, we must go to the Balustrade Theatre, which was my theatre you know, where Jane Fonda is making a speech. She has been trying to see me all week.' Outside the restaurant were cars with flashing blue lights into which Olga, in her kindly way, piled Francis King and Diana Petre, part of English PEN, our guests. But we walked along with the President (thank God this time my heels weren't too high!) across the Karl Bridge. Václav: 'My first walk across the Karl Bridge since I am President.' It was a full moon with racing clouds, the castle wonderfully lit up behind us. Václav: 'We must look and see if the flag is still flying, it means that I am still President. If not, good, I can go back to the theatre. Ah, it is still flying. What a nuisance.'

A group of youths on the bridge call out a greeting and make V signs (Francis King told me that there were many V signs and cries of 'Olga' to the flashing cars: she's already extremely popular and instantly recognizable with that lovely face and snow-white hair). At the end of the bridge, a group of youths stop us. They take out a guitar. They proceed to sing in harmony to Havel. The tune is the 'Ode to Joy' from Beethoven's Ninth. The lighting: Havel's face in profile with his dark coat, the faces of the men and girls, the large guitar, it was all like something directed by Ingmar Bergman. The idealism of the young faces, the tenderness of the older one. These were – all of them – the people who had made the Samet (Velvet) Revolution.

At the theatre, Jane Fonda is surrounded by a huge entourage of extremely amiable people brought from California: Jane's personal photographer, etc. etc. Harold, who claimed to know her, embraced her warmly. She asks me: 'Are you an actress too?' When an aide tries to correct her, I reply with sincerity: 'Don't worry. I'm delighted to be taken for an actress. Who wants to look like a lady writer?'

10 February

Frantisek Fröhlich takes us up to the Cathedral which Harold is anxious to see in connection with his projected screenplay of *The Trial*. He points to the soldiers patrolling the Castle grounds as he drives us up the hill. 'Before, they patrolled with big dogs. Now, no dogs, by order of the President.'

Like all our friends here, he emphasizes the dream-like quality of all that has happened. 'No dogs' seem to stand for a lot, that and the singing students.

11 February

We arrive in East Berlin from Czechoslovakia for a film festival: Margaret Atwood's *The Handmaid's Tale*, for which Harold wrote the screenplay, is part of it. We take the opportunity to go to the Brandenburg Gate, reaching it in fact by a muddy little path beside the blackened Reichstag, German flag flying, and saw the wall. Holes in it grilled over. Later we noticed an orderly procession of East Germans on foot coming in as pedestrians through a wicker gate. Also we see a double-file of very young, soft-faced, sweet-looking Russians soldiers in fur hats marching on their way somewhere or other; I feel rather sorry for them in this rapidly changing world.

Only one soldier guards the gate. But: 'I hear the sound of hammering,' says Harold, in a puzzled voice. And looking to the left, we see this amazing sight of people of all races and nationalities busily bent down towards the wall and hammering away with huge hammers in order to hack their own pieces off. For all the world like the Seven Dwarfs in the film, something comical at any rate, not the Nibelungen in *Rheingold*. Meanwhile in front of them were ten or so trestle tables on which lay pieces of the wall of all colours (bright blues, greens, as well as pinks, blacks) with enterprising lads selling them. Capitalism, quick off the mark! Harold bought me a pink-and-black piece looking like a jellied eel for about £6. Then I decide to do better myself and borrow a hammer from a dark-eyed energetic girl and hammer away. We photograph each other cordially.

Scrawled at the highest bit of the Gate were the words: '*Vive l'Anarchie!*' But it was far from being anarchy we saw here, a new kind of order rather.

21 March 1990

Havel's visit to London. We are asked to a small, i.e. non-State, lunch at Buckingham Palace. I wear my impractical white suit, bought for Anne Somerset's wedding and more or less on hire from the cleaners ever since. A loyal crowd of Czechs, many in national dress, flowing red ribbons, outside the gates. Homemade banners. Other guests: Phyllis (P. D.) James in an elegant beige straw hat, Sir Charles and Lady Mackerras, various kindly attendants such as Sue Hussey.

When the Queen arrives with the Duke of Edinburgh, into a small sitting room decorated with pictures of the daughters of George III, she looks very like Phyllis but smaller and prettier. I find myself with the Duke of Edinburgh. He asked me what I was writing – I was dreading that. When I revealed that it was *The Six Wives of Henry VIII*, he said quite angrily and looking irritable too: 'Why do people always say "Henry VIII and his six wives" as though it was all one word? There is plenty more to say about Henry.' Me, cravenly: 'Oh yes, sir, there is, I mean he was a wonderful musician.' The Duke, sounding even crosser: 'He was a wonderful military strategist, a fighter, he bashed the French.' He repeated the words with great emphasis. 'He *bashed* the French.'

At lunch the Queen is notably sympathetic, says Harold. She expresses interest at the change of Havel in his life from being a playwright to being a head of state. 'But of course you were always working with your head?' And she sort of mimed it. In the middle of lunch Václav leant across the table and said: 'I never thought to see an unofficial playwright in Buckingham Palace.' Pause, while everyone is slightly surprised at his choice of the word 'unofficial'. Then: 'No, Harold, I mean *you*.' The men from the Foreign Office are convulsed.

Later Václav answers questions brilliantly at the ICA. Czechs now have liberty, he says, but with liberty comes the need to make decisions – for them to make the decisions. 'Freedom means what it says. Now *you* decide. You don't ask me whether there should be a cable car from Mountain A to Mountain B. That's not my job.'

Throughout our summer holiday in Corfu in 1991, Harold had been cracking away at his screenplay of Kafka's *The Trial*, to be directed by David Jones. He lurked in the little white annexe to the modest low-built villa, which we called the Cowshed. My mother actually did a watercolour of him at work: Harold was oblivious. He said that he wrote his early plays with his son crawling over him, and simply didn't notice such things. It is fair to say that when Harold wasn't working, he was as cranky as most other people when there was noise, maybe more so.

5 May 1992

In Prague again: the third time in less than three years. This time it is for the shooting of *The Trial*. To the Barrandov Studios on a hill, built by Havel's family. Harold feels strongly that *The Trial* is about man's spiritual relationships, his search for God (like *The Hound of Heaven*, I add) i.e. not political.

At this point Harold wrote in my diary: 'Quite right! H.P.'

5 May cont.

Later: Havel actually comes to watch the night-shooting when his immense work for the day is over. Harold is delighted. 'I came to see his work,' he says. 'So he came to see mine: that's how it is between us.' I see Harold's and Havel's faces, close together, dark and fair, in the lighting of the street amid pools of darkness, like a picture by Rembrandt; both animated, and animated also by the human condition.

Chapter Twelve

STAGE WIFE

Harold, I noticed, felt a kind of existential despair in the mid eighties. It was partly the state of the world. Giving up smoking – from sixty Black Sobranies a day – no doubt added to it in the short term, although the trauma gave way to a permanent state of what one might call non-addiction and quite soon he said that he never felt the slightest temptation to regress. He had done this after Hugh died of lung cancer in March 1984. Hugh was a heavy smoker of the wartime generation which was unaware of the dangers and as a young soldier probably wouldn't have cared too much about the prospects of a long life on the eve of a parachute jump. He also had a family blood condition which made smoking specially dangerous: but these things were not known then.

1984

9 July

Harold in a mood which I can only describe as savage melancholy. Directing seems to take more and more out of him. He is infuriated by the mainly adverse critical reaction to Simon Gray's play *The Common Pursuit*, the whole episode exacerbated by his lack of smoking. Perhaps no one should accept to direct under these circumstances, especially a play by Simon Gray, the celebrated smoker, but it is easy to be wise after the event. Harold had admired the play even if he didn't get the best out of it. Harold, leaving the Lyric, Hammersmith, hears a woman shout: 'Harold Pinter, why don't you write about the workers?' Fatally he goes back. Further cries from this woman: 'What about Chile?

What about South Africa?' As though *One for the Road* was not about Chile and the whole damn thing. This play had after all been on at this very theatre only a few months earlier as Harold's attacker appeared not to know. The point is that the ridiculous incident got to him. Sometimes melancholy spreads across the waters of Harold's life like black water lilies. At such moments he is always careful to except me from his cares. Sometimes when things are dire, he writes a poem to make the point as when he was visiting a relative in hospital.

DENMARK HILL

Well, at least you're there,
And when I come into the room,
You'll stand, your hands linked,
And smile,
Or, if asleep, wake.

1985

Harold started the year in better nick since he's going to direct Lauren Bacall in Tennessee Williams' *Sweet Bird of Youth* at the Theatre Royal Haymarket. Also there will be a production of his *Old Times* with Michael Gambon, Liv Ullmann and Nicola Pagett at the same theatre.

8 January 1985

Tenth anniversary of our fatal meeting. Harold gave me an enormous Georgian paste ring, pale golden stone set in subtly gleaming dark paste diamonds and masses of white flowers. I gave him two silk shirts from Angelo's. Personally, I allowed myself to be cheered up by the progress of the Arms Talks in Geneva. I mean on TV, the Americans, even Reagan, were issuing statements of compromise about Star Wars and Gromyko was quite gracious, if that's the right word. Harold:

'Listen, I adore you, that's my position, and if Reagan and Gromyko make you happy, they're my boys.'

———

The significant event in Harold's change of mood, however had probably taken place the previous autumn when we went to New York and Harold gave an enactment – as opposed to a reading – of scenes from six of his full-length plays at the YMHA, on the Upper East Side, a great venue for such things. I noted at the time that his melancholy was much alleviated. Harold: 'I was especially proud of my women.' He was right. His Ruth in *The Homecoming* was a triumph, Anna in *Old Times* no less so. I sat next to Jeremy Irons, however, fresh from his own triumph as the lover Jerry in the film of *Betrayal*. I was amused when amid his generally lavish praise, he commented in his precise, elegant voice: 'I don't think he got *Betrayal* quite right though.' Harold himself, it was fair to say was dissatisfied with his Davies in *The Caretaker*. 'I was too ferocious. I didn't have the charm.'

I believe it was this return to acting, as opposed to simply reading, which prompted Harold to return to the stage the next year. Up till then he remained periodically depressed.

30 June

Harold had a sleepless night over money. It seems awful to me that he, who earns a great deal of money, who has a wife who does all right by most standards, only one grown-up child to support, parents he happily and successfully cares for, two plays in the West End, directing another, a film opening, *Turtle Diary*, about to play a nine-week season as author/actor in Los Angeles, should have financial worries to keep him up at night.

———

Harold entered as I wrote this and I read him the sentence. He seized the Diary and wrote in enormous letters: 'I love you wildly and that is my solace.' Perhaps everybody nice worries about money – and probably everyone nasty too. It's just the human condition. It's odd that Harold worries so much more, for example, than my father, who has never had any, let alone made any.

Later: Harold thinks he has an ulcer or an ulcerette and again talks about money. Then – miraculous to behold! The first night of *Sweet Bird of Youth* starring Lauren Bacall is a triumphant success and the pain has completely disappeared. Nor is money further discussed. At the first-night party Betty Bacall glitters in a white top, tight white satin trousers, showing off her superb figure; she dances away. Harold too dances away extremely energetically, Hackney style, he says, as usual. I dance away – South Kensington style is probably the right description.

———

Directing Betty Bacall in Tennessee Williams' masterpiece was both a rewarding and an entertaining experience despite gloomy prognostications to the contrary. I record that Harold adores Betty and rejects stories of her being difficult with scorn. 'She's just professional' – that's always a term of praise with Harold where actors are concerned. Bob Gottlieb was the one who got the future of their relationship right, the less talented doom-mongers wrong. Bob had edited her autobiography: *Bacall by Bacall*. 'Betty' he said 'is a good pal.' And indeed we formed an enduring friendship with Betty thereafter. When directing I always thought that Harold felt himself to be on the actors' side because he identified with them; where there were differences it was to do with his perfectionism, his attention to the text, rather than to something more aggressive like natural impatience. Throughout his long career in that sphere, I got used to tributes from those concerned, often said in a slightly surprised voice, to be honest: 'Harold is so sweet as a director.'

Harold's decision to take on the part of Deeley in *Old Times* in the US led to a considerable change in our way of life ten years into our relationship. There had, he said, been a gap of seventeen years since his last foray on to the stage. It arose because Michael Gambon, who had been so wonderful in it – a mixture of bear and big cat with his rugged appearance and extraordinary grace of movement – wasn't able to go to the States. Throughout rehearsals in the early autumn of 1985 Harold was, I noted, in a remarkably sunny mood, despite the world being in its usual parlous state. He worked with the director David Jones, and the actresses Liv Ullmann and Nicola Pagett, who are Snow White and Rose Red, respectively blonde and dark.

3 October

Harold: 'The sexual attraction between Deeley and Anna is now very strong. One possibility at the end of the play is for Deeley to go off with Anna, which we'll explore.' Yes, I bet, given the magnetic beauty of Liv! (She's all the more attractive for being very active over human rights as well.)

5 October

Harold: 'I'm doing my violence in Deeley quite coldly and quietly.' (Mike used to roar.) He talked of the frightening feeling of seeing the two women's faces turned towards him, blank, close together, when he comes back from giving himself a whisky. He's happily having singing lessons for those snatches of song. But where text is concerned, Harold always stumbles in the same places as Mike Gambon did, according to the ladies. When I tell this to Claire Bloom, she wrinkles her lovely face just slightly – except it has no wrinkles – and says: 'Perhaps that's where the author didn't get it quite right.' Harold loves this.

10 October 1985

Harold's fifty-fifth birthday. I give him a black kimono lined in red for his theatrical tour: he looks like something in a Japanese print, or perhaps a Kabuki actor. Everybody spontaneously says to him: 'You look ten years younger.' It's true that there has been no nicotine in his system for eighteen months (he could never have taken this on without that abstention) and there is all the new exercise thanks to tennis at the beloved Vanderbilt Club. But fundamentally it's the acting. After all, that's the profession he chose, as I used to remind myself, whereas poetry and writing plays had, as it were, chosen him. And he loved it. For the rest of his life there would be many such forays on the stage, as well as acting on radio and cameo roles in film.

Old Times opened in St Louis, as a try-out before Los Angeles and San Francisco. Unfortunately Harold trod the boards officially for the first time in seventeen years on the night of the World Series in which the St Louis Cardinals were featured. Unhappy husbands listened to the results on headphones during the performance, having been dragged to the show by culture-conscious wives. While these same wives put on expressions thought suitable for Pinter: wistful *ennui* just about sums it up. There were sudden eruptions of violent unlawful sounds from the headphones.

25 October

St Louis. Paid a visit of respect together to Tennessee Williams' grave as a tribute to *Sweet Bird of Youth*. The Catholic cemetery has the penitential name of Calvary, but the day was so incredibly beautiful that the green swards rather resembled a Hollywood version of eternal glades of happiness. Having recently read the Donald Spoto biography of Tennessee, I uttered the sincere prayer: 'If he's anywhere, O God, let him be at peace.' On the way home Harold shows me one of his cards, written at the graveside while I was praying: he's had an idea for a piece using a sudden ending to a young man's life: a fierce white light. (This was the first intimation of the play called *Party Time*.)

We both liked writers' graves. Once when we were in Zurich, visiting a performance of *One for the Road*, we went on a pilgrimage to find the grave of Harold's hero James Joyce. First we were informed by the poetry-lovers Geoffrey Godbert and Tony Astbury exactly which restaurants Joyce liked, and what he liked to drink: we followed instructions. Harold sipping white wine and overlooking the water: 'Joyce liked his bourgeois comforts.' Now we toiled high, high above the city to the cemetery, where Joyce was reported to lie. We arrived, we stumbled up icy stone steps, white frost everywhere amid heaths and heathers still flowering and carefully chosen trees, all Zurich laid out before us. I bent my nose towards the various frosty plaques on the ground. Suddenly a cry from Harold: 'Here he is!'

And there he was, Jimmy Joyce, modelled in bronze, life-size but only three-quarters of him. I imagine him with his specs, his open book, his ash plant and his cigarette ... looking towards us. I had actually seen this figure in the grass but somehow thought he was a real man encouraging us forward. Back at the hotel I checked in Ellmann's biography and learned that Nora said about the cemetery's proximity to the Zurich Zoo: 'Jim can hear the lions roaring, he always liked lions.'

27 October 1985

Los Angeles. Bel-Air Hotel (where Betty Bacall insisted we stay, which was a mistake because I felt isolated). The real thrill was seeing my youngest daughter Natasha, who was aged twenty-two, living and working in LA. She looked like a Stuart beauty with her lustrous black hair, white skin and huge blue eyes: Charles II would have gone mad for her.

30 October

Harold went for broke, no, went for bankrupt. David Jones told him in the interval, 'Be wicked' – and he was. His humour, his confidence, apparent or real, made Deeley's sobbing at the end of the play extraordinarily compelling: as a result Liv was even more incandescent than she had been with Gambon, performing amazing gyrations with her black sheeny legs and Nicola found full authority, especially in her last speech. Afterwards Duncan Weldon, the producer, asks Harold what other parts he wants to play. We got into jealous males such as Robert in *Betrayal* and James in *The Collection*. Harold kept saying: 'I am too old', but at this moment he could play anything. First-night party at the Polo Lounge. Waiter to Harold: 'So you are in a play? Claudette Colbert is in a play.' Harold: 'Well, I'm not Claudette Colbert, in case you think I am.' Later the waiter is brought back by head-waiter. He apologizes gravely for mistaking Harold for Claudette Colbert.

31 October

Hollywood! Went with Duncan Weldon to a performance of *Aren't We All?* with Rex Harrison and, guess who, Claudette Colbert. Backstage *before* the performance there was a party of Mr and Mrs Frank Sinatra, Mr and Mrs Kirk Douglas, Mr and Mrs Gregory Peck and Mr and Mrs Roger Moore. Then they were joined by the stars who were supposed to be performing in the play. It was by now 7.55 p.m. Thanked God Harold was on a stage elsewhere, not directing these insouciant creatures.

I couldn't really enjoy Los Angeles, despite meeting the famous as above, until I started to work on my new book on Warrior Queens in the library of UCLA. I simply wasn't used to a life of doing nothing in a hotel and it produced melancholy, even though Natasha was there as a solace and drove me about in a stately fashion in her large dusty, second- (or third-) hand Mercedes. It was a city, we found, where people worked hard on films and went to bed early; it didn't suit our way of life of roistering and relaxing after the theatre. In fact the tour was cut short, thanks to the illness of one of the cast. Harold, having proved to himself that he could act again, said that he was happy to return home.

18 November

Met Faye Dunaway after the play because Harold hopes to direct her back in London in Donald Freed's thrilling, menacing play *Circe and Bravo*. Quite lovely in the flesh: daffodil hair, masses of it, pale face, white mac, yellow jersey, slender legs and body. These stars! Nobody knows the stars I've seen. These ladies size me up at the first meeting with their shrewd (and beautiful) eyes and give me a character. After that I obediently stay in the character whenever I'm with them. Betty told me I was so funny (although she is really the funny one) so now I'm quite hilariously witty with her. Liv told me I was serene so naturally I compose my features into a tranquil blancmange whenever I'm near her. We shall see what character Faye gives me.

The fact was, once I had got over – or rather coped with – my obsessional need to work, I found being the wife of an actor an exceptionally happy role. Although actors sleep late, writers (or me anyway) get up early. Writers then have a cheerful day working incredibly hard, at least in their own opinion, before joining the actor after the show for an invigorating supper.

Sometimes I went to the theatre or the opera by myself before joining Harold. I loved this: the anticipation of meeting him; plus the pleasure of going to the show or opera without, to be honest, bothering about his reactions.

1986

24 January

Lunch at Kensington Palace with the Prince and Princess of Wales for Shimon Peres, Prime Minister of Israel. Philip Roth in his waggish way: 'Of course Harold hasn't been invited: he's Jewish.' Like the child who goes to the panto, I was ready at an early hour – green suede dress, black patent shoes, pearl necklace. I was much too early and had to sit by Kensington Public Library for ten minutes, then realized I would be late. Felt very nervous, amid the immense security precautions (for the President, not the Royals). Inside, saw a tall crimson streak who proved to be the Princess of Wales. Gazed into the famous face. A perfect pale pink complexion, pale rose colour, not pink or white. Azure-blue eyes, even bigger than in her cartoons, ringed with what looked like kohl. Her voice has that light rather flat upper-class quality I have noted on TV, but what I hadn't appreciated is that she's extremely vivacious, eager to please, rattles on: 'Are you writing a new book? Oh, I do hope so.' And so on and so on. To Peres: 'Yes I'd love to come to Israel. Anything for some sun.'

Princess: 'I always used to believe what I read in the media until I was in the media.' She shook her beautiful head mystically. Peres: 'I want to say what inspiration you have given to children all over the world.' Princess: 'They always expect me to have a crown on.' (I guess that's her stock remark.)

Magic moment when Princes William and Harry rush in. The Israeli Ambassadress is enchanted: 'Children break down all barriers.' Prince William would certainly break down any barrier. He's quite marvellous, tall, straight, thick glossy hair. Totally un-shy. Ran about. Then looked up at Noel Annan and pointed like the Duke of York at Richard III at the opening of the Olivier film: 'You've got no hair.' Intense pleasure of other guests. Princess collapses in giggles. Noel attempts to be good with children and drops artily to his knees: 'The wind blew it away' – said in an exquisite voice. Prince William: 'Where to?' Prince Charles, at the end: 'Is your husband all right about not coming?' Harold had not been asked because we were supposed to be historians, to please Shimon Peres. Prince Charles adds concernedly if not accurately: 'I expect he is eating scrambled eggs at home?'

A new vista was shortly to open up in my own work, thanks to a chance visit when I was in New York. In 1988 when *The Warrior Queens* was published, the third history book published during my twelve years with Harold, I see from my Diary that I was casting about for a subject for a new book. I contemplated writing about Madame de Maintenon, last mistress and maybe wife of Louis XIV. I thought I could sink myself in the court of Louis XIV and the fortunes of this odd woman, and do something interesting and original, if not particularly popular. To dig and not to count the cost, to adapt Elizabeth Barrett Browning. Harold always applauds non-commercial decisions, to his great credit, and applauded this one. Although he's deeply proud of my commercial success, as and when it happens (from time to time, but not every book every time), he would have made a good husband to a reclusive lady scholar of impeccable integrity, indifferent to sales. The interesting thing about Harold and money is that every now and then he decides to worry about it, as part of a general *cafard*; but fundamentally he's not interested in it. Certainly, in the years I have known him, he's never taken on anything for money.

April 1988

An exciting thing happened when I visited Bob Gottlieb, now editor of the *New Yorker* (office newly kitsched up, according to Bob's taste, two lamps made of ballerina's legs in pink tights and shoes). I was supposed to go to Philadelphia to be interviewed but the journalist broke her arm so I seized the opportunity to see Bob. Talked about my future plans for a book. Bob: 'Well, I have an idea, but maybe it will sound stupid to you. It's just come into my mind: THE SIX WIVES OF HENRY VIII. Me: 'That is certainly not stupid, Bob, that is an idea of genius.' And equally immediately, I saw how that might be really very interesting for me, the types of women, the period just before mine. I felt good about it. And I could complete it to be published for my sixtieth birthday in August 1992. Told Bob: 'That fact wouldn't sell one copy. But it would make me feel good.'

Recently my books hadn't sold particularly well, although I was extremely content with what I had done. But the fact is that any book on Henry and his six wives sells. As a young publicist said to me on the day of publication in England, on the way to a radio show, when I suggested that the book appeared to be subscribing well: 'I think it's the subject, isn't it?' Maybe she wasn't destined for a life of diplomacy, but the fact is that she was right. Biography in my experience, however brilliant, rarely transcends its subject in terms of sales. The quality however soars or sinks with the writer.

Whenever required, Harold entered enthusiastically into my expeditions on what I called 'optical research', the term invented for tax purposes, which could be put in another way as 'Going to places and looking at them'. Even though I never quite cured myself of impulsive gestures such as ushering Harold on to turrets of perilous height or worse still, into claustrophobic dungeons ... Sometimes his visits to what he called 'your own world ... the world of history which you love' coincided harmoniously with his own film work. This happened when Harold was invited by Canadian director Patricia Rozema to play Sir Thomas Bertram in a version of Jane Austen's *Mansfield Park*.

It was set, for reasons which seemed good to the director, in an early Jacobean mansion in Northamptonshire. Even though one of the points of Jane Austen's novel (hence the title) is that Sir Thomas has built his house himself with money he has earned. And he has earned it from the slave trade, as was certainly stressed in the film. If ever there was a case for the usual graceful Georgian mansion, this was it. But apparently 'that had been done before', as reported by Harold, presumably in *Pride and Prejudice*.

Never having read the novel, Harold was tickled with the script because the part of Sir Thomas was such a good, meaty one. My historian's yap about the date of the house did not bother an actor with a good part one whit. Like most actors in films, I imagine, Harold's complaints were mainly about his stockings with garters not staying up.

Nor did he mind the inevitable delays. He stayed in his caravan 'thinking about cricket', in his own words.

So I went to Oundle where Harold was staying in order to be with him while he was filming. It was golden autumn weather. An amiable round of historical sight-seeing followed. We looked at four churches and one cathedral, Peterborough, where I was delighted to see that the tomb of Catherine of Aragon on which I had reverently placed flowers when I was working on her life, even now had a huge bouquet. Then I took Harold with me to Fotheringhay where Mary Queen of Scots had been executed in 1587. It was what Henry James called 'the visitable past'. For although essentially the past of the tragic queen, it was also my past, thirty years ago at the time when I was working on my biography, in a different life before I met Harold. Fotheringhay looked of course exactly the same, the surviving lump of masonry more like an asteroid which had landed from space beside the River Nene, than the last remnant of a once great castle. The thistles on the mound were grown high. I remembered picking a huge bunch in the sixties; I also remembered the story I had picked up of a Highland piper who used to come and play a lament in memory of Queen Mary on the anniversary of her execution in February. No sign of a piper now, but I gathered another enormous bunch of thistles for remembrance. We both contemplated the mound in silence.

After that we went on to the eighteenth/seventeenth-century Kirby Hall, and to Harold's twentieth-century caravan. It was surrounded by trailers, sheep and a huge fire engine. He donned his full billowing shirt, his flowing brocade dressing-gown, his nightcap, and striped waistcoat and the famous unreliable white stockings. Looking suitably menacing, he strode off in the big black buckled shoes of Sir Thomas Bertram.

Chapter Thirteen

MARRIAGE – AGAIN

In the summer of 1990 Harold and I began to have talks about the possibility of getting married – or rather having a ceremony of validation – in a Catholic church. In one sense, the strict Catholic sense, the deaths of our previous partners in 1982 and 1984 respectively, had left us free to marry. I see from my Diary that I must have mentioned it in passing in late 1984.

22 December

I told Harold lightly that I sensed a reservation about our getting married in a Catholic church. Harold: 'That's very perceptive of you. It's my parents. They just wouldn't understand. And they are not going to last many more years.'

That made complete sense to me and the subject was dropped. After all, the senior Pinters had been through a lot, one way or another, the price of being parents of an only child who was Harold, proud of him as they were.

Now the subject re-emerged. Of course we considered that we had been married in the eyes of God, if She/He exists, in November ten years earlier. What we discussed was a mixture of reaffirmation, as Christian couples sometimes do renew their vows at appropriate anniversaries, but also something more practical. I thought that if I died suddenly it would be an unnecessary grief for my children to have to deal all over again with my situation vis-à-vis the Catholic Church.

They might have to ask: is our mother entitled to a Catholic Requiem Mass? Questions of that order. In the meantime I had returned to the practice of the Catholic religion, attempting to attend Mass regularly.

By a happy coincidence, we were enjoying a friendship with Father Michael Campbell Johnston SJ, formerly in El Salvador. Like many Jesuits, he was a leading supporter of Liberation Theology in South and Latin America. I had always been emotionally prone to the Farm Street Jesuit Church, where my father had been received as a Catholic in 1940. And I had worked on documents there for Mary Queen of Scots, thanks to my friend the Archivist Father Francis Edwards SJ. Attendance by Harold as well as myself at the première of a film commemorating the murdered Archbishop Romero – the party was actually at the home of the Catholic Archbishop of Westminster – led to a propitious atmosphere.

It may seem odd to relate that Harold, a determinedly non-believing and non-practising Jew, and I, an aspiring if extremely imperfect Catholic, should have lived together for thirty-three years in perfect amity where religion was concerned. We had lots of discussions about religion, always the spiritual side (he wasn't interested in doctrine), very occasionally about the social decisions of the Church – and no rows.

That could not be said about our political discussions, where as the years passed I decided to my own satisfaction that Harold really enjoyed a good political argument, didn't he? So I gave it to him. Only our firm rule that we should not, as in the Bible, let the sun go down upon our wrath made sure that, even if there were pretty late sundowns, dawn at least always found us reconciled. Religion was different. Harold had a deep sense of the spiritual, hence his love of such poets as Eliot, and when we were abroad liked to sit in dark churches while I tried to brighten them up by lighting candles to St Antony.

1 April

The Beckett memorial evening at the National Theatre. What I got from it again and again was 'I must go on, I'll go on.' Not the so-called despair with which Beckett is too loosely credited. Other impressions: how no one is ever dead in the Beckettian world, particularly not Beckett and particularly not the dead. The seriousness of Harold's old friend, Delphine Seyrig, in *Footfalls*, an existentialist nun in black trouser suit, white collar, black-and-white spotted coif.

I remember Harold's grief when he heard of Beckett's death at Christmas 1989; Harold had visited him in his Paris nursing home earlier in the year and they had spoken on the telephone only a short while before (Harold was excited that Beckett told him the Kafka screenplay was beside his bed). At the time I drew attention to Beckett's lack of despair – 'I'll go on on' – to Harold.

20 May

I tell Harold in a conversation on our balcony after Mass, aided by a convivial glass of champagne, that I went and wrote to Father Michael Campbell Johnston, wanting at least to know if a Catholic marriage is possible. Me: 'The idea was originally that we should wait for your parents to die because it might upset them, but now I do believe they would accept anything we choose to do, and secondly, I am glad to say they are not going to die. They're both extremely well.' Harold: 'It's not as if I have to be a Catholic.' Hardly!

1 June

Went to Catholic Institute for International Relations Third World Mass, concelebrated by Cardinal Hume with numerous Third World priests. Red vestments. The Cardinal waved his crozier about most skilfully; it occurred to me that it was a tradition going back to Cardinal Wolsey and beyond. Harold commented afterwards that he was impressed by the multiracial nature of those on the altar (although after Mass I often report that impressive fact back to him about the congregation at the Carmelite Church). 'And how everyone knew exactly what to do.' Told him, with hyperbole I dare say, that I would know where I was in the Mass if plonked down blindfold anywhere in the world. Cardinal Arns, from Brazil, preached; this was a great thrill for Harold who had just been reading about his courageous stand in logging the names of the Disappeared. The Cardinal related the work of the CIIR (on it's fiftieth anniversary) to that of the Holy Spirit and Pentecost – the ecumenical nature of Whitsun.

At the reception afterwards we were received by Cardinal Hume, who behaved as an Ampleforth gentleman to me, apologizing for not recognizing me (actually we had never met). I asked him about Communion in two kinds which I hadn't taken as, apart from anything else, I was feeling faint from taking cortisone for my skin allergy: 'We don't have it generally, such a big place, so many people, but it would be expected by the CIIR people from overseas.'

Later supper party at home to celebrate PEN's Writers' Day. Cold salmon and salad. A visit to the Super-Study after dinner where Harold read James Fenton's *Ballad of the Imam at the Well*, that wonderful disquisition on the ascending growth of prejudice. Then Bernice Rubens persuaded him to read it again. Nadine Gordimer was tiny, calm, poised, friendly. Then there was Larry McMurtry, to whom I had taken a great fancy at a previous PEN conference at Maastricht, also to his works, another happy coincidence of the person and the prose.

2 June

Nadine Gordimer spoke marvellously well and clearly; she has such elegance of language, which is what I've always adored about her books. Larry managed the difficult task of both being funny (fundamentalist story of the 1850s in Texas) and serious. Both never stopped bringing in Salman Rushdie, which was *good*. Questions 99 per cent favourable to Salman this year. (Last year many more hostile to him.) Only one foolish woman talking about the 'need for self-restraint' we all have in our lives. But people generally seem to have settled into an understanding that for writers this is *the* serious issue of our time. William Shawcross told me at lunch that he would have withdrawn

The Satanic Verses if he were Salman. Me: 'But you're not Salman, you're not a creative writer; you're a brilliant polemicist.'

8 June

Went to Farm Street to talk to Father Michael Campbell Johnston. Felt rather nervous. Harold: 'Finally I would do it because I want to make you happy.' Father Michael greeted us in grey shirt and trousers and sandals, although the weather was very cold. 'I can't get used to jackets or even shoes after so many years abroad,' he said. We chatted about Harold's recent broadcast concerning Latin America which has made him the hero of the hour in these circles. We discuss the question of the marriage. Father Michael: 'For an unbaptized person [i.e. Harold] you get a dispensation. On the subject of privacy, you could get married in our chapel.' I was extremely excited by the idea of a chapel and even more so when I saw it. The upper room of Catholic history! I felt emboldened to say: 'Father, would you marry us?'

Luckily Harold did not feel later that I had jumped the gun, perhaps because most of the rest of our conversation was about the murdered Jesuits in El Salvador (I had read a most affecting pamphlet on the subject by Father Jon Sobrino SJ). I told Father Michael that Harold had come to respect the Catholic Church through its work in South America: indeed we were on the cover of the *Catholic Herald* that very morning, seen at the CIIR reception, the Cardinal beaming at me. A good omen? Discussed telling Harold's parents. Tell them long, long after, if at all, was my advice. As to telling mine: fear of Dada's publicity-mad streak prevented me; this really was a private matter for us both since all too much of our lives hitherto had been lived out, however reluctantly, in public. I would tell my mother in time, when it was all over, and she could then please herself by telling my father.

11 June

Theatre Museum, Covent Garden: Labour's reception for 'people in the Arts World'. The first thing which struck me about the Labour turn-out, male and female, was how smartly dressed they were. Has the word gone out? 'Look successful! So we can Be successful.' I really like Glenys Kinnock: a great person, direct, decent and intelligent. Neil Kinnock embraced me: 'Hello, love.' Me: 'I thought you'd given all that love stuff up – glad you haven't.' Glenys: 'All that is just a silly Southern reaction.'

15 June

We visit Father Michael together. One moment of nerves when reading out the provisions of the ceremony from the form, he says to Harold: 'You are supposed to have instruction.' Harold's eyes glitter. 'But I'm sure your wife can do it,' he continues smoothly. Equally, at the age of fifty-seven, I had to sign a statement (like Sarah in the Bible) promising to bring up 'the children of the marriage as Catholics'. At the CIIR meeting afterwards, everyone congratulated Harold on the various stands he has taken about Nicaragua and Latin America generally.

22 July

In New York. Harold talked proudly for the first time of the *Pinter Review* (American-based periodical of the Pinter Society). He is youthfully boastful about it. I think this is because it includes an article in this issue about 'Harold Pinter, Citizen': the thing which concerns him most these days being the-artist-is-also-a citizen. (He still doesn't read the literary stuff, but then out of choice he never does that.) I am reminded of Simon Gray's joke: Simon declined to contribute to *Pinter Review* I on the grounds that he was founding his own English Pinter Society. This imaginary society duly got acknowledged in *Pinter Review* I as 'our sister organization', since Harold forgot to tell the editor that it was all a joke. There were more acknowledgements in *Pinter Reviews* II and III. Future scholars in the British Library will never believe it didn't exist and will comb the records endlessly. Now Carlos Fuentes, who is doing a piece for *Pinter Review* IV, proposes to sign it: 'Carlos Fuentes, President, Mexican Pinter Society'.

27 August

The day my dream – fantasy as it had seemed for a long time – came true and in a ceremony of 'grave simplicity' (Harold's words) we had our close-on ten-year marriage 'convalidated' (Father Michael's words) in an upstairs chapel at Farm Street. I learnt later from Diana Phipps that it had been the chapel used by the gallant Czech airmen in the war. Edward Fitzgerald, our newish son-in-law, and Rebecca were our witnesses; their daughter Blanche, aged three months, was parked in a suite at the Connaught Hotel the while, with an appropriate carer. The fact it was my birthday solved the problem of two wedding anniversaries: we shall continue to celebrate 27 November. So now I am well and truly in a state of grace!! A lot of my feeling of fulfilment and happiness was due to the quiet, dignified benevolence of Father Michael, his absolute consideration of Harold's feelings in the texts he used: we were referred to as being a fruitful life and also continuing a fruitful life.

I bore a wedding bouquet of white roses, freesias and myrtle – picked from my own myrtle, grown from a cutting from Mummy's wedding bouquet. In an access of discretion, Rebecca insisted on carrying it for me across the road 'in case anyone should realize you are getting married' although an unlikelier scenario – a middle-aged woman and man not in bridal clothes – is difficult to imagine. No one else was invited other than Diana Phipps, who had intended to come from Czechoslovakia, but at the last minute Olga Havel came to stay.

Harold had cogitated in advance whether he would join in anything (nothing he didn't agree with) but in fact as the ceremony progressed, joined in more and more, I noticed. Rebecca read from the Song of Solomon, Edward delivered St Paul to the Colossians with its admonition about 'forbearing one another': 'And above all these put on love, which binds everything together in perfect harmony'. Then we all declaimed Psalm 148: 'Praise him, sun and moon, Praise him, shining stars.' And this is where Harold began to join in, for as I pointed out, this is *your* Old Testament. The Gospel was the wedding feast at Cana, chosen by me because it seemed so absolutely right for us – the best wine left till last.

After it was all over, we went to the Connaught and drank a great deal of champagne. Little Blanche attempted to gnaw my knobbly pearl ring which Harold had given me as birthday present-cum wedding ring, blessed by Father Michael. The huge blue-green eyes which would make her a great beauty in eighteen years' time were at present fixed avidly on the sanctified jewel.

Later Harold and I went to see the Turners in the Clore Gallery: that was an extension of the beauty of the day, a day which had begun with good wishes from Salman Rushdie and Olga Havel (it transpired that Václav Havel had visited the 'Czech' Chapel when in England). Then Harold watched the English team save a cricket match and I fell asleep.

The advent of Edward Fitzgerald into our family circle had brought happiness to every single member of it, starting with my father, who found in Edward the soul-mate he'd craved in his work for prisoners generally thought to be beyond redemption. That side of Edward – which enabled Harold to quote Yeats to him many years later: 'He served human liberty' – was immensely appealing to him. Then there was a personality rightly termed 'genial'. (Edward's favourite word.) A radical lawyer, he had been described to me before we met as looking like Dionysus and working for every good – if hopeless – cause, quite apart from having a double First in Classics at Oxford.

As for Harold, he had been especially touched when Rebecca invited him to give her away at their wedding. Pouring himself into a hired morning suit for her sake, he reflected: 'I haven't worn one of these since I acted Sir Robert Chiltern in *A Woman of No Importance*.' The other eternally happy event in the family circle occurred the year before when Flora gave birth to Stella.

15 May 1987

Having been invited to attend, about 1 a.m. I received a call from the hospital – the baby wouldn't come before breakfast. I was curiously wakeful, most unlike me at that time of night, and thought I might just as well get up and go to the hospital; I wore my Tree of Life brooch (lucky). Walked into the room in St Mary's. 'You're just in time,' said Sister. It was an amazing sight, one of the most thrilling, unexpected moments of my life, the emergence of a tiny human being into a new world. It was an experience I'd had six times myself but never witnessed. (It was my mother who witnessed the births of my children.) There was so much going on, the baby was so small. Then Sister said: 'It's a lovely little girl.' The young father said to the young mother: 'All this happiness and she's a girl.' So Stella Elizabeth Powell-Jones, the first grandchild, later to be known for this reason as Senior, illumined our lives from that spring night onwards.

This first stage in the welcome enlargement of the family circle was completed in late 1990, when Benjie brought his new girlfriend to play tennis with us at the Vanderbilt Club.

We had joined the Vanderbilt five years earlier: we liked the fact that the décor of the bar resembled the Carlyle Hotel in New York but the whole structure was actually perched on top of a railway hangar at much less chic Shepherd's Bush. I knew it was for Harold when I saw the notice: 'Members Personal Laundry Done'. Harold said: 'As I pull a muscle every time I play cricket [he was fifty-five], I shall concentrate on active tennis.' There were those that maintained Harold remained a maniacal squash-player to the end of his days on the tennis court. The art of serving certainly eluded him: as against that, he had been Pinter the Sprinter at school – as he often reminded us – and could outrun many younger men. All in all, many of our happiest leisure hours were spent at the Vanderbilt.

14 December 1990

Lucy Roper-Curzon, aged twenty-one, looks like the nymph Ondine, tall and slender with fair floating hair, enormous almond-shaped blue eyes, translucent complexion fresh from some spring and wears nymph-like clothes to play tennis: a long trailing diaphanous skirt which contrasts strangely with our rugged tracksuits. She proves to be by far the best player on the court, her long skirts no obstacle to fast running, her slender arms capable of the most swingeing hard strokes.

Lucy and Benjie got married the following July at Pylewell, the Elysian country house of her parents John and Elizabeth Teynham. The magic setting on the Solent, combined with the family life all round – Lucy had nine siblings including musicians and a sculptor, and there was even a cricket pitch – made this a favourite place for us to visit.

By the time of Harold's death twenty-one years later, Stella had become Senior to sixteen other grandchildren; the last born that he knew was Ruby, who contributed a memorable photographic image (which he had on his desk) of Harold dangling a toy before her. The baby with her angelic white-blonde curls and wide blue eyes gazes in polite amazement at the strange behaviour of a grown-up man. It was actually a rattle he had brought from Nicaragua to amuse Stella all those years ago: known as 'the revolutionary rattle'. Harold adored small babies; all round he loved the relationship of quasi-grandfather (the children's real grandfather had died three years before Stella was born) terming himself 'Grandpa' with zest. Benjie's three sons, close together in age, Thomas, William and Hugh, getting up at first light to play cricket together on a lawn outside some holiday house, recreated his own childhood obses-sion. Later it dawned on the grandchildren that 'Grandpa' was a name with which to impress their teachers: 'Oh, really, not *the* Harold Pinter ...' would be said with thoughtful interest in reaction to the throwaway line from a grandchild which introduced the name. As Harold's plays were regularly set for public exams over the years, I guessed that his reputation soared upwards in the eyes of the younger generation.

On the subject of family life, Harold and I had once discussed the matter generally when we were in Venice. We both had a sense of Armageddon, brought on by Margaret Atwood's extraordinarily prophetic novel-of-the-future *The Handmaid's Tale*, for which he had been asked to write a screenplay. The book haunted my dreams in the most terrifying fashion: every 'intelligent' woman's nightmare, complete powerlessness, total subjugation of one sex to another for breeding purposes as well as giving me fresh insight into what it was like to be a seventeenth-century woman. We get on to the discussion of the family. Talked of the break-up of the wide, warm, family circle of his childhood and what had been lost. Harold: 'You're different. You've still got one.'

Perhaps it was relevant that Harold was beginning to lose touch with his son, who was living in the country; he once said about the relationship that he felt 'a great sense of failure'. Eventually in about 1993 Harold stopped having personal contact with his son altogether (although he continued to support him). There was no actual break-up so far as I know, merely a distancing. It seems that they both preferred it that way. Instinctively I could see that it was not easy for anyone to bear a famous and distinctive name – which is why Harold's son had chosen to give up the Pinter name before we ever met. Unfortunately, unlike a name, the burden of being a son of a famous man is not so easily put aside. Nevertheless Harold's son had the right to choose to pass from his father's story, a right I will respect.

At the time, as Harold discoursed on the loss of the family circle of his childhood, I made a different point: 'There is another side to the family too. You wrote the most chilling and discerning play about the subject once. I think it's called *The Homecoming*. We have to ask ourselves: Why on earth did Teddy choose to come back to that nest of vipers? He just couldn't resist it.' Harold quoted Lenny's welcome to Teddy with a smile then wrote it down for me in my Diary: 'Hello, Lenny.' 'Hello, Teddy.' 'I didn't hear you come down the stairs.' 'I didn't.'

Our shared life with children and grandchildren was mercifully nothing like as dramatic. As to family holidays, in the eighties up to the mid nineties, they were once summed up with the following Pinteresque comment reported in my Diary when we were in the Algarve with my mother: 'As Harold says about our conversations here, two people here call me Mummy, and one person calls her Mummy, and two people here call her Grannie and I call three people Darling, and she calls three people Darling (but not the same three people).' Or then there was a passionate poem written in Paxos in August 1987. What actually kicked it off was passion of another sort: Harold's rage against the Italian tourists who defiled the beach below our rented house with raucous goings-on in the small hours and caused him much helpless anguish as he brooded in the darkness above, refusing to go to bed with the words: 'I'm guarding the house.' But as ever with Harold, the original touchstone soon became quite irrelevant compared to the joy of creation. These lines referred back to his first poem to me, 'Paris', written in 1975, quoting the last line at the start.

TO ANTONIA

'She dances in my life'
Still you turn in my arms
Still we clasp
Still you swim in the big and brilliant bay
And come backing the wave
To my side
And you dance in my arms
And you turn
And stay in my clasp
Where I found you forever
In the only first time in my life
Which calls out again and again
In the light of this moon on our sea
In our fierce and young and tender tide
My dancer my bride.

A feature of these holidays were the play-readings which reached their height of excellence, surely, when something we dubbed the Playwrights Express landed in Paxos: the Simon Grays and the Ronnie Harwoods.

We address Simon and Ronnie on arrival; they had both written published Diaries in the past: 'When are you going to write the Diary of this week?' we ask. Simon, casually, lighting a cigarette: 'Oh, I've written that in advance.'

There was much planning of walks round the island but Ronnie says he must work, referring to the 'scorpions in my mind'. 'Oh well,' says Simon, 'that leaves adultery for the rest of us.' Later I suggest a play-reading, tossing up between the works of Simon and the works of Ronnie. Simon: 'As a matter of fact, I did bring a couple of copies of *Otherwise Engaged* over on the boat.' He looks for a laugh. Me, smoothly: 'That makes five copies, because actually I took the precaution of bringing with me three copies each of *Otherwise Engaged* and *The Dresser*.' In the event we read both on successive nights. At the end, we agreed that it was miraculous that six people, three of them playwrights, in a rented house in Greece, could enjoy themselves for a week in harmony. After all, we were on an island. It could have been an Agatha Christie situation . . .

At this auspicious moment we decided to plan for the time when the auguries would not be so favourable.

19 March 1992

Feast of St Joseph. I have long been concerned that for people who cared so passionately about graves, beauty and history, we don't have graves which we can, as it were, look forward to occupying. We are forever visiting writers' graves: Tennyson, Williams, Joyce, Philip Larkin when we were in Hull. (At the latter grave, shortly after Larkin's death, we had seen a deadish fuchsia, really dead cornflowers in a glass and some perky flourishing scarlet geraniums. Harold hissed: 'No flowers on *my* grave.') Coincidentally I read about Trollope's grave in the magazine *The Trollopian*, together with an account of Kensal

ᴛ: East Coker church containing the memorial to T.S. Eliot where Harold recited 'Little Gidding' by
ᴛake.
ʜᴛ: Listening to Eliot.

As Goldberg in a TV production of *The Birthday Party* including Julie Walt[ers,] Ken Cranham and Joan Plowright. Harold inscribed the[se] photograph himself: 'Uncle Cuddles ... l[ove] H'.

Love
G

Uncle Cuddles

Harold, Liv Ullman[n] and Nicola Pagett, *C[alls]? Times*, Los Angeles, 1985.

OPPOSITE PAGE:
Antonia, George Galloway and Harol[d] releasing 'the Black Balloon' and carryin[g] crosses symbolising [the] Nicaraguan war dea[d] outside the US Emba[ssy,] Grosvenor Square, 1987.

Harold and Václav Havel, 1989.

...vel interviews Harold about theatre.

...ga and Václav Havel, Rita ...mova and Diana Phipps ...lcome us with a Union ...k outside Havel's house, ...adecek, Czechoslovakia, ...89.

Harold greets Daniel Ortega, President of Nicaragua, on his arrival at Campden Hill Square, 1989

Listening to Daniel Ortega

At Cibo's restaurant for Harold's sixtieth birthday party, 10 October 1990.

Venice in January: sunshine and Corvo Bianco.

Green Cemetery, still run by the General Cemetery Co. after 150 years.

I made an appointment and told Harold what I had done. Me: 'Will you drive me to my grave or I drive you?' Then a burly man of suspicious aspect drove us through the long avenues of the graveyard in a decommissioned taxi of ancient date. As a metaphor for death, a dusty black taxi, left ticking over while we inspected areas, was something Cocteau wouldn't have dared. At one point, he poked his head back through the glass partition and asked: 'When did the deceased pass away?' 'We are the deceased,' we replied, merrily.

I asked for somewhere secluded, adding, 'We're writers,' as though we would be toiling away in the future and need some peace. Thus we strolled and clambered among the most beautiful mausoleums, ivy-covered columns, Gothic, oriental oaks, birds; all with a splendid secular early nineteenth-century feel to it (the cemetery was founded so that people of all religions – or none – could lie together in it, which suited us). Afterwards we went for an exceptionally jolly lunch à deux, which also suited us.

Chapter Fourteen

———

MOONLIGHT AND ASHES

Harold and I both voted Labour in the 1992 election, having supported the party at the previous one, and counting ourselves as supporters of the new leader Neil Kinnock. As always seemed to happen to me (call it prejudice!), I was an even stronger supporter of Glenys Kinnock, but then she was not actually the candidate. Reading the newspapers we noted that words like 'a new era' were being bandied round.

9 April

Polling Day. Ended up at Melvyn and Cate Braggs' house in Hampstead. I was quietly confident that Labour would win. Therefore the behaviour of various important TV executives after 10 p.m. and mutters like 'It doesn't look good', passed me by completely. Lots of departures by other people also failed to make a mark. In the end Harold and I were left looking at the television in bewilderment – the results seem to be perfectly all right to us. The room was empty except for a couple of cheerful men. They proved to be Salman Rushdie's bodyguards. I suppose in the world of bodyguards, business is always good, whatever the outcome of the election. We trailed home to Notting Hill Gate listening gloomily to the radio as we went. It was shaming to have the defeat of the Tory, Chris Patten, in his Bath constituency, hailed as some kind of Labour victory: he is after all a decent, liberal man, and it's sad he's not in Parliament, whatever his allegiance. Afterwards we learned that certain Tories were supposed to have rejoiced as well. A depressing business.

Five years later, by which time the Labour Party was being led by Tony Blair, we both voted for the party again. I had listened to Tony Blair speak to the Fabian Society shortly after the unexpected, sad death of the previous leader, John Smith, and had been deeply impressed by his sincerity. After all the so-called sleaze swirling around in politics at the time, here at last was a straight man. I liked his smile. It was an enthusiastic, boyish, above all an *honourable* smile. Such a man could not lie. So I joined the Labour Party on the day he was elected leader (as it happened, in spite of living in and around parliamentary politics for the first forty-two years of my life, I had never joined a political party; although party workers of all persuasions were always among the people I liked most).

1 May 1997

Polling Day. Voted, with Harold, at noon up at Fox Primary School. Only one teller, a Tory, a jolly blue-rinser who bemoaned the lack of tellers for the other parties: 'Once we tellers had such wonderful talks ...' The truth is, we are now a small safe Conservative seat. Later we went up to Melvyn and Cate's in Hampstead as before, in a hired car. Me to Harold: 'Would it be the height of radical chic to ask for a driver who is a Labour voter?' Melvyn beaming and friendly as usual, but that means nothing: he was beaming in 1992. Michael Foot, who was ostensibly co-host (as in 1992) very frail, there with his dog, Dizzy, aged seventeen, also very frail. A touching sight. I sat next to him on the sofa. Michael Foot didn't quiver when the various TV programmes referred insistently to his 'disastrous leadership'. Others present included Salman as before and his wife Elizabeth West, expecting a child imminently, looking like a Madonna with her mystically beautiful and tranquil face. Also Kathy Lette jumping up and down like a sexy frog as – at last! – the results came in and this time it really was going to be a victory. No, a landslide.

We decided to indulge ourselves by going to the BBC party.

Christopher Bland, Chairman of the BBC, very bonhomous. *Enormous* security to get in (the IRA does not go away). It was another kind of rout. Such delight as the Tory grandees crumbled on the screen and crumbled in our sight at the party. Allegiances were being hastily shuffled. For example, I like to think that John Birt's face shaded from blue to pink as in a Disney cartoon, while I was watching. Later we had yet another party at home with the cats, Catalina and Casimir, strong Labour voters both of them, and champagne. By three o'clock in the morning everything was a blair, I mean a blur. Memorable day to be compared with that marvellous summer's day in 1945 when following the landslide victory of Labour, my father's friends predicted to this awed, happy schoolgirl that Labour would 'rule Britain for fifty years'. Of course it was actually six . . . but this time it was going to be different.

The chart of Harold's loss of faith in the Labour government began with the situation in former Yugoslavia. Along with many others, including me, he disapproved strongly of NATO's action against Serbia following the failure of the Rambouillet Agreement starting in March 1999. This NATO campaign had of course the full support of the British government. None of this was easy, starting with the situation in Kosovo. What action, if any, should be taken by outsiders when atrocities were taking place? There were after all atrocities by Albanians as well as Serbs. What was the role, what *should* be the role of the all-powerful US? Personally I rather agreed with a letter in the *Guardian*, rather rude, saying that Kosovans didn't give a toss about US foreign policy: they just wanted to be rescued.

Yet under any circumstances, it was difficult to see that NATO bombs constituted any solution to a place already tormented by so many historical, tribal issues. Bombs, after all, are no respecters of persons.

8 May 1999

We get the news of the NATO bombing of the Chinese Embassy in

Belgrade. It is announced 'with regret'. Just one of those mistakes. Oh, so that's all right. To say nothing of a cluster bomb in a market, grandmas and grandpas bestrewed about, dead amid their vegetable stalls. This week has naturally been dominated by the war. Harold's broadcast on Tuesday was icily brilliant, pale (chest infection), all in black (natural plumage) and then he spoke the now famous words: 'What is moral authority? Where does it come from? Who bestows it upon you? . . . It is *power*.' Then he clenched his fist very slowly. Letters are flowing in via the BBC. I try to persuade Harold to find some way of answering them. 'People feel powerless, so they write to you and thank you for speaking up for them. They mustn't feel they've reached another void.' All this time he has felt quite ill, but is resolute.

———

Harold remained a resolute defender of the Serbs as being unfairly victimized, held solely responsible for a ghastly situation in which many others were equally guilty. In later years, he was informed he had become a hero to the Serbs, which he found unexpected and gratifying. In later years, also, Harold and I came to disagree on one aspect of this war and its consequences. That is to say, the trial of the Serbian leader, Milosevic for war crimes. While I had deplored the bombing of Belgrade, I supported this trial. Harold, on the other hand, disapproved of it strongly, signed letters protesting against it – in his opinion there were many other 'war criminals' and he was generally extremely active on the subject.

For a long time he never argued the point with me, but in the face of all Harold's activities my silence was no doubt eloquent. Harold did finally raise it at dinner one night. He explained that he did not (necessarily) believe Milosevic was innocent but that he thought what happened was illegal: the Court of Justice was in essence just NATO – his enemy. I put my opposite point of view: that it was good to try war criminals and although this court, like Nuremberg, was not perfect (think of the USSR then presiding over a court condemning atrocities!) yet it was better than no court at all. You will never have perfect human justice at a court run by imperfect humans. I pointed out the case of Pinochet: there had been something uncomfortable about a Spanish judge, a member of the former imperialist power, doling out justice to a Chilean. But it was still the right thing to do.

The radical and surprising action recently taken against Pinochet, indicted while in England by a Spanish judge for what he had done to a Spanish citizen in Chile during his 'reign' as leader, was dramatic and encouraging, unlike the whole situation of former Yugoslavia. Harold's sympathies for those who had suffered after the fall of the Allende regime – the 'Disappeared', many of them very young who had been first interrogated, then tortured, then eliminated – remained as acute as ever. In 1998 he wrote a poem on the subject, inspired as it turned out by a visit to the Sainsbury Wing of the National Gallery to see an exhibition of the Dutch painters of Utrecht, entitled 'Masters of Light'.

19 July 1998

Extraordinary daring effects; all the painters had been to Rome and there was a strong Caravaggesque feeling.

We liked *The Denial of St Peter* especially, the amazing construction, the arm blocking the candle completely, the candle which illuminates the girl's face. Then Harold gave a sort of groan; 'I haven't got any paper.' But I had some at the back of my little diary. Ripped it out. So he sat down there and then in the National Gallery and wrote a poem which came to be called 'The Disappeared'. He told me later that a large image of Samson, the shackles especially prominent, was the key inspiration. What did people think of this dark figure scribbling furiously? I did not wait to find out but went and shopped for Art Kitsch upstairs.

THE DISAPPEARED

Lovers of light, the skulls,
The burnt skin, the white

Flash of the night,
The heat in the death of men.
The hamstring and the heart
Torn apart in a musical room,
Where children of the light
Know that their kingdom has come.

In October 1998 an enormous amount of time was consumed talking about General Pinochet, rejoicing at his detention, worrying at the result of the judgment in the House of Lords. Harold was philosophical: 'At least things about Chile in those days have been aired. People of twenty-two who have never heard of Chile, let alone Pinochet, and the tortures which were administered, now know all about it.'

25 November

Pinochet judgment in the House of Lords due at 2 p.m. We settled ourselves in front of TV, focused on BBC 24. View of the House of Lords totally empty, then a few peers saunter in, followed by the five Law Lords, who all seem to be very tall. Perhaps becoming a Law Lord makes you grow. We watchers have been coached in what will happen beforehand by Joshua Rozenberg, BBC legal correspondent. If the appeal is 'Allowed', then Pinochet is in trouble. So when the first Lord gives a 'Disallowed' to the Appeal, I put my thumb down to Harold beside me. Lord Lloyd also indicates 'Disallowed'. It seems all is lost (as we had expected). Then: Lord Nicholls: 'Allowed'. Then Lord Steyn: 'ALLOWED'. Lastly Lord Hoffman, a grim-looking man, but how we loved him! Because he indicated: ALLOWED. It was, so Rozenberg told us from the box, the first time such a judgment had been televised. We drink to the ruin of dictators starting with Pinochet.

Later the sight of the relatives of the Disappeared weeping on TV is immensely moving. Others scream and leap for joy. Pro-Pinochet women in Chile, mainly blue-rinsed, are seen to lunge at reporters.

Harold agreed to go on *Newsnight*. He was quite nervous, he admitted later. He looked calmly vengeful on screen and saw off Norman Lamont, who said that the Chilean people had given Pinochet immunity. Harold: 'No, *Pinochet* gave Pinochet immunity.'

All the time the shadow of the coming (First) Iraq War was falling athwart the British political scene. There was, for example, an Emergency Committee meeting about Iraq at the House of Commons early in 1988.

12 February

There were extraordinary scenes outside St Stephen's entrance, big crowds, flaring TV lights, policemen pretty stroppy. As 'speakers' we got in with some difficulty. (We learnt later that neither Valerie Grove of *The Times* nor Adrian Mitchell, poet and protester, got in at all, being sent to 'the back of the queue'.) Packed meeting in a large committee room in the far corner of Westminster Hall. As we crossed the Hall, I found myself treading on the plaque to Sir Thomas More – another man of conscience. Tony Benn batted off and was excellent, clear, firm. Stated that he was not in favour of Saddam Hussein, but in his meeting with Iraqi dissidents he'd found that none of them were in favour of any kind of invasion since it would merely strengthen Saddam. Harold was good, short and to the point. He, too, although he had demonstrated against Saddam and his treatment of the Kurds, did not think that bombing civilians was the answer. Diane Abbott, an impressive figure, large, beautiful, high rounded forehead, spoke with authority and verve.

As an example of a situation developing in a different, more encouraging direction, we visited Belfast (first time for both of us) in the same year.

2/3 December

Nothing prepared us for the Terror Tour – local black phrase of taxi drivers. The sheer narrowness of the districts we have heard about on the news. Little Protestant streets, so close to famous Catholic streets. Huge graffiti, but that is not the right word for these awesome artworks on walls: the Red Hand of Ulster or Cuchulainn. We were driven by the distinguished poet Michael Longley. The first police car we saw was like something out of *Dr Who*: heavy, dark grey all over, an armoured pill box on wheels, narrow slits instead of windows.

But Michael is actually reporting progress. 'A year ago there would have been policemen everywhere in the streets, grilles, bricks fortifying every shop, practically no windows. The building of the new centre by the docks is a sign of hope because it has glass. Mind you, the strongest glass they could find, but still glass.' We liked both the two young writers that escorted us: Colin Teevan, writer-in-residence at Queen's University and Glen Patterson. Michael Longley is a big, fine-looking man, huge brown eyes, white hair and beard, tweed jacket, rough scarf. I was ignorant of his poetry but Harold has always admired it and read me several poems. Michael Longley told us that he had been offered creative writing courses in America 'but it's just too interesting to leave'. I noticed how all of them, including Edna Longley, Professor of Literature, felt they were contributing something to the country – that something being moderation.

In view of Harold's general preoccupation with politics and the oppressed in many, many countries, it should be recorded that the first play he wrote in the nineties could not possibly be argued to be political even by the most wily interpreter of his art. This was the play he called *Moonlight*, written in late 1992 and first performed the next year. In my opinion it derived fundamentally from another very different human experience, his mother's death, peacefully in a nursing home in Hove in early October, at the age of eighty-eight. *Moonlight* is redolent of death;

it is the story of a dying person, actually a man nursed by his wife, whose sons refuse to come home to say goodbye to him. What tipped Harold into writing a play was, I believe, the fact that he was actually rehearsing to play the part of Hirst in his own play *No Man's Land* at the Almeida Theatre at the time. Having spent most of his time with his mother in the summer, now he had to interrupt rehearsals to rush down to Hove at the end. Thereafter, even more importantly, he was closeted in a dressing room with three other actors, Paul Eddington, Gawn Grainger and Doug Hodge. This comradeship was very important to him. Going down to see his father, now alone aged ninety, Harold began scribbling in the train. He gave me the odd bulletin: 'A mother, a father, two brothers.' He began toiling throughout the frosty nights, in his Super-Study across the garden. 'Maybe a daughter,' he said one evening. The characters were, as usual despite my protests, known as A, B, C & D. Now we had E.

January 1993

Mauritius. Royal Palm Hotel. Harold has hired a 'manual typewriter' (last of a dying race) and last night got back to the yellow pages, scrutinizing the airline paper he had scribbled on in first class all night on the way here. This was because the noise from the headset worn by Lester Piggott in the row ahead was extremely loud: Lester is deaf but we are not. It proved however creative. More characters have entered. The play begins with a daughter called Bridget. Now Harold types and types and is totally happy. I hear the rat-tat-tat of the typewriter even when I'm swimming in the ocean.

13 January

Even a cyclone, hoving somewhere in the Indian Ocean near us, does not disturb Harold's rhythm. In fact it rather inspires him. Read *Moonlight* as it has become. School of *No Man's Land*, if one can talk like that. Harold even scribbled away on his little pad at dinner. I didn't mind as I was trying to think of a way to scrape acquaintance with Lester Piggott, my hero forever. All my life I always used to bet on him.

15 January

Did the timing. Fifty-four minutes. Harold very firm: 'This *is* a full-length play.' But later more scenes come to him. We're up to sixty-one minutes. And we're going to have dinner with Lester tomorrow night! With all my timings, Harold calls me his editor. Not so. I was the midwife saying, 'Push, Harold, push,' but the act of creation took place elsewhere and the baby would have been born anyway. Harold very firm that E, now Bridget, who is a ghost, is dead because she has committed suicide.

3 February

Doug Hodge 'crazy' about *Moonlight:* wants to be involved. And Ian Holm has put himself forward as Andy, the father, which touches Harold very much, with their shared history over *The Homecoming* so many years ago.

7 September

The first night of *Moonlight*. Harold, typically, found himself near a woman at the first preview who sorted through her Sainsbury's bag of shopping throughout the play. The next morning (after the first night) Harold said, 'Let's face the music', the familiar phrase, and went downstairs to fetch the papers. 'Good God, it's on the front page of the *Guardian*!' And so it was. A large photo of Anna Massey, Ian Holm in bed, and a rave review. Benedict Nightingale insisted on saying he was so pleased Harold had deserted politics – because frankly nobody can possibly pretend *Moonlight* is a political play. Harold delighted, unequivocally delighted. The Sundays less good although we were both amused when Michael Coveney called, as I predicted someone would, for 'hard-edged political plays' – instead of, presumably, boring things about life, death and loss.

4 November

Moonlight transferred to the Comedy. Even better than at the Almeida. Boys speedier, wittier. Half the critics think it is a tragedy of a mother alienated from her sons, the others think it's a father ditto. Why not both? Anna Massey's Russian husband says triumphantly: 'Ah, I get it at last. The boys have AIDS.'

———

Harold continued to enjoy life on stage as well as behind the scenes. The summer of 1995 saw a particularly happy combination, as I saw it, of Harold directing and acting, and me working on a historical book. My book *The Gunpowder Plot*, which I had long wanted to do, explored the world of the Catholic recusants – refuseniks as they would be called today – in the Elizabethan world, the factors which led to that great (unsuccessful) terrorist plot in November 1605. It was a subject which had fascinated me ever since my arrival at St Mary's Ascot. As a Protestant girl of Anglo-Irish and Nonconformist ancestry – about to be converted to the Catholic Church – I there encountered the famous, revered names of England's Catholic past. It wasn't a project with built-in commercial appeal, although incidentally it appealed very much to Harold: I had to change my American publisher to persist in the project across the Atlantic.

In the meantime Harold was delighted to be asked to direct Ronnie Harwood's new play *Taking Sides*, about Wilhelm Furtwängler and his relationship with the Nazi regime. He was full of admiration for Ronnie for handling the theme of art and collaboration so well. It was a good year altogether: two grandchildren born, William and Honor, and even our cat, beloved Catalina, gave birth to two kittens under my bed: Pushkin and Placido (Placido is with me as I write).

*

At the beginning of August, we rented a house, allegedly near Chichester, which turned out to be near Petworth. Harold acted the tyrannical part of Colonel Roote in his own play *The Hothouse*; I worked on revising *The Plot* and was driven over the darkening Sussex hills in the evening to join him for dinner after the theatre. It was a magic time.

27 August

My sixty-third birthday. Dada has just told me on the telephone that, at this age, Churchill had yet to become Prime Minister and Attlee did become Prime Minister and so forth. Me: 'I shall expect the call at any moment.' Dada continues: 'And I resigned from the cabinet, and Newman wrote *Apologia Pro Vita Sua*.' He added kindly: 'It's a zenith.' Ronnie and Natasha Harwood stayed here, to see *The Hothouse*. Ronnie on his success with *Taking Sides* (which Harold had directed): 'It's so extraordinary at sixty when one is declining.' Me: 'One is *not*.' And Ronnie certainly isn't. Amazing lunch party to which all the actors and their families came, as well as Betty Bacall: always a great hit with staff because she not only is famous but looks famous. The actors ate and ate and ate. They stayed till about six although Harold stumped off for a siesta before that, and issued some Roote-like instructions out of the window for some quiet (which everyone ignored, unintimidated, I was glad to see).

Harold's next play which became *Ashes to Ashes* first emerged in my Diary in 1996.

25 January

Harold told me at dinner that Judy Daish (his agent and friend) had almost choked on the telephone when he said: 'I'm writing.' Me: 'Do these people *move* or is it a radio play?' Harold did not accept the distinction, saying: 'Don't forget that *Landscape* began as a radio play.' Harold, having read it through, reported: 'It's a plant. It's alive. Now I shall see whether it wants to grow or wants to remain as it is.'

He was referring to the fact that none of his recent plays – since *Betrayal* in fact – had been long. There had been *Party Time*, for example, timed by me on my stop watch at the first reading by Harold in the drawing room at thirty-three and a half minutes. Harold was happy with that: they were the length they were, as he was fond of pointing out to managements; the latter were faced with the problem – if it was a problem – of the public expecting a full-length evening. I believe that *Ashes to Ashes* was in some way sparked off in Harold's imagination by Gitta Sereny's life of Albert Speer, which he had read with total absorption the whole of one holiday.

19 January

Harold: 'I've just realized that I would have been dead if the Nazis had invaded. Aged ten.' Me: 'Have you never thought this before? I used to look at your parents having lunch at Eaton Manor Gardens in Hove sometimes, your father so feisty, your mother so gracious, and think that these two decent, dignified people would have died in conditions of unspeakable humiliation and terror.' We then discuss whether the ten-year-old Harold would not have been shipped off by his parents to relatives in the US, fare provided perhaps by Uncle Coleman. Harold warms to the theme: 'And then I'd probably have grown up to vote Republican. A Reaganite.' The alternative Harold? Like the Oxford don that never was, the one that drank claret and played cricket and never lifted up a pen.

24 January

A and B are stalking the land again! Harold started to scribble. He came over for supper having written a scene of great power which he read to me. A man and his wife. He then wrote on until after one. Rather erotic. Rather horrible. So far.

28 January

Harold wrote madly on Thursday, seven hours yesterday. He's very excited about it: as he said. It came to him just as he was talking to Tom Rand, so he bustled him out. (Tom Rand was doing the costumes for *Twelve Angry Men* which Harold was about to direct.) Now that I have heard the whole thing, it may come from *Speer*. But the first image is never the point with Harold. It's now taken quite a different path, i.e. it's set in the present day.

30 January

The play has grown. Scenes came to Harold in the middle of the night. I found notes scribbled in the bathroom. He even wrote during breakfast.

25 February

Harold read *Ashes to Ashes* (which will probably be done upstairs at the Ambassadors Theatre – suitably small) to Salman and Elizabeth West. Everyone deeply moved but Salman suggested he put 'Time: present', since even Salman hadn't understood that. And it's vital. This is taking place now, not in Nazi Germany.

———

Later, Harold talked about the play to the young foreign playwrights at the Royal Court. This was a gig organized by Elyse Dodgson that Harold took part in annually. The presence of serious young – twenty to thirty-five, at a guess – people of an extraordinary variety of nationalities, Israelis and Syrians, Serbians and Croatians, Chinese, Americans, often brought out answers from him about the meaning of his plays which he would decline to offer to English audiences. Although it should be recorded that on one famous occasion, a man declared himself as a playwright coming from Uganda, then added, 'I earn my living as a dentist.' With his scalpel, as it were, he proceeded to dig into the fact that Harold had been writing plays for forty years. 'So why don't you retire now and make room for younger people like me?'

On this occasion however, there were no such enjoyable diversions. Harold said an interesting thing about the character of Rebecca in *Ashes to Ashes*, 'She is the artist who cannot avoid the world's pain', and he equated himself with her (this was the time of the savage war in Lebanon, for which Harold, at a time of great physical weakness, was being asked on every side to speak; sign petitions, etc.). Devlin stands for the rest of the world who ends up by being brutal towards her. I ask him afterwards: 'But isn't there another side to Devlin? He is trying to help Rebecca to stay sane and have a normal life, i.e. those references to Kim and the Kids.'

Whatever gloss may be put on it, *Ashes to Ashes* – whose clear narrative was not fully understood at the time, I thought – ends on a note of savage despair. Harold's own *weltschmerz* was very marked at times. This was quite different from our occasional arguments which one might even call rows. After all, these resulted in some of the most passionate love letters he ever wrote as gestures of reconciliation: certainly the smooth side of the rough, to adapt Harold's favourite phrase.

21 October 1996

In New York with Harold. I am on a book tour for *The Gunpowder Plot*, here called *Treason and Faith* ('Americans know about treason,' says my publisher Nan Talese, 'they don't know about the Gunpowder Plot'). Harold does a reading of *Ashes to Ashes* at the YMHA which has a bizarre beginning to question time: the essential comic note, perhaps, to give relief in a deeply serious occasion. First questioner, female dressed in a navy-blue uniform of some sort, cropped blonde hair: 'Mr Pinter, do you approve of sado-masochism?' Harold startled, makes some bonhomous reply which, he hopes, neither hints at a taste for whips nor the desire to feel their impact. On she went: 'Speaking as I do as a professional dominatrix . . .' Lugubrious man, monk's face, very tall, who runs the Y: 'Thirty years of poetry readings, and this is the first question from a dominatrix.' All this puts Harold in a very good temper and he indicates he may after all come to New York again.

This was in contrast to the night before. He had had a spat with a political commentator on the right at *my* publishing party which may have pleased the commentator as fulfilling his expectations, but greatly displeased me. We had the kind of row at the end of the evening which no doubt marks many of the happiest of marriages. Harold said he would never come to New York again and I said that was fine by me. Etc. etc. Even Harold's usual mantra, 'We are two strong characters in the same marriage,' did not assuage my wrath and the sundown must have been one of the latest ever. We were finally reconciled. His very frequent telephone calls to me as I carried out my subsequent book tour amazed my various publishers' escorts, one of whom asked me: 'How long have you two been together?' Actually my mood was of the sunniest by now because while in Canada, quite aside from Harold's assiduity, I received a wonderful telephone call: Flora and Peter Soros were planning to get married, an event which was celebrated the following January in a style worthy of Louis XIV (to whom, with his sense of style as well as his magnificence and his generosity, I would often compare Peter in future years).

13 June 1997

Harold morose – you have to use the word – at lunch. He is seldom like this. We didn't seem to be able to talk. At dinner the next day he explained it to me: his overwhelming sense of the sorrows, and thus the evils of the world. I thought I must put my point of view. Which was that this awareness of world-wrong should not spill into our relationship.

Harold: 'It doesn't! You're the one thing . . .' Me: 'But it does when we have a lunch like that one. All I can do is shelter you under the wide umbrella of my love.' All the same, I have to accept that this too is part of Harold's character – twenty-three years after 'Must you go?' it will never be eradicated, and why should it be? So long as the sorrows and evils are there in the world.

———

The other side of Harold's character, which was perhaps less publicly appreciated than it should have been (because the political outbursts were, so to speak, much better copy) was his generosity: a young poet, an older lady living alone in bad health who had years ago been his valued patron, an actor in trouble, a radical magazine . . . these are only a few of those that come to mind. In particular Harold remembered the acts of generosity which had been shown to him at the start of his career and either consciously or unconsciously (probably the latter) decided to act similarly. He never forgot that the American producer, Roger Stevens, whom he had never met, came to his aid after the fiasco of the first *Birthday Party*; this was at a time when he had a young family and he had no work. Jimmy Wax, his first agent, arranged it: a thousand pounds in about 1959 (a huge sum then) which was like manna in a very desert.

Then there were charities in favour of liberty and against torture, to say nothing of presents and entertainments for the family, or provision of comfortable transport for my parents, indomitable but frail in their nineties. Rather like his courage, Harold took his own generosity for granted, just as he took for granted what we might euphemistically call his outspokenness and could not quite see why other people sometimes objected.

As to patriotism, it might surprise people who only knew of Harold's criticisms of the government to learn that by his own standards Harold was extremely patriotic. I do not mean the sporting test – although naturally Harold had backed the English cricket team since youth. He also, for example, felt strongly that his manuscripts should go to the British Library, whatever the lure of well-endowed American universities which some of his contemporaries had felt. Thus he began by letting his papers go on loan, and ended by selling them not long before his death for a handsome price with which he was more than content. As for me, just as I wanted to lie one day in the next-door grave to Harold, I decided that our papers should lie together too. So I joined him.

25 July 1994

We decided to pay our manuscripts a visit. Harold's were in the familiar, and efficient, green box-files. Mine were in a smart woman's shopping bags: Jean Muir, Ferragamo, The White House, Christian Dior, stuffed with tacky and tatty proofs and papers. I couldn't resist it: I took out my phial of Miss Dior perfume from my purse and *sprayed* my manuscripts. Harold looks up from his inspection of his early works, which he has quite forgotten about: 'That is the most impressive thing I've ever seen in a library. I shall never forget it.' I'm hoping the perfume will steal upon the sense of some researcher in a thousand years' time.

In the high summer of 1997 Harold's father, living in a nursing home since Frances' death in 1992, began to go downhill – health-wise, that is. He was ninety-five. Mentally he had remained astonishingly vigorous, one might even say combative, well into his nineties. One famous New Year's Day when Frances was still alive we went down to Hove to see them both. 'You'll find my father rather frail,' said Harold. Actually we'd hardly sat down in the restaurant before Jack was at it hammer and tongs about Harold's visit to the Israeli Embassy to protest about the solitary confinement of Vanunu: they'd read about it in the *Jewish Chronicle*. 'When are you going to do something to defend Israel?' 'I am defending the rights of an Israeli citizen.' And so on and so forth, Jack getting visibly more forceful with every minute. In the end, I said placatingly to Frances: 'They are so alike, aren't they?' Knowing this was a peace-making appeal that her loving mother's heart could not resist.

8 September 1997

A message to say that Jack Pinter is fading fast. Harold saw him a few days ago and Jack said: 'I just want to get into that bed and fall asleep.' And that I suppose is what he is doing. In a strange re-run of Frances' dying days in 1992, it is now the TUC Conference in Brighton, just as it had been the Tory Conference then. So we are surrounded by police at our hotel, due to the presence of Tony Blair, otherwise many big, burly trades unionists, mainly male, smoking cigars. But this time the *Guardian* is outside every door in the morning when I go to swim, not the *Telegraph*.

When we saw Jack, he had a look of peaceful determination on his face. He died in the small hours. The next morning Harold had an encounter at the Town Hall trying to register the death, which, he said, put up his blood pressure. A maddening bureaucrat kept saying, 'You need an appointment,' as he sat idling behind his desk although there was no one else present. 'But you're free.' Bureaucrat: 'That's because the next person will not arrive for half an hour.' 'Then you're free.' 'But you do not have an appointment.' Etc. etc. In the end Harold got his certificate and rushed back to the hotel.

But it set him off, and he has written a poem, one of his best, I think. It was odd seeing him sit in the hotel amid the suitcases and the trades unionists with his pen and yellow pad, earnestly writing: the best example of art not being part of life but working through it. At the end of writing it, all Harold's agitation with the bureaucrat had disappeared, forgotten; thus you might say the bureaucrat had been the opposite of the person from Porlock who interrupted 'Kubla Khan' forever. Harold's grief for his father remained but had been subsumed.

I have since come to treasure this poem more than any other of Harold's poems with the exception of those he wrote to me. He incorporated it into his Nobel Speech, and I had it read, the very last words of the brief ceremony to mark his burial.

DEATH

(Births and Deaths Registration Act 1953)
Where was the dead body found?
Who found the dead body?
Was the dead body dead when found?
How was the dead body found?

Who was the dead body?

Who was the father or daughter or brother
Or uncle or sister or mother or son
Of the dead and abandoned body?

Was the body dead when abandoned?
Was the body abandoned?
By whom had it been abandoned?

Was the dead body naked or dressed for a journey?

What made you declare the dead body dead?
Did you declare the dead body dead?
How well did you know the dead body?
How did you know the dead body was dead?

Did you wash the dead body
Did you close both its eyes
Did you bury the body
Did you leave it abandoned
Did you kiss the dead body

Chapter Fifteen

FRANCE: CELEBRATION

I can pinpoint the exact moment in 1995 when I decided to take Marie Antoinette as my new subject, thus impelling me towards what would turn out to be ten years of French research, first on the eighteenth century and then a hundred years earlier for Louis XIV. I was in a taxi on my way to give lunch to my goddaughter Helen Falkus in order to dispense sage advice about A-levels, as godmothers are traditionally supposed to do. The moment I arrived at the restaurant in Portland Road, I brushed aside all questions about A-levels, saying in a rush of excitement: 'Helen, you've just got to listen to me, I've suddenly had the inspiration that I'm going to write about Marie Antoinette and I have to talk to you about it.' When I got home I marked the date in my Diary: it was 16 October, the anniversary of the Queen's execution in 1793, which I subsequently came to mark with Masses offered in many places in the world.

So this, which became the most personal of all my books with the exception of *Mary Queen of Scots*, my first love, began with an expedition-that-failed to give advice to a young girl; there was a certain synchronicity here, since the most touching aspect of Marie Antoinette's life (one that was subsequently stressed by Sofia Coppola in her poignant film based on my book) is her need for advice on arrival in France aged fourteen – and her failure to receive it.

On the whole the press now left us alone except over matters of legitimate comment such as Harold's publicly expressed political views. The publication of Michael Billington's authorized biography (for which we had both contributed interviews and which we both liked) did however provide a brief flurry of the old kind of interest, not really experienced for many years.

21 September 1996

Michael Billington biography: press are in a tizzy about the revelation of Harold's affair with Joan Bakewell in the sixties. 'Family and friends' as the saying is, think that Joan has made rather a meal of the whole thing in the book ... Whereas I know that Harold had a more intimate relationship at the same time, with the woman he called Cleopatra. Harold indifferent to the whole thing: 'It's all a long time ago.'

Seven years later – in 2003 – he was not indifferent to the whole thing when Joan published her own memoirs which, following the failure of her second marriage, she called descriptively *The Centre of the Bed*. In a draft which she sent to him, Joan interleaved her own account of the affair with pages of dialogue from Harold's play *Betrayal*. Harold was furious at what he termed to me the 'claiming'. I pointed out that, however unpleasant it was for him, Joan had a right to tell her own story: 'In her words, however, not yours.' So the unauthorized Pinter pages were duly removed and there was a truce. It was endangered, however, according to Harold, when Joan quoted to him the comment a woman journalist friend made on the book: 'You managed to humanize Harold Pinter: I always thought he was just an angry and aggressive man ...'

I myself had found Joan's original reaction in 1975 – sensitivity on the exposure of her private life however great the work of art – very sympathetic. And she had been completely honest with Michael Billington in 1997, the first the world knew of the relationship. Now I felt she was distracting attention from her own remarkable achievements by too great an emphasis on a long-ago affair: when there was after all so much more to be said about her career.

However by then, working on *Marie Antoinette* as I had been doing, gave me quite a different perspective on press scandal and satire. The pamphlets attacking her in the Bibliothèque Nationale were so gruesome in their (invented) salacious detail that one could only sigh with horror:

and then grapple with the biographer's problem of how to quote them in sufficient detail to make the point of what Marie Antoinette had endured, and not so much as to coarsen the whole tone of the book. Compared to this vitriolic campaign, the serialization of Joan's harmless memoirs in the papers seemed very small beer. Harold wrote her a letter expressing his unhappiness: 'You should register the fact and take it on board.' And there the matter rested. There were, as there had always been on this subject, two fundamentally different points of view, that of the artist using some elements (not all) from real life to create fiction, and that of the actual person, some of whose life was used.

16 October 1998

Vienna. Anniversary of the execution of Marie Antoinette. It seemed an appropriate day to visit the Imperial Crypt. (The Blue Guide inaccurately says *La Reine* is buried where she was executed, whereas in fact she was moved to Saint-Denis after the Revolution was over.) Took Harold. 143 Habsburgs and one commoner: Maria Theresa's governess who died in 1750. Harold was impressed by this respect accorded to a governess. I was struck by how much life, as it were, there was in the Habsburg crypt, flowers, messages, compared to the crypt of Saint-Denis where the Bourbons lie, frozen and apparently unvisited (I was certainly the sole visitor all three times I went there).

Here people throng reverently. Instructions are reverent too: 'Please take off your hat. No Photos. No young children.' Masses and masses of dried flowers in bouquets with ribbons of the imperial colours and also some fresh flowers. White carnations for Maria Theresa by her vast connubial tomb, roses and piles of bouquets à la Princess Diana for the Empress Elizabeth, lots of flowers for Franz Josef, lots for Archduke Rudolf. Crowned figures of death, skulls grinning under their diadems, remind me of Mexico. But outside the magic circle of royalty, there is a great deal of appropriate dust and darkness. Harold very thoughtful. He sees the light of 'walking around a bit' in my eye – this is my euphemism for sight-seeing, a word which causes him to shy like a nervous horse – and quickly says: 'I'm going back to the hotel to read *Mary Queen of Scots.*'

He'd never read this, my first historical biography, published six years before we met and took this opportunity of leisure in Vienna to do so. It made for odd conversations in the evenings when I tried to tell him my discoveries about Marie Antoinette and he tried to tell me his discoveries about Mary Queen of Scots . . .

I would like to report our foreign travels to be one continuing progress of triumph and acclamation but honesty compels me to admit that it was by no means the case.

October 1998

Vienna. Visit to Shakespeare and Co. bookshop. My researcher, Jessica Beer, admirably efficient and intelligent, who helped me cope in German, said: 'They will certainly be delighted to see you.' We found a very pleasant shop in the old quarter of the town, small, absolutely crammed with English books. However in the large theatrical section there was only one copy of Harold's work, a dusty little edition of *A Slight Ache*, obviously left over from the theatrical season of ten years earlier. To make sure, I enquired of the assistant if there was anything more. I added: 'This is Harold Pinter.' But there was nothing else. Then the proprietor, a large blonde lady, appeared and freaked out: 'I am nearly sixty and this is the happiest moment I have ever had.' She even added: 'And you are certainly Antonia Fraser.' Joy, joy, ecstasy, ecstasy. But – she didn't have any of our books for all this, and capped it all by praising Harold's *Proust Screenplay* to the skies, how wonderful, how absolutely brilliant: 'Yes, yes, after a while I had to put it in the remainder tray, someone got that really cheaply, I can tell you.'

Our new shared French lives – because Harold decided to direct his own play *Ashes to Ashes* in Paris – got off to a flying start with Natasha's marriage to Jean-Pierre Cavassoni in July 1997. Natasha had invited Harold to give her away and he accepted with much pleasure. He did not however bargain with Natasha's French-acquired expertise where spectacle was concerned. In short when he found himself escorting Natasha across the bridge from the Crillon Hotel to the church of St Clothilde in a bright pink Cadillac, this was surely a dramatic experience for which nothing, no rich full life of acting, had prepared him. I asked Harold later if they had been cheered by the populace as they crossed the bridge. He gave me a look. It was my turn to quote his favourite phrase: 'You have to take the rough with the smooth.' Once in the church, in his black shades and his pale blue-grey morning suit, he looked more like the Godfather than the stepfather of the bride.

Both my parents, aged ninety and ninety-one, actually made the journey to see off Natasha, my father with the lure of making a speech, my mother with the lure of having fun. I had emphasized to Harold that speeches must take place. He gave in and made a charming speech saying quite truthfully that Natasha was the most beautiful bride he had ever seen. He might with justice have added that Jean-Pierre was, with his film-star looks, the most handsome bridegroom. My father accepted his bribe of making a speech with equal grace: the only untoward moment came when the bridegroom Jean-Pierre in true French mode tried to embrace his new grandfather-in-law at the end. Dada ducked. 'I may be old-fashioned,' he said loudly, brushing himself, 'but I don't kiss men.'

Unlike the wedding of Marie Antoinette and Louis XVI at which large crowds were crushed to death in the mêlée surrounding the fireworks, Natasha and Jean-Pierre's wedding was harmonious as well as picturesque at all times. I was reminded of the scene on the eighteenth-century fan Harold had given me for my birthday when I first decided on the project: it showed Montgolfier displaying the ascent of his famous azure and yellow balloon to the enraptured French court in 1783. We were all similarly enraptured by the dashing style of this thoroughly French wedding although the real star (apart from Natasha) was not

French at all: Joan Collins. I met her in the ladies at the Cercle de l'Union Interalliée where the reception was given. She was in shades of cream including a cream straw hat, with matching creamy face, quite perfect. Delicately, the brims of our huge hats touched as we tried to kiss. She told me her daughter had got married, courtesy of *Hello!* Magazine, three weeks before. Joan: 'Oh, Antonia, your *Hello!* people were so much less intrusive than ours . . . I mean ours even came on the honeymoon.'

All the time I worked on Marie Antoinette, it was strange to find that I was immensely helped by hostile French reactions to the French Queen from intelligent, cultured, sensitive people. For example the chic and essentially benevolent French producer who shrugged her shoulders: 'Ouf! She has certainly not helped the monarchy very much.' This scapegoating inspired me: I wanted to avenge it. In New York, for example, I was able to harangue my publisher Nan Talese about the sheer misogyny of the treatment meted out to Marie Antoinette. (Of course dislike of Marie Antoinette was not limited to the French. My father gave me lunch at the House of Lords with his new friend Ann Widdecombe. She had loved *The Gunpowder Plot* as a recent Catholic convert, but snorted when I mentioned Marie Antoinette: 'That dreadful woman!')

Yet in general, proceeding round galleries, museums such as the Carnavalet, I was amazed at the total denigration of Marie Antoinette I heard from teachers with their flocks of children: '*La reine méchante*' was about the best of them; 'She was responsible for the whole Revolution,' was quite commonly said. Because Marie Antoinette was after all Austrian, French people often added patriotically: 'The King was not really to blame.'

At the same time the months I spent in France gave me an insight into how these people had lived under the *ancien régime*, just because of the arts-and-fashion world in which Natasha moved. She passed on to me an invitation from Karl Lagerfeld to lunch at his house, an *hôtel particulier* on the Left Bank. Karl Lagerfeld was, I realized, a highly cultured eighteenth-century aristocrat in a twentieth-century disguise. Every single one of the gorgeous rooms had pillars of books, no other word will do. Karl: 'I sometimes knock them over in the middle of the night.' At first I didn't believe him, then I saw more pillars by his bed: actually a wonderful French bed which had belonged to the Comte d'Artois, brother of Louis XVI. At least there would have been some eighteenth-century action in the Artois bed, I reflected, since the dashing Comte, unlike poor Louis XVI, was a ladies' man.

1 March 1998

Visit to Versailles. Our guide, President of *Les Amis de Versailles*, Vicomte Olivier de Rohan, had been introduced to us by our French friend Laure de Gramont. He was highly energetic, in his marvellously well-cut grey suit, his English included old-fashioned slang learned from his nanny like an aristocrat in a Nancy Mitford novel. 'I will take you at once to what no one can see . . .' Magic words. So we were taken to the Queen's Theatre which fairly ravished the eye with its blue and gold, its celestial air. Harold deeply impressed but whether by the opportunities for performances here or just the beauty I wasn't quite sure. I really felt a strange feeling standing on the stage where Marie Antoinette sang Rosina. I would have sung a note if I could sing a note. So I sang a note interiorly. Olivier took us everywhere with one sorcerer's key. But what struck me most forcibly was the complete lack of security, let alone privacy, with which eighteenth-century royals loved. Their travails in the marriage bed took place virtually – not quite – where the public could gawp.

We retreated with relief to our rather scruffy apartment off the Champs Elysées, picked so Harold could walk to the Rondpoint Theatre where he was directing; there we ate pork pies bought from the supermarket next door. Far more fun to research and write about Marie Antoinette than to *be* Marie Antoinette.

A few years later, I was able to expand that statement: far more fun to make a film about Marie Antoinette than to *be* her. For Sofia Coppola took an option on the manuscript of *Marie Antoinette*, six months before British publication. It had been sent to her by my American publisher Nan Talese, a friend of her mother Eleanor Coppola who knew of Sofia's obsession with the subject. She wrote me a gracious letter referring to her own upbringing as a young woman in a strong family, which had provided the original inspiration. It was all very exciting for two reasons. First, I had been foolishly disappointed when William Boyd's exciting, religiously challenging script of *The Gunpowder Plot* failed to get made into a film despite the gentle warnings of Harold, the veteran of these situations. The Omaha bombings in the US convinced the producers 'that the subject of terrorism was not currently suitable for US audiences' – whereas from my point of view you might have drawn exactly the opposite conclusion. Secondly Harold and I had much admired the originality of Sofia's first film *The Virgin Suicides*, and would find her second, *Lost in Translation*, made during the five-year period of the on-offs, even more stimulating.

Our warm alliance with a proper French family in the shape of the Cavassonis gave me new confidence in our French life – up till then I had always been rather frightened of the French. This was based on my unfortunate memories as a British schoolgirl in 1948, going on an exchange visit to a château near Bordeaux: here everything, including my wardrobe and my French accent, was found wanting by cruel French teenagers. My feeling of acceptance was reinforced by the subsequent birth of the Cavassoni twins, Cecilia and Allegra in 2001. Harold, whose works had been done early and done very well in France – they continued to be extremely popular – had had a different experience. Now we both shared the pleasures of a life which veered between Versailles and the supermarket pork pies. We received generous hospitality and there was also much political accord as the shadow of the second Iraq war grew closer and finally enveloped us all in a culture of protest.

In the same way, the marriage of Damian to Paloma Porraz del Amo in Mexico and the births of Ana Sofiá, Oriana and Miranda, transformed us into Abuela Antonia and Abuelo Harold (whereas we were Grand-mère Chat and Grandpère in France) but also, we felt, gave us an interesting perception of Mexican society. For Harold, with his keen interest in Latin American politics, a first-hand experience of Mexico, the country once described as 'so far from God, so close to the United States', was a boon. Then there was his deepening affection for the Porraz family, including not only Paloma, a serious museum curator, who actually had the graceful looks of an Infanta painted by Velasquez, but her parents Rosa and Alfredo.

January 1994

Mexico. Our first visit together (Harold had been on stage at the time of Damian and Paloma's wedding). While we were at Oaxaca, we stayed in a hotel which was a converted convent. Sight-seeing, or rather 'having a look round', although in this case, it was really having a look up. We both climbed up Monte Alban. Two things made Harold laugh in the midst of his exertions. 1. Loud, very loud American voice echoing reassuringly through the clear air: 'Henry, I'm on top of the next pyramid along.' 2. Me to Harold briskly: 'OK, now it's *tombs*,' as I shut my guidebook in a purposeful manner, following our rest under a tree. In the mornings I swam in the icy pool (the only person ever to do so, so far as I could see).

———

It was while we were there that I received that long, carefully worded, sensitive but inexorable message which all pet-lovers know must come one day unless their pets happen to survive them. Rowley, our cat aged sixteen, was dying. 'Unlikely to survive,' said the vet, 'until you return.' Although there were various options which might have staved off death for a little while, all of them put the feelings of the owner above those of the cat and could not humanely be contemplated. I knew I had to take a decision. Rowley must go to his last sleep even though I am not there to hold him. Rowley: one of the kittens we acquired when we first lived together in Campden Hill Square. In his prime, he reminded me of the Persian saying: 'God created the cat so that man might have the felicity of caressing the tiger.' When my basset hound died in 1968 I didn't believe that animals had souls. But now I do. If there is a heaven, how on earth could God's creation not be fully represented? At least, if we cannot be with Rowley at the last, we are in the right country, as Harold, who was extremely comforting, pointed out to me. In Mexico, death is not sentimentalized, but it is understood and in a certain way celebrated. So: many candles for Rowley in Mexican churches.

1 February 1994

Palacio del Artes, Mexico City. Vast Art Deco building. Harold gave a poetry reading. Contrary to all our expectations, and their general rule, the Mexicans were all totally punctual. We learned later that there was a simple explanation for this. Damian had announced beforehand to all his friends: 'My stepfather is a very violent man and we must respect that.' The Mexicans all nodded sagely. While peaceful themselves, they understood violent men. 'And what makes him violent,' Damian went on, 'is people who come late to his speeches or poetry readings. Very violent,' he emphasized. So the Mexicans were all on time. Nor did the press bulbs flash unduly, since that was apparently another phenomenon calculated to provoke violence . . .

The hall was packed. Carlos Fuentes, our friend, introduced Harold with a speech in Spanish which we understood to be very gracious, before reading with much spirit some of his own translation of *No Man's Land*. Then a languid Mexican actress read a poem with much tenderness followed by Harold reading it with much passion. It was 'Paris'. I wanted to dig Silvia Fuentes in the ribs and say: 'That's written to me, you know.' I felt an extraordinary tingle when my eyes met Harold's at the end of this, first poem, written during our first 'honeymoon' at the Lancaster Hotel in 1975 and he gave me a small private smile. Afterwards Harold was very pleased and moved by the mass of students who emerged to talk to him, and told him of his works which they were studying, not only *Betrayal* but also his sole novel *The Dwarfs* which is virtually unknown even in England.

31 December 1997

In Mexico at Puerto Vallarta. Damian and Paloma and little Sofi are in a neighbouring seaside flat. In our hotel, to our delight, are Carlos and Silvia Fuentes, Arthur and Alexandra Schlesinger, and Eric and Marlene Hobsbawm. We come down to lunch at the little café on the beach and champagne is being drunk. Eric has been made a Companion of Honour. Arthur Schlesinger, *sotto voce:* 'Nice to see an old Communist so pleased with an honour.' He revealed that they had been friends – and disagreed – for sixty years, having been at Cambridge together. Eric explains benignly: 'It's all right to take this. It's from the people. A knighthood would have been all wrong.' Later Harold, who heartily agreed, told Arthur and Alexandra that he would take the Companionship of Honour if offered as it was not political.

The two Dublin festivals of Harold's works which took place at the Gate Theatre, promoted by Michael Colgan, were not exactly new territory in the same way that Mexico was. I was Anglo-Irish (Irish, my father would have said, while resolutely remaining in England in order to serve in the British government) and with my brother Thomas had visited Ireland all through our shared youth, including wartime. Thomas was destined to inherit a large Regency Gothic castle in Westmeath from my father's elder brother Edward – who by a strange coincidence had actually owned the Gate Theatre and showed far more interest in it than he ever did in the family estates. Harold had spent much time in Ireland as a young actor which was enormously important to him, working for the travelling company run by the actor-manager Anew McMaster. He had written a fine short memoir about it called *Mac* which he had given me when we first met. On that occasion I couldn't help thinking that in his few pages he had evoked the man quite as vividly as I had in any of my long, long biographies.

8 May 1994

I realized I hadn't been to the Gate Theatre for fifty years, since my uncle Edward Longford stood outside, before and after the play, with a begging bowl. The play in question was a terrible adaptation of *Carmilla* by Sheridan Le Fanu, by his wife Christine. Superior fare this time: a whole Pinter Festival. In the city itself we are surrounded by families celebrating First Communions: everywhere there are little brides in white dresses and veils which remind me of Larkin's poem 'The Whitsun Weddings'.

15 May

Run-through of *Landscape* directed by Harold in an empty room at the Shelbourne Hotel on Sunday morning for the Reiszes who have to return to London in advance of the play's opening. We trail through desolate banqueting suites to get there, a room containing nothing but a wooden table, a teapot and a mug. Only audience: ourselves and Michael Colgan. It was the most appropriate setting: the couple somewhere alone in the big house, in this case the big hotel. And wonderfully done. Penelope Wilton so tender, so lost, Ian Holm beginning tender, finally so violent. Could there ever be a finer performance?

20 May

After the first night of *Moonlight*, directed by Karel Reisz, there was quite a roister. Hangovers all round the next day when the weather is freezing. Everyone, but especially Alison Lurie and Diane Johnson, visiting from Paris, are rushing out and buying scarves and shawls. We too rush out and spend a fortune on a set of Waterford glass at

Blarney's Woollen Mills in Nassau Street. As Harold tested the weight of the glass in his hand – the heaviness is so lovely – he said sadly: 'I only wish this glass had a drink in it now.'

———

Our stay near Chichester when Harold was acting in *The Hothouse* had been such a success that we decided to enjoy merry England rather than merry airports in the summer in future. Thus for ten blissful years we rented a house near Dorchester called Kingston Russell, in essence a late seventeenth-century hunting lodge transformed into an elegant if slightly bizarre country house, like a stage set, only a single room thick. That is to say, at one moment you were gazing at the amazing façade and the next moment you had already stepped into the back garden. Harold was captivated by the natural beauty of Dorset since he loved anything that could be construed as 'England' – which was perhaps why cricket appealed to him aesthetically so much, the cricket on the village green, the cricket match of a David Inshaw painting (the most famous one was actually painted in the neighbouring village of Long Bredy so that we were able to contemplate the celebrated pitch with reverence).

In 1999 Harold was toying with a play tentatively entitled *Restaurant*. He had begun it late one Saturday night when we had been unlucky in our very, very loud neighbours at the next-door table in a famous West End restaurant. It was not going well.

16 August 1999

Little Hugh Fraser is three and we are at Kingston Russell. He came into the kitchen in Lucy's arms, fair and small and snuggly and said in a very loud voice: 'Look out! I'm the birthday boy.' The next person to come in was Harold who was none of these things just extremely dejected. He said that he had chucked in *Restaurant* because the people in it were just too nasty. He didn't even let me read it. 'You'd hate it. Just letting off some bile.'

But later that night, when we were feeling rather exhausted, what with the birthday breakfast and a lot of people over to lunch, the subject came up again. By now the only adult guests left were Benjie and Lucy. For want of anything else to do, I suggested idly to Harold: 'Why not read it to us?' So he did. And it was hysterically funny, if only for Harold's brilliant enaction of the so-called nasty people.

Benjie: 'You should have some criminals coming in and interrupting it all.' This was uncanny because that had been Harold's original plan – but he couldn't get 'the ideology of it all'. So he rushed away to his study at the side of the huge, rather empty house, which looked out to trees and the night sky. He worked very late. The next night he read us more; the people who interrupted were not terrorists, but a maître d' such as Jeremy King at the Ivy and a maîtresse d' such as Carol at Lola's, in Islington.

18 August

Harold worked on the play, which is now called *Anniversary*. At 1 a.m. he came into our room in his robe. Took off the robe. Got into bed. Got out of bed. Put on the robe again. He said: 'It's no good. It won't let me rest. I've got to go downstairs again.' Apparently he worked till 5 a.m. and finished the draft.

Harold read it to me in full, as he then thought, as I lay in bed in our rose-chintzy bedroom. There's now a Waiter, the best character in the play. It's brilliantly and savagely funny, Swiftian, one might legitimately say, and I laughed a lot. Privately was depressed by the man–woman relationships of all three couples. Managed not to say so. Later Lucy in a letter recalled Harold's original title of *Celebration* and that became the title. Harold told me that the Waiter had talked about Nicaraguan figures like Sandino and Ernesto Cardinale but then he decided that he was planting his own words in the Waiter's mouth, which he never intended to do to his characters. So now he must listen to the Waiter. It transpired that the Waiter wanted to talk about Gary Cooper, Hedy Lamarr and T.S. Eliot.

12 September

People ring up about *Celebration* choking with laughter. It will be done at the Almeida, paired with Harold's first play *The Room*. Apparently this was my suggestion: I think I must have counted up the characters and found they fitted. Harold to Jeremy King at a party for Ed Victor's sixtieth birthday: 'It's about a restaurant, Jeremy, but nothing to do with the Ivy.' May God forgive him. Harold said himself: 'I'm slightly high on all this.'

4 November

Felt so proud of Harold and then 'swooned' when he gazed at me and recited the three love poems, ending with 'It Is Here'. This was at the British Library, an evening for the American Friends. What a charming, civilized group! Harold himself rejected reading his strident poem 'American Football' (thank goodness) only to have a delightful, older lady hiss: 'I hope you're going to read "American Football".' But he didn't. It would have been his definition of bad manners to suggest that this cultured, philanthropic group was in any way responsible for the crimes of the American government – as though all Americans were bad Americans, the sort of crude generalization which did not belong to serious debate. Back to the swooning. It was an extraordinary moment. He faced me at his table across the large room, our eyes met and he read . . . twenty-four years since 'Must you go?' and I still swooned.

20 March

Celebration and *The Room* have been received with ecstasy! No other word for it. The atmosphere on the first night on Wednesday was, as all agreed, extremely benevolent, even with all the critics there. And the laughter! A murmur of a special sort when Tom Wheatley entered as the 'Jeremy' character, Jeremy King himself having elegantly chosen to be present. Both have the same lofty, handsome appearance. Later Harold and I decided to tough it out and go to the Ivy. Game, set and match to Jeremy who had his maître d' say, like the Waiter, 'May I interject?' before plonking down a saucer of complimentary gherkins in front of us in another reference to the play. Jeremy sees it as 'an affectionate portrait' and that is of course absolutely true. Simon to Harold: 'If you had to guess the play written by the seventy-year-old, and the one written by the younger man, you would guess the other way round.' Certainly *The Room* is a savage, melancholy play which ends in appalling *on stage* physical violence (something Harold never repeated, as though learning to do it better with words, although plenty of violence is suggested off stage). The melancholy of *Celebration* is existential. Mick Goldstein, Harold's old friend: 'It's the last play the world would expect from you now. They expected *Retribution* and they got *Celebration*.'

John Peter got it exactly right when he wrote in the *Sunday Times*: 'Harold Pinter is in a frisky mood. Imagine an ageing lion, the great yellow eyes aglow with a wicked twinkle, the huge paw might even be about to stroke you. And still you feel a certain unease, a shivery sense of apprehension.'

Ten years later I still think this is the best verdict on *Celebration*, which turned out to be Harold's last play. It includes the shiver brought about by the Waiter's last speech after all this raucous materialistic jollification: 'My grandfather introduced me to the mystery of life and I'm still in the middle of it. I can't find the door to get out. My grandfather got out of it. He got right out of it. He left it behind him and he didn't look back. He got that absolutely right. And I'd like to make one further interjection ...' The stage directions read: 'He stands still. Slow fade.'

PART THREE

Chapter Sixteen

THE STEPS DOWNWARD

Harold was diagnosed with cancer of the oesophagus on 13 December 2001, and died almost exactly seven years later. Before that date, which changed our lives forever, we had a prelapsarian summer in New York at the Pinter Festival which came originally from the Gate Theatre, Dublin. I call it prelapsarian, because all our lives were in a different state after 11 September 2001: the Fall.

Harold acted in his own play *One for the Road* with Indira Varma as the poignant, tragic Gila. There were plays galore, interviews, talks, even films connected to him. We stayed in a high-tech hotel called Parker Meridien which had a glassed-in swimming pool on the roof – the forty-second floor. As I travelled up early each morning from our thirty-fourth-floor suite, looking way over the tops of the trees of Central Park, I meditated that anywhere else, in the present state of the world, there would be colossal security risks; but this was the United States, so we were safe. Thus I swam confidently, soaring above the towers of Manhattan.

It was a time before the Fall, also a time of epiphany. Immediately on arrival, we found ourselves resuming the New York life we had always liked so much: dinner with Bob Silvers, Barbara Epstein, James Fenton and his partner Darryl Pinckney. Very jolly. On the way home Darryl said: 'For scary people, you're really a lot of fun.' Me: 'Oh, but underneath we are really much scarier than you think.' Harold: 'Nonsense, I intend to be a pussycat, Uncle Cuddles.' And so he proceeded to be.

I was too busy to write more than impressions in my Diary. First of all, there was the success of the festival, in honour of a living playwright who has himself acted in one play, directed another (*Landscape* with Penelope Wilton) as well as writing the whole shooting match, to say nothing of three symposia about Harold and one interview conducted by Mel Gussow. There were fabulous reviews for *The Homecoming*, with Lia Williams as Ruth, in the *New York Times*, the best review I have ever seen for anything anywhere. There was Harold's personal success with the dreaded Nicolas in *One for the Road*. I was touched when Harold revealed to Rosa Porraz del Amo, Paloma's charming and cultivated mother, that it was painful to enact him; at least he knew what we, the audience, suffered. I had sometimes wondered.

One man said to his wife on leaving the press night: 'To think that a guy could *write* a play like that and then to think that he would want to act in it!' It was not intended as a favourable comment in either case.

There was a lot of late-night carousing with the actors, night after night, in the Parker Meridien bar, which is partly outside, virtually on the pavement. In the heat and semi-darkness of a New York July we congregated with a changing cast of actors and their families: Lia and Guy Hibbert, with Josh aged eleven and Guy's mother. In the pool on the forty-second floor I used to meet Anastasia Hille who was playing in *Ashes to Ashes*, a tall streak of pale blue, with a round little baby, and the director Katie Mitchell, sleek and wiry in a black athlete's suit. I even managed to have tea with Sofia Coppola when we discussed Marie Antoinette's female relationships: how these relationships were all-important to her due to her upbringing among a gaggle of sisters, but she was not a lesbian.

The first Fall was in fact that of an oak tree – my father – who died at the age of ninety-five, five days after our return from New York. Having arrived overnight, I had hesitated to go round to the nursing home where both my parents were installed, on Sunday morning. The heat was intense and I told myself: 'tomorrow'. Luckily my conscience would not let me stay lounging in the garden, so I went round to the nursing home just in time to comfort my mother, left behind as she watched my father vanishing. It was an inspiring death, serene and befitting a great man, not forgetting the fact that he had made a speech about prison reform in the House of Lords only a couple of weeks before.

During the autumn, Harold's health was, presumably, declining but any check-up was delayed until after he had opened *No Man's Land*, which he directed at the National Theatre with Corin Redgrave as Hirst and Andy de la Tour as Briggs. I made one or two dabs at persuading him to go to the doctor about his indigestion, without success. 'I'll wait till the play has opened.'

But this was a horrible time for the whole world.

11 September

We were at Florence Airport: Harold having received an honorary degree at the university and made a speech in which he denounced American foreign policy, when I idly noticed rows of people staring glazedly at the TV in the Exit Lounge. Two English lawyers, father and son, recognized us and told us the unbelievable story. Images sprang up: Independence Day, Towering Inferno. Thereafter we sat more or less in silence on the plane for two and a half hours, the memory of Harold's recent speech with us both. In addition I realized that my son Damian was almost certainly in New York where he worked half the month in the financial sector. This was no doubt a common thought to all the people on the plane: Who is in New York? And where? It's the first primitive thought of human beings.

When we reached home, Harold rang up his Italian translator, a close friend: 'I want to withdraw my speech from any of the websites who asked for it.' Damian had left me a message: 'Like a war. People weeping in the streets.' I managed to reach him on the telephone and he told me that in his mid-town office, 'I look out on the Twin Towers and now they are not there.' Then he told me the sort of personal details about people in his office and their losses which stab you. After that we just sat watching the TV screen. Harold's speech lay heavy upon us because although there are rational arguments to be marshalled against US foreign policy, to say nothing of Iraqi casualties, nothing, but nothing, could alleviate the sheer horror of what had happened, the unalterable tragedy for those left behind.

Later Harold made a press statement pointing out with regard to his speech: 'I use words not bombs.' Then he maintained silence out of respect for the bereaved. My own private reaction was to cancel my projected book tour of the US to promote *Marie Antoinette*. 'She had her sorrows too' – perfectly true, but I couldn't and shouldn't say things like that at such a time.

15 November

Harold has not felt well since he returned from Canada, a month ago, absolutely exhausted, no energy. Both of us, in it together, feel a kind of despair which luckily we can discuss. Naturally I get nightmare scenarios in my head in the night hours. I don't know how to combat them.

25 November

Harold feeling better. It's just indigestion. We discuss Harold's idea years ago for a play as a sequel to *One for the Road*, in which the wrecked parents Gila and Victor, together at liberty but of course without Nicky, meet the torturer Nicolas at a party. He had even started to write it, when I reached Chez Moi restaurant at 10 p.m. after a film. He has not written for over two years. It makes the whole difference to his spirits as ever. Harold on the problem: 'There will be no confrontation. At least I don't think there will . . .' Later: 'No explicit allusions.' It takes place in an embassy, possibly in America – the UN? – and the characters are, as before, called Nicolas, Victor and Gila.

27 November

Our wedding anniversary – twenty-first. The hopeful entry above about a sequel to *One for the Road* has to be completely contradicted. Harold found 'nothing' in the ten or so pages he had written, had violent indigestion at Sunday lunch and felt incredible lassitude on Monday.

12 December

No Man's Land having opened, Harold is off for an endoscopy. He feels generally better.

13 December

Oh, the optimistic tone of that entry yesterday morning. Everything has changed. Harold came back from his endoscopy and buzzed me in my Eyrie. I found him in the drawing room looking rather white. And I knew. What Dr Westaby said was: 'There is something there and I don't like the look of it. I suspect cancer.' Later on I looked up oesophageal cancer on the internet on Flora's computer. I weep a bit in the car outside her house where I'm going to tea with the Soros boys, Simon and Tommy, to play Scrabble, my weekly pleasure. Flora very supportive: 'It's only what someone has put on the net,' she tells me when I found out that the mortality rate was 92 per cent.

14 December

Today Harold goes for a scan to see it 'from another angle'. And then to an oncologist. Wish it wasn't the eclipse tonight. And I thought it would be poor Mummy . . . (My mother had been very ill with a series of strokes but had recovered.)

Harold tremendously calm. Asked what could be done. The answer: 'An operation or chemotherapy or a combination of the two.' Late, late last night, Harold: 'I just can't get used to the notion of death in my early seventies.'

———

In the event the decision was chemotherapy followed by an operation if the tumour was shrunk or at any rate not increased. So months of chemo followed.

14 December cont.

Harold had the scans, saw the consultant and was then given his programme. He's also given a printed list of possible side-effects: 'You won't necessarily need a wig.' Suggest that Harold has a trendy short haircut, like David Beckham, before the chemo kicks in.

Everything is cancelled, Ireland, Paris, Barbados. Harold very sweetly keeps apologizing. As if I cared a hoot about any of that! The sheer shock of the verdict, though. I fear my lip trembled. I realized that a small part of me, I suppose it's only human, had hoped that the consultant would spread his arms and say: 'It was all a mistake.'

On the whole I haven't cried very much, only on the telephone breaking the news to very sympathetic people like my children.

19 December

Odd thoughts. I gave Harold my usual early-morning kiss, and then wondered: 'Is this the spot where the tumour is?'

22 December

Harold, although feeling very weak after a procedure under anaesthetic (thank God no spread!), persisted in his plan to go and buy me a Christmas present at McCarthy's jewellers in Artillery Row. We found a jade bangle, thick, bright spring green, full of light. I am giving Harold a DVD of the work of Frank Auerbach that he likes so much.

25 December

All in all, despite dreads (like: I won't have the energy to carry this through) it was a lovely Christmas Day. Harold made a touching speech about the power of human support, especially the children. I drank a toast to Dada and the past, but the star was Thomas Fraser who had written both an earnest and considered speech and a Viking poem. Also Phoebe Fraser who recited 'Away in a Manger' in a strong voice, aged three, word perfect. A tiny star.

27 December

Harold's first go of chemo. Tests, tests, tests. I visited Harold at 8 p.m. The hospital at night quite sinister, the smell of chloroform. Told myself: 'It's the smell of cure.' Harold very positive: 'I only have four goes and this is number one.'

30 December

Took Harold up to the Serpentine as we had had a terrible night of worries, both of us, which we could not somehow seem to control, and I thought air would be beneficial. We sat in the bright winter sun, huge ducks and geese being fed, light on the water. I went for a brief walk while Harold reflected. Alternative was going to Mass, but good deeds preferable.

2002

1 January

Palindrome year as Simon Gray points out last night. I shall be seventy in August, I said. Simon: 'What's a girl like you doing being seventy?' Gallant. I feel a hundred and seventy.

Lack of courage this morning and a few tears of which I feel ashamed. No way to start the New Year. Not fair to Harold, to put it mildly, and to have provoked the sleepy words 'I am so sorry' made me even more ashamed.

4 January

Harold read me 'a sketch' – former Minister of Police becomes Minister of Culture. He said: 'It's very crude.' It was. I got upset: the death of a child being described as 'educational'. I realize that it's the relic of the play he began once as a sequel to *One for the Road*. Still, the energy is good.

5 January

Harold announced he was going to perform his sketch, now called *Press Conference*, twice at the National and within days of the third bout of chemo. 'I know you don't like it.' We didn't pursue that point: it wasn't to do with *liking*, more with my generally fragile state. But I did question his decision to take this on. I was thinking of all the instructions we've read about leading a very easy life while you're having chemo. Is performing a new sketch on stage at the National an easy life?? Harold: 'I'm not just sitting here waiting to die.'

8 January

Twenty-seventh anniversary of our first meeting. Surgeon has outlined the procedure for the operation. He has also okayed Harold's two performances, delaying chemo a little to accommodate them.

27 January

The week after this chemo was horrendous; I suppose it was only to be expected. Harold feels cautiously more human this morning. The hair, the blackness of it, characteristic of his appearance, has gone. Everyone says it will grow again but perhaps the blackness, phenomenal at seventy-one, will change, and he will be a Godfather silvered like Al Pacino in *Godfather III*. In which case I'm glad I did a Delilah seventeen days ago and cut off a black lock. (I still have it today.) Harold, who has no personal vanity, doesn't care a bit. He minds, sensibly, about other things such as the sickness, which is getting worse. Baked potatoes, soup and ice cream: the valiant trio will be familiar to all those who have been through this. I comfort myself by reflecting that the Irish nation survived for hundreds of years, strongest of the strong, on potatoes.

28 January

Someone told poor Mummy in her nursing home about Harold despite my explicit instructions to the contrary. (At the time I sought to comfort and sustain her so far as I could, following my father's death in August; I didn't see that knowing about Harold's cancer would help her – or me.) I was extremely upset by this. It got worse when Mummy was then helpfully told it was only a rumour, Harold was all right. I couldn't bear this travesty of the truth, given Harold's current ordeal. Went round after Mass and told her it all. She wasn't as devastated as I expected, given her affection for Harold: of course she lives in a world of the dying, and the person she loves most in the world is dead. She was very sweet and murmured: 'Is there anything I can do?' Me: 'Pray. But you do that anyway.' Stumped away home in the wind and the rain. Benjie and his children to lunch. Eliza got Harold a plate of ice cream: a first for him at a family lunch and the children were duly impressed. Thomas aged nine then asked Harold what *sort* of plays he wrote, which Harold found unanswerable but amused him, both at the time and in recollection.

1 February

Front-page news this morning: both *The Times* and the *Daily Telegraph* (I believe) saying: 'Harold Pinter has throat cancer.' Well, it took six weeks to reach the press. Not pleasant to read it but let's face it, press attention is not the problem. Harold, I note, is wonderfully open about the whole thing: 'Yes, it's true,' he says instead of denying it; which rather destroys the story. I worry that Harold will do *Press Conference* twice out of bravado and then collapse. But I don't voice this. I've been reading about the last months of the great Duke of Ormonde (I was contemplating a book on the Battle of the Boyne), who said that for him the time for field sports was past: 'The steps downwards are very natural from a field to a garden, from a garden to a window, from thence to a bed, and so to a grave.' Actually this is true about Mummy, if you leave out field sports. But it is also a powerful image in Harold's situation, he who has been an athlete all his life, his buoyant, dashing if unorthodox tennis style being the wonder of all players at the Vanderbilt Club.

5 February

New endoscopy. I collected Harold at 10 a.m. after his early start. The news was good. No spreading. The pain probably caused by necrotic shards of the tumour being sloughed off. So IT is responding. Quel relief.

Later we visited Dr Westaby. I spied photos upside down. Insisted on looking and after a bit Harold did too. IT looked 'like something on a rock,' says Harold. 'An evil oyster,' say I.

8 February

After some rough days and tests, Harold is feeling better. Saw the oncologist in the morning, who confirmed things are moving in the right direction. In the evening to a packed house (nine hundred people) he gave a magnificent performance in *Press Conference*. He looked elegant in grey shirt, black tie, formal black jacket and the new trousers from M&S: he's lost so much weight that we had to make a rapid expedition there, despite his sickness. (Harold kept trying to pay more money at the till as he couldn't believe how cheap everything was compared to the trendy Italian shops he patronizes.) His splendid newly revealed skull most impressive, highly suitable for this horrible governmental character, and so was his voice – which grew – and his ferocious glee. It was a triumph for a man undergoing chemo or indeed any man. I was quite wrong to try and persuade him not to do it because it has boosted his morale enormously. I'm learning as I go: the demands of the body, the needs of the mind . . . trying to balance them.

9 February

Harold totally exhausted and the bloody indigestion acute.

11 February

Another triumph for *Sketches II*. Harold possibly even better – less nervous. And I adored Doug Hodge and the lovely Catherine MacCormack in *Night*: I used to think that it was the only happy thing Harold had written when I first met him. Harold's skull beneath the skin, as Webster would put it, even more noble.

Some terrible days followed of sickness, the problem of eating and so on. It was the most brilliant weather, crisp, blue skies. Camellias started to flower in the garden, and I was able to bring in my favourite Amaryllis Appleblossom from the greenhouse. Otherwise I just read and read and listened to opera on Radio 3 wishing I could do something, bear something for him. Harold has been told he will probably need more chemo after the operation: not good news and I know his morale is low though he is staunch in not talking about it. The arrival of food supplements, little infant-looking packs with plastic straws and flavours like 'Peach' and 'Cherry' give a nursery air to the dining room.

20 February

Harold's supper was two scoops of ice cream and three grapes. A friend, whose husband has recently died of cancer, says: 'I hope Harold is not very cross with you.' (I imagine her husband was.) Me: 'No, Harold is *saintly*.' True enough. Keeps worrying sweetly about me: 'I want you to have a nice time.' As if I could!

2 March

Harold a little better on the potatoes and ice cream diet, awaiting the fourth chemo session. We went to the Olympia Fine Art Fair on Tuesday to see the Keith Vaughan exhibition, an artist we both admire: I have a small, multi-coloured male figure bought in the fifties. Left Harold at the champagne bar and went a-wandering. Vaguely I was looking for my jewellery (I had been robbed in April 1999 and the police had advised me to 'keep an eye out'). Rounded a corner on the ground floor – and there was a large stone font full of primroses. Knew I had to buy it, it was waiting there for me, and I would put it in the middle of our rather scrawny lawn as a visual attraction. 'From an East Suffolk Church 1781': where the Pakenhams came from before they set off for Ireland with someone called Oliver Cromwell. 1781: a date when Marie Antoinette still held sway at Versailles. Harold slightly surprised to hear we had acquired a font but readily agreed to pay half when I explained that it was an 'affirmation thing, an affirmation of life'. After all, life begins with a font – well, some lives anyway.

11 March

Bad day after the night-long chemo session. I dashed to No. 10 Downing Street to a Prisoner of Conscience Appeal party held by Cherie Blair, out of guilt as I'm a patron but a useless one. Cherie much prettier than her pictures, most beautiful creamy complexion, and very warm and friendly. The photos of prime ministers all down the stairs all gazing at one with earnest solicitude: 'I've mucked up the world to the best of my ability, but you do admire me, don't you?'

14 March

Harold's poem, inspired by a remark of 'a senior nurse called Sue' to him at the Royal Marsden, 'Cancer Cells', appeared in the *Guardian* and it was subsequently printed by Bob Silvers in the *New York Review of Books*, to his great pleasure.

CANCER CELLS

'Cancer cells are those which have forgotten how to die' –
Nurse, Royal Marsden Hospital
They have forgotten how to die
And so extend their killing life.

I and my tumour dearly fight.
Let's hope a double death is out.

I need to see my tumour dead
A tumour which forgets to die
But plans to murder me instead.

But I remember how to die
Though all my witnesses are dead.
But I remember what they said
Of tumours which would render them
As blind and dumb as they had been
Before the birth of that disease
Which brought the tumour into play.

The black cells will dry up and die
Or sing with joy and have their way.
They breed so quietly night and day,
You never know, they never say.

Harold is I think fortunate to have been able to write two great poems
at critical moments in his life – 'Death' when Jack died being the other.
Come to think of it, what about 'Paris' in May 1975: 'She dances in my
life'? He had worked on this poem since his return from the hospital
which has brought him much pleasure.

17 March

Innumerable children racing round and round the new font (thirty-five
apparently). Like the tigers in *Little Black Sambo* I thought they would

turn into ghee. The occasion was the christening party of Natasha and Jean-Pierre's twin daughters Cecilia Antonia and Allegra Giovanna. Harold managed to make a well-turned speech at the godparents' lunch beforehand: he invented the Twinnies' conversation with one another, half in English and half in French. It came to an end at the age of eighteen when one says to the other, 'It's a funny old life,' the reply being '*C'est une drôle de vie.*'

22 March

Went with Harold for a 'family conference' to the Royal Marsden to see the oncologist following the endoscopy which had showed a 'reduction'. Dr Cunningham was extremely cheerful: it was good news and they were recommending an operation. Harold remarkably calm at the description of the operation and its results in full detail including the comment: 'You'll never be fat again.' But as to the next batch of chemo, post-operation, he says he will make up his own mind about that.

25 March

Saw the surgeon Jeremy Thompson. He drew maps for us of what he was going to lop off from the stomach(!) He called it high-risk surgery and referred to 5 per cent mortality, as he was bound to do. I think we were both quite shocked by the reality of all this. As Harold said later: 'I've been pretty broody ever since.' Harold: 'I never asked what would happen if I didn't have it,' so he rang up and asked. The answer was that the tumour would regroup and spread ... Anyway, on a lighter note, Jeremy Thompson had on his desk a copy of Harold's poem 'Cancer Cells' which he had sent him. We'd both been eyeing it and in unspoken accord longed to know what he thought of it. 'I got your poem,' he said at last. 'Very enjoyable,' he said with a humorous, almost indulgent smile. It was the most wonderfully inappropriate word, surely, for such a poem. That at least cheered Harold up.

7 April

Dedication of the plaque to my father in the local Hurst Green church. Harold gallantly elected to come despite a bad attack when he tried to eat, failed, took refuge in the kitchen and was fed ice cream by the aged Bernhurst staff Gwen and Ellen. But he did manage to have some words with Mummy, not seen since 3 November. They discussed Peter Stanford's book on Heaven and Mummy told Harold that she thought he would be a very exciting presence in Heaven. Later Harold wondered aloud in the Chez Moi restaurant in Holland Park Avenue what would happen if there was no death, no one ever died. So perhaps there had to be death to prevent the planet overcrowding. I composed a haiku and wrote it on my napkin:

> If there was no death
> How in all the crowds
> Would I have met you?

Harold answered it initially but being a real poet was dissatisfied and corrected it in the middle of the night.

> You'd find me turning from the long bar
> Glasses raised,
> One for you, one for me.

11 April

The destruction of the lofty – twenty-five foot – olive tree in the garden is the worst thing that is happening to me emotionally apart from THE thing. The evil, indifferent squirrel bites off vast silver branches evening after evening in front of our appalled eyes, and stripped of leaves or not, they lie pathetically abandoned on the terrace. It stands for absolute helplessness. The tree, the myrtle bush from my wedding bouquet (also stripped), me, we're all helpless. And the squirrel is energetic, playful and a killer.

16 April

We took a break in Torquay for Harold to try and get some strength back before the op. At lunch in a country pub (Harold's favourite thing – not that he was able to eat) we argued about a line in W.S. Graham: was it the 'shining' sea as I thought, or the 'silent' sea as in Harold's version? Harold is always right about these things which doesn't stop me gamely arguing. So when at dinner he pronounced, 'It's actually the *speaking* sea,' it was a touching demonstration of his weakness, that he had forgotten one of his favourite lines.

23 April – St George's Day

To my amazement Harold had agreed to my idle suggestion as to how to spend the last night before his enormous operation to remove the tumour: 'Let's have a party.' Suddenly it was boiling hot, unbelievably so, and under a convenient full moon, lighting by Mick Hughes as it were, we held the entire party in the garden. The whole wonderful evening was a tribute of affection to Harold. Even Peter Hall and Trevor Nunn came, the busiest people we know, and at prime theatrical time. All the children of course and afterwards Peter Soros, ever practically generous, took us for dinner.

It's odd how anxiety blinds you to some things, while exposing you to others. It never occurred to me that the reason why all these busy people took the trouble to come was that they feared the end was coming and wanted to say goodbye. I only understood this when Edward blurted it out to me, following the happy outcome: 'I never thought I would see Harold again.' I also took a lot of photographs of the scene in the moonlit garden. Much later Harold looked at them and said curiously: 'Who is that?' He did not recognize himself with his mysterious Jacobean skull.

25 April

Harold rang me at 7 a.m. before the operation as promised. I had told him, 'On no account do a Louis XVI on the eve of his execution,' i.e. fail to call in order to spare me, as Louis XVI, sweet but insensitive to the last, did to poor Marie Antoinette and the children. They just sat there waiting for the promised summons until the roll of the drums from afar told them that the King was dead.

Continued. Well, it's over and Harold has survived. No roll of drums. This morning (26th) is better than yesterday when I sat all morning trying to read a book about Danish Regiments at the Battle of the Boyne. Then Rebecca thoughtfully offered to come and sit with me. On the dot of three, I rang the Clinical Nurse and she said Harold was OK. Went there at five o'clock. He was still unconscious. I was handed over to Staff Nurse Steve: a very nice man. Sat in the Relatives' Room, a small octagon. Later I was allowed to give a reverential kiss to this Pietà figure and so some squeezing of the hand; Harold's eyes opened and he definitely knew me.

———

Days followed in intensive care with me visiting Harold three times daily. He wanted, he said, the pleasure of looking forward to my arrival. Which he couldn't do if I just stayed there. As I shuttled to and fro from Campden Hill Square to Chelsea, I took to speculating what happened to people who had *no one* to visit them: because surely cancer doesn't spare the lonely. There was a strange period when Harold started to hallucinate, a temporary consequence of the anaesthetic. It began with 'awake dreaming' as he put it: he had a lovely dream that we were both in California and there was sunlight and leaves and I looked very beautiful. I think I had been swimming and my hair was shining. Then it got more serious and turned to bugs, Harold's bane, infesting the (immaculate) telephone. This was fearful – literally so – for him but I was able to remain optimistic in what might otherwise have been a desperately worrying situation because by an extraordinary coincidence this had happened to another member of the family after a major operation a year or two back. So I knew Harold would recover his wits. In the meantime, the fears included a gentle black man with a crown – a king as in the Three Kings of the Orient – residing in the television so his face had to be extinguished with a towel, although unlike some of the visions, he was not menacing.

This led to a hilarious situation as Harold began to recuperate and the hallucinations at last faded. I arrived for my morning visit quite late on in his stay and Harold said: 'I must warn you there is a very tall black man in the bathroom.' Oh God, I thought, here we go again: my heart sank. And lo and behold at that moment the door opened and out came the cleaner, an Ethiopian perhaps, of about 6'8" . . .

7 May

I can't believe it, I took Harold out to lunch at Le Colombier! (the restaurant next door to the Marsden Hospital). Gaunt, fragile, all in black, he then proceeded to eat liver and bacon, the first real food since forever.

8 May

He's coming out at noon. I am to spring the prisoner. I can't believe that either.

I did spring him. On return home Harold behaved like Hector, Damian and Paloma's golden labrador in Mexico who was kidnapped for a week; when recovered, he just rushed up to their bedroom, went under the bed and stayed there for forty-eight hours. Except that Harold got *into* the bed, he behaved exactly the same. I stayed downstairs and answered the doorbell to flowers. Finally I opened the door to Mr Nader, of Savile's Cars, who had been so tremendously staunch in times of need, driving both of us to and from hospital endlessly; he had a huge bouquet 'from all the drivers'. At long, long last I burst into tears which I didn't try to stop.

Chapter Seventeen

———

THE NEW DEAD

In the course of the summer Harold cautiously began to say that he felt better.

15 May

Alexandra Shulman's tenth anniversary party as editor of *Vogue*. A touching occasion, full of Alex's old friends, most of whom I have known throughout their lives. Nigella Lawson was tenderly sympathetic about intensive care at the Royal Marsden where John Diamond had died, and the holy character of Steve the male nurse. At this point the photographers descended on her in droves as if she were Princess Diana and perforce snapped us together – if only they knew what her perfect lips were discussing.

25 May

Took Harold to Holland Park and we sat looking at the irises and the water sculpture. This was the first time he had walked properly and it was real progress.

———

There were milestones, like the day that he was pronounced 'clear' of cancer: so no need of further chemo – the chemo he had announced beforehand he would not have. I might have disagreed but we had no need to go that route. He was once again a man with black, curly tonsured hair – it did not grow back silver as I had expected. He fell into a routine of lying in the drawing room like a leopard – a convalescent leopard – on a branch, then going out for a couple of hours at night.

I found that the subsidence of one anxiety, the major anxiety, led to the emergence of another much smaller professional one, which had been concealed by the traumatic events of winter and spring 2002. I was no longer convinced that I could write an interesting book about the Battle of the Boyne – and who wants a boring one? Of the two principal antagonists, I admired but disliked William III and simply disliked James II without admiration. My pulse quickened only when I had to think about Louis XIV, who backed James II and later gave him refuge in France.

9 June

Over five hours in a car – to Ilminster and back where I spoke about Marie Antoinette – led me to say to Harold on return: 'I'm going to Bin the Boyne.' I told him: 'It was learning the Irish that did it. I thought – why am I doing this? To give depth to something which is fascinating in itself but doesn't have depth in me. Never mind the Irish books, the Irish lessons, the prints. Away with them! Versailles here I come (back).' And furthermore Sofia Coppola's Marie Antoinette project does not seem quite dead.

10 June

Sofia Coppola came to tea. Tiny, lithe, very well-proportioned in her black leggings and little black jersey, shivering in the cold June rain. 'Flaming June,' as Harold said, leading her to the French windows where rain was sploshing down into the garden. Sofia and I have an interesting discussion about playboys and the attraction they have for women who know they are destined to be unfaithful, yet can't help believing 'I am the one'; this is in relation to Marie Antoinette and Count Fersen.

15 June

Harold delighted with the reactions to his award of the CH. *The Times* runs a leader which mentions Gaieties CC and states: 'No one who loves cricket can not be a gentleman.' Splendid old-fashioned stuff. About six years previously, he had rejected a knighthood: 'I can't make the sort of speeches I do and be introduced as "Sir Harold",' he told me, but he felt the CH was different. I am certain that, whether consciously or not, Eric Hobsbawm's acceptance in 1997 had influenced him. His only regret about the knighthood had been that it would have pleased his father – then in the last year of his life.

19 June

Determined to give Harold treats insofar as he is up to them. I decided that the Lucian Freud exhibition opening at the Tate would be a treat – it might not be everybody's idea of a treat but it is certainly Harold's: we have been to at least two previous Freud exhibitions. Harold havered more about the need for a wheelchair than about the treat. It was odd pushing him, I must say, as in spite of Harold's colossal weight loss, he's still an adult compared to tiny Mummy. Also it was a reversal of our roles; I felt rather uncomfortable being the director of our progress. But it grew on me, I found. I was soon whisking Harold past huge pictures of full-frontal naked Leigh Bowery in favour of a tender, even beautiful one of Bindy Lambton in a butterfly-strewn jersey.

28 June

Visit to Professor Cunningham. Harold is cured of cancer, it was all got out. Cunningham looked at Harold's body, the war wounds and said: 'Yes, I can see Mr Thompson has been here.' He then told Harold he had benign leukaemia of the mildest sort, but people often lived for ten years . . . This struck a chord with me although I did not say so. I had been saying to myself, 'Give us ten years, when Harold is eighty-one and I am nearly eighty . . .' and copying the message to God.

4 July

End of a Diary. I am resolved that the next one will record happier times. Harold and I love each other more than ever, now and forever. That's the Royalist slogan of the Battle of the Boyne: 'Now or never. Now and forever'. The Protestant one was: 'No surrender'. Both seem appropriate.

5 July

Harold read my Diaries having gone over to the Super-Study for the first time for months (always a sign of his mental as well as physical health to take the short walk down the garden). He has never read them in depth before, made the occasional jocular interjection when in the mood. But if you live with someone, you keep a diary at your own risk – see Count and Countess Tolstoy who left messages for each other diary-wise. I told him that the Diaries did provide a day-to-day picture of his illness. But of course reading them meant that Harold lived through the whole thing again, all he suffered, all I suffered, which he says he knew but we didn't discuss. Harold very, very moved, and still in quite an emotional state, which having written the things, left me proud but to be honest a little embarrassed and just a little self-examining. (Did I go on a bit much about my own sufferings? Diaries are self-pitying instruments. Did I criticize Harold? Diaries are also self-justificatory, q.v. the Tolstoys.)

12 July

The great news is that Harold is officially cleared of the oesophageal cancer – no trace and no treatment needed for leukaemia. Professor Cunningham told Harold that his poem 'Cancer Cells' was quoted from at a recent oncologists' conference. 'So you've made a pretty good thing out of it.' Scottish twinkle.

24 July

Thrilled with the arrival of *Pinter Poems* which I edited for the Greville Press at the request of Anthony Astbury. Four copies. Harold gave me number one, I gave him number two, and we gave number three to Edna, the dedicatee, and number four to Victoria and Simon. Harold and I managed to go to the Picasso–Matisse exhibition at the Tate – no wheelchair this time.

1 August

Kingston Russell. Benjie and Harold had a session over Benjie's poems. Harold finds this an extraordinarily exciting development: he loves the poems and helps Benjie choose some for a little book also to be published by the Greville Press called *City Poems*. At the end Benjie touchingly says: 'I think this has been the happiest hour of my life.' Later still I thank Harold for making my son so happy (he's half asleep but smiles). Lucy reveals that Benjie always wrote poetry, even on their honeymoon, but it was previously 'unresolved'.

17 August

Harold wrote a poem. A perfect image of an embrace.

MEETING

It is the dead of night,
The long dead look out towards
The new dead
Walking towards them
There is a soft heartbeat
As the dead embrace
Those who are long dead
And those of the new dead
Walking towards them

They cry and they kiss
As they meet again
For the first and last time

—

We met Norman Mailer later in the summer and he told Harold he didn't like the poem. Too soft! But he liked everything else Harold had written. Harold actually delighted with both comments.

26 August

Harold gallantly came to Edinburgh Festival where I was booked to speak, and did a gig himself. He was interviewed by an Australian journalist. To my surprise, she began right in about cancer, reading the poem. Harold then talked about it, very frankly, including a tribute to his 'brilliant' doctors, ending on his wife. Felt tears coming but saw granddaughter Eliza's little face beside me and thought: No. Of course it wasn't all about that. Much vigorous political discussion as Harold defended his position on the Serbian leader Milosevic: he just wants him to have a fair trial.

27 August

My seventieth birthday. Turned out to be the happiest day of my life – so far. Part of this was relief, of course, the great unbelievable happiness that Harold is all right, and in fact seems to have been given a great fillip by Edinburgh. Then there was the ineffable happiness of the FamPicnic at Hampton Court followed by dinner in our garden. I am the luckiest woman in the world (Harold can no longer claim to be 'the luckiest man'). In my speech, I determined to embarrass my children as what is otherwise the point of being old if you can't be roguish? Told the story of the immortal courtesan Ninon de Lenclos, of extreme longevity in her career. She was pursued by a young gallant, but she wouldn't say yes and she wouldn't say no. Then one day she named a

264

ABOVE: I bring down the Berlin Wall. Photographed by Harold, February 1990.
BELOW: Harold at James Joyce's grave, Zurich.

ABOVE: Salman Rushdi
the West Indian fast
bowler Ossie Gooding
and Harold, before the
Guardian match.

At the Comédie França
for *Le Retour*.

Harold and the grandchildren.

RIGHT: Harold and Blanche, Dorset, 1998.
BELOW: Ruby is not impressed by the 'revolutionary rattle', 2007.

In front of Harold's 1992 portrait by Justin Mortimer at the National Portrait Gallery.

If there was no death
In all the crowds
How would I have ?
               near you.

You'd find me turning
    from the long bar
Glasses raised,
One for you, and
            for me.

7/8 April 2002

The two 'Haikus' we wrote in Chez Moi restaurant when Harold was about to have an operation for oesophageal cancer.

ABOVE: Tom Sternberg, producer, Harold and Jude Law, during the planning of the film *Sleuth*, Dorset, 2003.
BELOW: Edna O'Brien and Jude Law, Dorset, 2003.

Dominique de Villepin, Prime Minister of France, presents Harold with the Légion d'Honneur at the French Embassy, London, 2007.

The last photograph
us taken together.
...'s, July 2008.
...zy Fraser

...on and Victoria
...y.

Harold's seventieth birthday, 10 October 2000. © *Susan Greenhill*

date three weeks ahead. The day – or rather night – arrived and it was the best night of the young gallant's life. Towards dawn, however, he did ask: 'Out of curiosity, beloved Ninon, why did we wait so long and why this precise date?' 'Oh, darling,' she replied, 'I just wanted it to take place on my seventy-fifth birthday.'

12 October

Shortly after his seventy-second birthday Harold played tennis again, forty minutes, a real breakthrough. I never ever thought this would happen. He slept like a top but no ill effects.

23 October

Mummy died peacefully at Bernhurst, as she would have wished. We were there, with the Billingtons and Thomas. Later Kevin said: 'The Meeting must be taking place about now.' He was referring to Harold's poem alluding to the meeting of newly dead Mummy with long (fifteen months) dead Dada. But if I believe anything about the after-life, I believe that Mummy and Dada will be united forever; unlike in the poem, there is no last embrace. Just an eternal one.

26 October

Thomas is an extraordinary person. We gave him a copy of the *Pinter Poems*, originally given to Mummy, and as he was about to register the death, advocated reading Harold's poem 'Death' as a preparation. Thomas: 'I shall read it to the Registrar.' And blow me down, he did. And the registrar, a woman, duly asked for a copy.

20 November

Reading my mother's Diaries, kept in the last seventeen years of her life, which have come to me as her Literary Executor. Amused rather than anything else to see how wrong her judgments were in 1975: they were based on erroneous statements by people like Malcolm Muggeridge who said that Harold was like Peter Sellers: 'Not husband material'. In fact Harold is the most uxorious person I know. But then Malcolm never actually met Harold but was inclined nevertheless to hold forth to his wondering Sussex neighbours, Mummy and Dada, in his role as a man-of-the-world.

The last months of 2002 and the spring of 2003 were dominated by the possibility of war in Iraq. Increasingly people used sentences like 'When the war comes', especially our French friends and family. We both felt passionately on the subject: Harold was in fact one of the people who spoke out publicly who never varied in his view from the pre-war period until the time of his death. He felt from the first that the invasion – if there was to be one – was being done in the oil interests of the US, not out of fear of al-Qaeda who were not even in Iraq (Afghanistan was a different matter). And he was not afraid to say so. For one thing he could shrug off comments that he was supporting a dictator in Saddam Hussein. After all, he had denounced Saddam's treatment of the Kurds for years, demonstrated on the subject and as usual spoken out.

27 November

University of Turin. Harold made a stirring speech in exchange, as it were, for an honorary degree in a style described by the Italian paper *Manifesto* this morning as *sobrio e secco* – sober and dry. At dinner he was neither! The hours dragged on and the later it got, the more he prophesied doom, the end of the world by 2007 in a messianic style. The speech went down tremendously well; unlike Florence last year when an American diplomat walked out, there was no American diplomat present. I speculated that a round-robin of an email is sent to all American embassies at the present time: 'Danger! Alert! Do not attend Pinter's speeches! Danger, alert!' Students all thrilled. The

speech itself was along familiar lines (to put it mildly) but then that's
the point of a campaign: you keep on at it, so gradually people find your
views less shocking, and finally realize that they agree.

I quarrelled with one word however. Harold all too presciently referred
to the possibility of an attack on the London Underground, saying
'the responsibility will rest *entirely* on the Prime Minister's shoulders'.
I queried 'entirely'. 'No, it won't,' I said, 'it will be shared. It will also
be the responsibility of those who order it and those who do it. Free will
and self-determination can never be eliminated from calculations of
responsibility.' I see that Harold himself wrote in my Diary: 'I accept
this point!!'

29 November

We celebrated our wedding anniversary two days late: Harold gave me
a new Enitharmon edition of David Jones' wedding poems with
woodcuts.

9 December

St Paul's. In the icy dark an absolute throng of people trying to get in
to hear the Great Noam Chomsky speak. Two thousand people inside,
I believe, and another thousand outside. It was the tenth anniversary of
the Bar Council's Kurdish Human Rights Campaign. Chomsky, last
heard by me and Harold at the Almeida some years back in dialogue
with John Pilger, did brilliantly with notes at a lectern and a large
audience. Very well-constructed talk, bringing in not only Turkey,
which he had bravely visited to get a treason charge against his
publisher dropped, but Colombia where he had recently been. Smallish,
battered corduroy jacket, smiling fresh face, slightly baggy trousers, he
looked the epitome of the liberal academic.

23 December

Resurrection Day. I took Harold to Wilton's for the celebration of a
year to the day of his diagnosis with cancer. It was terribly expensive
and I loved doing it. After all Harold is still having the odd 'hit' at
tennis.

———

He subsequently gave it up with great sadness: 'Just too exhausting'. At
the same moment our beloved Vanderbilt Club came to an end, as
though in mourning.

2003

1 January

Harold took me to *Anything Goes* at the National Theatre. Magic
evening. Me: 'You can have Ibsen, Strindberg, Miller, Beckett, even
Pinter . . . just give me Cole Porter.' Harold: 'I totally agree.' This year
I am looking forward to Natasha's biography of Sam Spiegel, Benjie's
poetry, working on *Love and Louis XIV* and going to Paris again – and
Harold's increasing energies. Not looking forward to the war which
no one wants, the grim world predicted by Blair today, financial
downturn, people's troubles all over the world in consequence.

15 February

The largest demonstration in British history: so said the papers, even
the hostile ones. One million? Maybe twice that. I am so proud for
Harold that he was one of the speakers. I think he was very nervous.
The park was full of scurrying and walking and pushchair-pushing
figures going to and from the large blue-purple baldaquin with its small
platform for speakers. Getting inside the wire fence to reach the
baldaquin was not easy. Once there we were herded into the 'Green

Room', actually a small chrome caravan, full of people. One of these was Jesse Jackson, the wide-apart deer's eyes of so many photographs. Naturally he was incredibly pleased to meet Harold and me, we got the impression that it made his day. Someone, probably George Galloway, was blaring away on the loudspeaker. Then Louise Christian, magnificent Brunhilde of a solicitor came in. Me: 'What is George saying?' Louise, cheerfully: 'Oh, I'm not listening. I've heard it all before.'

On the platform Vanessa Redgrave, Bianca Jagger and beyond them the great sea of the crowd, banners and all. Everybody perfectly attentive. Perfectly in unison. Laughing when laughter was due. Cheering and clapping ditto. Otherwise listening in silence. An ocean of faces as far as the eye could see. Harold got tremendous cheers for his poem 'The Special Relationship' beginning 'The bombs go off ...' Back to the chrome caravan while Harold spoke to *Newsnight* and thrill, thrill, I met Tim Robbins, he of the cherubic face, the curly hair and the devastating figure. Home, where Harold had a brief rest before setting off to address a demo about Cuba. Madness in my opinion. But admirable madness. I stayed home and listened to *Don Giovanni* from the Met on Radio 3 and thought about Tim Robbins.

23 April

Paris where I am researching for *Love and Louis XIV*. Professor Bruno Neveu, a portly fellow in his sixties, of great professorial dignity and charm, took me to see the Institut de France and showed me Mazarin's tomb. Before that there was an amusing incident when I gave Professor Neveu lunch. '*Je vous présente mon mari*,' I said, and idiotically never mentioned Harold's name (he was a last-minute addition to the party as he had bronchitis and couldn't go out). Harold and I are so famously married, to put it crudely, in England that I would not dream of mentioning his name at home. In fact the good professor had absolutely no idea who '*mon mari*' was. At the end of lunch he asked Harold politely what his work was. Harold, astonished but equally polite: 'I'm a playwright.' Bruno Neveu: 'And are your works performed?' Mutters from me of: 'Just the *Comédie Française.*'

24 April

Today Bruno had an elegant and perfectly prepared way of revenge. As we were in the great room where the new academicians are presented, he told me of an English man, an archaeologist, being presented and 'a little wife sitting there in an English woman's flowered hat'. It never occurred to anyone that this was actually Dame Agatha Christie, wife of Sir Max Mallowan. I took the point. Immediately I expressed my immense culpability on the day before in the matter of the flawed introduction, whereupon he expressed his, before we agreed that no one was really to blame.

Otherwise we had an extremely good time. Harold's professional career, which had been in the doldrums here since the death of his friend and translator Eric Kahane, has been given a boost by a big interview in *Le Monde* in which he praised the French stand over the Iraq war. A pro-French intellectual! Just what they like.

18 June

Our party for Benjie's *City Poems* (Benjie paid, we gave). I organized it brilliantly and unaided with the mere help of Amanda, a top-class caterer, Linda, my PA, Linda's stand-in Lesley, Benjie himself, Swiftprint, Teresa and Tina and twenty-five waiters. As you see, unaided. The real feature of the party for me was the praise people heaped on the garden with pink climbing roses and the orange blossom still flourishing, pink and dark red geraniums (Barbe Bleue), grey senecio and notes of blue plumbago. Lilies just beginning to flower. About fifty copies of the poems were sold because Eliza, adorably fey in her white muslin First Communion dress, her flaxen hair, her elfin looks, accosted each guest as they entered: 'You've got to buy a copy!' Who could refuse? Benjie thanked Harold for 'making him so happy'.

20 July

In Scarborough Harold gave a reading of *War* and was then in dialogue with the extremely amiable Alan Ayckbourn. Later he said he thought he must vary his act at Cheltenham in the autumn. We discussed returning to readings of his plays that he enjoyed doing so much. *Celebration*? Harold: 'I always fancied my Suki . . .' (the sluttish young wife). I wouldn't have raised it if he hadn't, but did feel that the Turin speech made on 27 November 2002 needed an updating, given the fact that the war had only been pending then.

August 2003

Kingston Russell, Dorset. The most exciting social event was the visit of Jude Law, who will star in the new film of *Sleuth*, produced by Tom Sternberg, directed by Ken Branagh, screenplay by Harold. Tom brought him down, arriving in a huge silver car which satisfied all expectations of glamour. As indeed did Jude himself, lying asleep under an apple tree in his swimming trunks like a young Apollo taking a nap. (Alas, Edna O'Brien, also staying with us, ordained that we ladies should not swim at the same time as Jude, lest we lose our mystery for him.) Harold worked with Tom and Jude on the script on and off all day. He's really enjoying himself. One forgets that Harold regards screenwriting as an important art, quite a separate one from playwrighting, it is true, but not just a 'my-house-needs-painting' exercise, as an extremely famous playwright once put it to us modestly, about his own screen-work.

24–28 August

Cornwall. Harold lurked at the Abbey Hotel, Penzance writing *Sleuth*; Rebecca lurked upstairs in the farmhouse she had rented working on the proofs of her masterwork *A People's History of Britain*. Edward and

I lurked round the gardens of many country pubs taking the girls out for lunch. All parties very happy.

———

October 2003. We went back to Paris for eight days for my research. Harold, owing to his political views being shared by the French, had a very happy time.

16 October

Harold read from the plays at Cheltenham, as planned, also three 'political' poems and three love poems. While he was enacting Gila in *One for the Road*, he had to suddenly shout back at the interrogator in a sudden fit of defiance from a helpless prisoner: 'As it was!' At which point a huge blond guide dog, sprawled fast asleep in the aisle in front of me leapt up and stood on guard against the attacks of the world. The dog remained extremely distressed until Harold's 'Gila' voice once again softened.

18 November

Scene outside Quaker Meeting House apocalyptic and rather touching. Flickering candles. Lots and lots of police everywhere: this is for Bush's arrival in London. The banner I liked best condemned Bush, Blair *and* Saddam. Harold made a short, passionate, well-thought-out speech on which he had toiled for nearly a week to get it right. Personally, however, I don't go for this condemnation of Bush and Blair as 'Christian gents' any more than you should condemn al-Qaeda for being 'Muslim gents'. It's for your works not your faith that you should be condemned. Best of all was a schoolgirl called Verity who made a short speech and ended: 'If I say any more, I'll be repeating what I've said already so I'll sit down.' And she did. I hope she goes into politics one day.

19 November

Ken Livingstone's Peace Party on the ninth floor of the so-called 'gherkin'. Ken made an excellent speech stressing the amount of Americans he employed and his affection for the American people as opposed to the government. Plenty of old thespian radicals present including Corin Redgrave, Ken Cranham and Roger Lloyd Pack. Caryl Churchill told me about her short play at the Royal Court with Vanessa Redgrave as Laura Bush, seated graciously at an Iraqi children's play group. Only all the children were dead. Laura Bush a.k.a. Vanessa: 'And *how* did you die?' Cooing at each one in turn. Vivid, horrifying – and not all that unfair.

2004

26 January

Coral Reef Hotel, Barbados. We spend most of our meals with the Grays. And then to everyone's delight, Harold proposed himself as director for Simon's new play about Berenson and Duveen, *The Old Masters*. It's also greatly to my surprise as Harold has persistently said he has no more energy left to direct.

—

Looking back, I see this as a halcyon time. It was not our last visit to Barbados – that occurred a year later under far less propitious circumstances. But here was Harold offering to direct a new play by his favourite living playwright and favourite friend. It could not get much better. Meantime I was able to go to Mass at St Francis Church, where Father Michael Campbell Johnston who had performed our ceremony of marriage, now retired, was the parish priest. Happy-clappy Mass is never my personal choice in London where Latin and music are two essentials for me. But here it is absolutely correct and harmonious. Leadership of a strongly built black woman with a number of very young women in attendance, extremely beautiful, tiny skirts, high heels, choir of angels. Only upsetting moment when Victoria, a great animal lover, threw a banana down from her balcony to a family of eleven monkeys which filed past the pool at breakfast. A circular was issued: 'Guests must not order extra bananas for monkeys ... Guests who feed monkeys on their balconies and then leave the hotel ... create unfortunate expectations ... Monkeys do not understand the change of guests and become extremely aggressive towards the next occupants.' Ghastly picture: bewildered and frightened guests, chattering disappointed monkeys. Question: 'What do monkeys want?'

3 February

The deal is done. Harold is going to direct *The Old Masters*. Conferences, faxes, emails, etc. round the pool. He is so pleased. Given Harold's level of exhaustion, Simon thinks none of this would have taken place if Harold had read the play in cold, dispiriting London instead of being surrounded by energetic monkeys.

16 March

Harold magnificent on Iraq in a one-year-on special on *Newsnight*. Pre-empted any possible statement to the contrary by saying how happy he was with the news given by BBC poll that the Iraqis now in principle content with their lot. His opponent, an American named Ken Adelman made the mistake of arming himself with lavish compliments to Harold's plays in order to lure him into complacency and then blast him. But Harold doesn't do complacency. 'My plays are irrelevant,' he snapped at the third lavish compliment.

17 April

According to an article in the *Guardian*, President Bush was asked at a press conference yesterday how history would judge the Iraq War. He replied: 'History? We don't know. We'll all be dead.'

25 April

Harold gave a Larkin reading at the British Library, courtesy of Josephine Hart, a truly beguiling person with a passion for poetry.

23 May

Harold rehearsing *Old Masters*. Gets very tired, especially in the morning and afterwards but perks up, he says, when he's actually working. His last direction. And this time he really means it. Actually he meant it last time but the excellence of this play, plus Barbados optimism, changed his mind. Harold: 'It's a wonderful play. And I can't wait for it to be over.'

31 May–5 June

Hyatt Hotel, Birmingham, for *The Old Masters*. A skyscraper. I felt as if I was in Toronto. Spent my time going to the cinema (*Troy*) and looking at pictures (Paul Nash), while Harold was working.

27 June

Harold has written a poem 'To My Wife'. He has circulated it to friends and relations. Two friends, one female, one male, said they had crossed out the word 'Wife' and substituted their own partner.

TO MY WIFE

I was dead and now I live
You took my hand
I blindly died
You took my hand
You watched me die
And found my life
You were my life

When I was dead
You are my life
And so I live

It was published in the *Guardian* a few days later. Originally Harold and I agreed it was 'too private' but apparently I rescinded that decision late at night. Delighted I did so.

18 July

Sudden return of The Great Fear. I came back from tea with Soros grandsons, playing a mythological quiz, to find Harold with 'abdominal pains'. We did go out and play bridge with Betsy Reisz and Haya Clayton, with me begging Harold to promise to call the doctor the next morning if he wasn't better. He wasn't and he ended up with an emergency appointment with the great Mr Thompson. Blood tests, etc. Tentative prognostication of scar tissue (there's so little of Harold's inside left, remembering the map Mr Thompson drew) bringing about problems. The pains got better slowly over the weekend, but the whole episode reminded me that, so far as I am concerned, The Great Fear is not dead but sleepeth.

7 August

Harold really pleased to be awarded the Wilfred Owen prize, specifically for *War*, the pamphlet and for his services to the anti-war cause. His pleasure is palpable – wrong use of the word but Harold uses it that way. He is so often accused of writing 'doggerel' in his anti-war poems. Personally, I make a distinction between his verse and his poetry. 'Death' for example is printed in *War* to give it gravitas, and that is a poem.

23 September

Harold at the Imperial War Museum in a debate on the war in Iraq.
Pro-War: John Keegan. A clever *Daily Mail* journalist called Melanie
Phillips then threatened all us women with burkas under a world-wide
Caliphate and then argued the next day in the *Spectator* for adultery to
have the stigma of public disapproval. Well, how about religious Islam
as an ally if that is what you want? On with your burka!

On our side Tony Benn was equally irritating by banging on about
the Palestinians which, like homophobia, changed the subject. Harold
got into full swing and spoke movingly about the actuality of death (re
the civilians) although I thought he was wrong to describe the American
empire as the most barbarous the world has ever seen: what about the
Nazis, Pol Pot, etc.? Questions from the floor. Far the best came from
Terry Waite: 'Is violence really the best way to deal with militant
Islam?'

12 October

Harold is extraordinary. He enacted *Sleuth* with Jude Law, playing the
Michael Caine part. Jude arrived from the airport exhausted but, said
Harold, his adrenalin visibly returned as the performance got under
way 'and his amazing eyes glittered'. They stalked each other round
the Super-Study.

15 October

Harold and I went to the David Inshaw exhibition. There was a huge
new cricket picture which we had been told David was keen for
Harold to have. I have no idea how much money Harold has, but if
he wants to buy a vast cricket picture, why not? He has every right
to do so as he is always doing things for other people. All the same,
I think he was a bit relieved when the picture didn't fit the
measurements of the Super-Study. Quiet supper. I watched two of

the David Starkey *Monarchy* tapes for review on *Front Row*. I found Starkey good, firm, lucid, interesting but the format so cliché ridden. A falcon flies, a flag flutters, the sea heaves, knights thwack ... Give me talking heads.

3 November

Too depressed to write.

The results of the American election when Bush was re-elected was the reason for my depression.

15 November

Depression continued. Didn't know whether to laugh or cry, on the whole I laughed when a huge parcel of my own books arrived from the US. No message. I assumed they were for signing but sent a message to enquire: 'To whom should they be dedicated?' Answer came back: 'They are not for signing. I have sent them out of disgust at Antonia Fraser's anti-Bush letter in the *Guardian*. I no longer want to possess them.' Had to repress an instinct to respond: 'Why don't you give the huge postage money to the Children of Iraq? And bin the books.' Resisted the temptation. Nevertheless I decided that I don't mind being attacked in a good cause; I don't positively enjoy it as Harold does, but after all my piece did contain the words: 'I am Philamerican since WWII when we children knew the American soldiers had come to save us.' Before denouncing Bush.

25 November

Feast of St Catherine. Decided the date was propitious to start writing *Love and Louis XIV*. I'm full of anxiety however. Can I bring it off? Wrote three pages of which only the first sentence pleased me. Harold suffering from diminished energies as he admits. He spends a lot of the day just sitting, not even reading. Worrying.

2 December

Everything is better. Michael Caine sends a message that he loves the *Sleuth* script. And I get positive messages from Sofia Coppola. She's still on track to make *Marie Antoinette*.

24 December

Met Harold at Le Colombier. He's *clear* of cancer and the leukaemia hasn't moved. It's wondrous.

Christmas Day

The youngest guest was Honor Fitzgerald aged nine and a half. As we were without babies, I seized the opportunity to have a proper poetry reading at lunch and No Speeches! Edward, who is a famous orator, did not like the ban. He said mutinously: 'I can start my poem with a long dedication, you can't stop me.' Harold read from his favourite *Gilgamesh* as the theme was feasting. I read the passage from 'The Eve of St Agnes' when Porphyro pops out of the closet and lays out a feast for the sleeping Madeline.

26 December

The 9 a.m. news tells of a vast underwater earthquake, the fifth biggest since 1900, killing thousands with tidal waves all round the rim of Asia and the Far East. Apparently it's called a tsunami. As I sometimes observe to Harold, even man cannot match God in destruction when he sees fit.

Chapter Eighteen

WORST OF TIMES, BEST OF TIMES

The dawn of 2005 found Harold in rather frail health for no particular reason since he had been found free of cancer comparatively recently and the leukaemia was quiescent. The Great Fear was therefore more like a figure at a carnival, masked and in the doorway; you're not quite sure who it is. Death, no, it can't be ... but it's definitely something menacing. But it all got much worse. Altogether 2005 was the most extraordinary year of our lives together, leaving aside our meeting and all that followed, thirty years earlier. I might quote Dickens at the opening of *A Tale of Two Cities* by the time we reached the end of it: 'The best of times, the worst of times'. Except that I think I would phrase the same words rather differently. Thus: it was the worst of times – and also by the way the best of times.

10 January

Barbados. Torrential rain. (This would turn out to be our last visit and it was, alas, dismal.) Harold developed a painful chest and heavy cough: he was tested for lung cancer on return which required hospitalization; mercifully that was one thing he did not have. My knee, following an operation the previous year, was extremely painful so I could not swim in my beloved sea, and hardly exercise in the swimming pool. The Grays came later. By the time they arrived, the rain had poured down on our enjoyment and we were seeking escape. But vainly. Everyone else wanted to escape. It was the epilogue to the tsunami, perhaps.

11 January

It *is* depressing, no doubt about it, when unordained rain comes to an ordained sunshine paradise. Pools everywhere, apart from cascading and dripping water. People who should be on the beach congregate inside and play noisy card games. Me, dourly to Harold: 'I am reminded of rainy Cornish holidays in my youth and the card games we played indoors, wet sand, our school macs over school shorts, all we had to wear.' Only a visit to St Francis where I heard Father Michael Campbell Johnston preach an excellent practical sermon, made a difference. 'The money collected today,' he said, 'will go directly to the Jesuits of Sri Lanka with whom we are already in touch: they plan to go where the political spotlight is not.' I had just found an unexpected hoard of US dollars in an old wallet and gave them freely, guiltily, instead of buying fripperies in the hotel shop. Father Michael also talked of orphans just gazing helplessly out to sea where their parents had vanished.

I am reading Margaret Macmillan's excellent book *Peacemakers* interleaved with Alice Munro's latest – she's the best! And Harold is reading Chekhov interleaved with Anthony Sampson on the oil companies of South Africa. Judy Daish (my dramatic agent as well as Harold's agent and our close friend) tells me from London that Sofia Coppola intends to start shooting *Marie Antoinette* the movie on 7 March. In my present mood, I feel there's many a hitch . . . (four years since she signed the first option). Except that I have just seen a rainbow. And I love rainbows.

All my gloomy predictions about Sofia – whom I liked and admired so much, and so did Harold whenever they met – were freely recorded in my Diary: they were wrong. She did start to shoot on 7 March, having always carried out everything that she said she would do, surely a record in the exciting, roller-coaster world of film, which normally I only knew about second-hand from Harold.

9 February

Sofia's final script arrived. Harold read it first and pronounced it 'brilliant, so economical'. I read it on return and thought: where people like me depend on the final gruelling scenes for evoking sympathy, she has the simple image of the sound of a guillotine falling. (Harold didn't tell me how it ended and let it be a surprise – an extremely effective one.)

10 February

The *Daily Express* rings me with the news that Prince Charles and Camilla will wed. 'Good luck to them! And the nation will heave a sigh of relief,' I say and ring off as fast as possible. After that I don't answer the telephone. I like my royals dead, I once flippantly said, referring to my historical works, in answer to those eternal demands for comments on this that and the other in the present royal family; then poor Princess Diana was dead and I couldn't use it any more. Just as the telephone stopped ringing for me, it began again for Harold, more significantly for the death of Arthur Miller. Harold was extremely sad. Me: 'You didn't lament for Beckett though you loved him too.' Harold: 'Beckett wanted to move forward towards death but Arthur was full of life and wanted to stay alive.'

2 March

Ran into Ian McEwan at a party for Ishiguro's superb, sad new novel about clones. Told him that *Saturday* had been a great solace to me, reading it when waiting for an operation because it's compulsive reading and you don't notice the hours passing. Ian's huge owl-eyes gleam behind his glasses: 'Was it a brain operation?' he asks hopefully. 'Was the surgeon drunk?' He is referring to the climax of his book. He is definitely disappointed when the answer is a modest knee operation and a stone-cold sober surgeon.

4–6 March

We both went to the Aldeburgh Book Festival, run by an enterprising and civilized couple, Johnnie and Mary James, who own a bookshop there. There was a blizzard on the way up, but once in the hotel we looked out at the sea from three huge windows; woke at 6 a.m., snow on all the car roofs, a vast grey flat sea. The view changed all the time as the sun came and went, now a Turner, now a more sinister Hopper. This was Britten country so we did some sight-seeing to feed our shared passion for his operas. My talk compared Mary Queen of Scots and Marie Antoinette. Harold enacted *Celebration* and was miffed because there were no laughs. Was it the bad language? Hugh Thomas, who had nobly introduced me, asked a local. Resident: 'No, that was just what we expected.'

3 March

Mary Nighy who is to play the Princesse de Lamballe, Marie Antoinette's favourite, came to see me. She told me to my pleasure that the producer Ross Katz was most enthusiastic about filming in France: 'They have châteaux out there! We don't even have to build them.' Pale and pretty, not exotically dark and beautiful like her mother Diana Quick; interesting to see Bill Nighy's wonderful raddled face transformed into that of an English Rose. Very bright, as she seeks information. But of course she's not at all my Princesse de Lamballe, who was six years older than the Queen, already a widow; and rather dull.

Suddenly I realized that she wasn't my Princesse de Lamballe any more: she was Sofia's. Did I mind?

8 March

The next visit, although extremely enjoyable, was even more disconcerting. Jason Schwartzman arrived from Paris (where he had left his beloved dog – I liked that pet-devotion which reminded me of Marie Antoinette and Mops). Bizarre-looking at first sight in bright chocolate brown suit, three piece, yellow open-necked shirt, longish black Beatle-style hair and black stubble. Quite short. Eloquent big black eyes (I had no idea that he was Sofia's cousin, the son of Talia Shire, the heroine-actress of the *Godfather* series). He told me he was half Polish-Jewish and half Italian. Well, Louis XVI was half Polish too. Otherwise, except for the marked black brows, there is no resemblance between this lively, attractive man and the fat slob who was Louis XVI. We get quickly on to his eating, how he's had to put on twenty-four pounds and wanted to do it 'organically' as he's a vegetarian. He has a list of questions in an exercise book. His main thrust is that Louis XVI was a shy romantic, pulsing with love for Marie Antoinette, not an obese oaf with sexual problems. I don't give in. He complains that he spends most of the film eating – except when hunting, which he likes: 'I have to eat mounds of pheasants and things which they don't make in tofu.' His accent to me is very Californian. And Mary Nighy very English. Whereas Kirsten Dunst is LA Valley Girl. What will happen about all that? Will it all be dubbed, as Bill Nighy speculated when I bumped into him?

29 *March*

Château de Millemont, somewhere near Paris, bought in a wrecked state by an American for film companies to use. My first visit to the set. Astonishing! A large painted backdrop outside the window makes it clear that this is Versailles. Marie Antoinette's bedroom is an exact replica of the one there: the bed, plumes and all, is perfect. Except that there are huge black cables and cameras everywhere. Me to Sofia: 'Think of all that did – and did not – go on in that bed.' I sit amidst swathes of feathers, gilt and taffeta, much created by laser, in a chair marked MARIE ANTOINETTE and while waiting for the shoot, I read *Tommy* by Richard Holmes, the story of the ordinary British soldier in the First World War. This tale of mud and blood seems peculiarly inappropriate to the scene before me. In my usual terror of being caught without serious reading matter I had stuffed it into my handbag. There is even a taffeta dog basket for Mops – and I later glimpse Mops himself being taken for a comfort break.

I love the scene in the canteen; men in white wigs, embroidered waistcoats and knee breeches sit indiscriminately among people in jerseys and jeans, with production mobiles trilling. Since no one pays any attention to their eighteenth-century fancy dress, these characters give the impression of being ghosts from another time. Except the ghosts are having some substantial nosh, lots of meat, and this being France, there are bottles of red wine on every table (apparently it's a French union condition). The first 'ghost' I talk to is Sebastian Armesto as the Comte de Provence, Louis XVI's brother, last seen at Eton as President of the Literary Society and with a patrician voice to match (accent again?). He is the son of the distinguished historian Felipe Fernandez Armesto. Sebastian tells me kindly that he enjoyed my book and that he finds his father's books rather boring. Charming! I hope my children don't go round saying that kind of thing to all the historians (I bet they do).

Then I see three geishas with huge be-rollered heads wrapped in black net and grey towelling robes over their taffeta skirts. Mary as the Princesse de Lamballe, the Comtesse de Provence, the gorgeous Rose Byrne with her rich auburn locks (she's allowed a red net) and perfect pout as the Duchesse de Polignac – what Sofia calls 'the party girl'.

Finally the filming starts. Kirsten Dunst, in turquoise with a little black lace scarf, takes my breath away. Not only does she look absolutely beautiful and natural (that fabulous pink and white complexion, wide-apart blue eyes) but she's graceful. Except that she's not disfigured by a big Habsburg lower lip – you wouldn't want that in a film – Kirsten is an exact replica of the young girl, as I imagined her. Sebastian Armesto asks me what he should call his wife. Me: 'Madame in public and Sweetie Pie in private.' I learn that the first seven-year-old Dauphin has been sacked. Well, that poor little boy never had much luck, did he?

28 March

Easter Sunday. France. We visit the country house of Laure de Gramont and her family, one of our favourite places (and families). Laure's brother-in-law Gerry Shea gets hats together with Harold over politics. Gerry says he is a coward when it comes to speaking out, unlike Harold: I must say I think this is modesty on his part. A critic might argue that Harold is not especially brave in speaking out since he particularly likes shocking and shaking. But later I say to Harold in the Dark Bar of the Meurice Hotel that he was certainly extremely brave over his chemo and his cancer operation when he faced death. In the real sense of the word, he is valiant.

Shortly after our return from Paris, Harold's health began to deteriorate again, with a severely painful throat. For a while I thought it was traumatic: Paris which had been so promising, ending in a devastating – for him – evening when the distinguished, ancient director Roger Planchon had elected to run together two of Harold's plays, *Family Voices* and *Celebration* instead of doing them separately. There had been rumours ... but Harold who had admired Planchon's *No Man's Land* years earlier, did not believe them. After this disastrous performance he left with dignity, as Planchon said roguishly: 'I hope you are not going to hit me.' Nothing causes Harold more pain than unlawful interference with his text.

I was absorbed writing my book called *Galaxy* at the time, which morphed into *Love and Louis XIV*. Harold admitted that reading it every three weeks or so when I had finished a new chapter, he found it rather muddling. I did not want to hear this: like everyone who asks their nearest and dearest for a candid opinion, I didn't actually want *that* candid opinion.

My Diary throughout the summer is dominated by observations about Harold's health, which is occasionally, but only occasionally reported to be better, generally worse: 'his depression is waning.' All sorts of verdicts (but not cancer). 'Viral bronchitis' is one of them. Better than lung cancer, we say to one another, the word emerging for the first time. In July things get worse. Harold's mouth is in agony and he feels ghastly. Visits to the dentist provide no relief or solution.

Then, after more hospitalization, 'inflammation of the oesophagus'. Oh for some relief for him! In mid July I record Harold as hollow-eyed after coughing from 10.30 p.m. to 9 a.m. (and for all I know after that).

21 July

Dramatic day. I was interviewed by Cherie Blair, assisted by Cate Haste, at No. 10 on the subject of prime ministers' wives for a TV film following their book (which contained much interesting, anecdotal stuff on the lives of the First Mates). Cherie, beautiful as she is in reality, not photographs, very sympathetic. I approve of her efforts to get the position of the prime minister's spouse defined, in view of the constant hostility of the press. At the end she leaned forward and asked me whether I would like to have been a prime minister's wife. I gazed at Cate and burst out laughing. 'What, Harold for PM!' and laughed some more. The bubble coming out of my head read: '*My* husband would like to indict *your* husband as a war criminal, so that's what he would do as Prime Minister.' What I actually said – perfectly truthfully – was: 'If he was Prime Minster, Harold would commandeer all the boxes at Lord's for the Ashes.'

Life's rich tapestry. I went from No. 10 (enormous security, which at the time I thought possibly overdone) to the Royal Court Theatre where Harold was being interviewed by young foreign playwrights, the annual date he much enjoys. Cuban, Finnish, Arab, etc. Naturally he was inveighing against Tony Blair . . . He also spoke passionately about the need for humour in plays. No one cracked a smile. Went out to pick up a taxi and found a traffic block. Then I heard of the four bombs and the dread words Shepherd's Bush (where two of my children and their families live). Found myself thinking that the police who had shot the would-be suicide bomber had been right, given his intentions and his desire to die, and I'm supposed to be a liberal! (I was of course totally wrong about this: here was an innocent man, the victim of police bungling.)

Harold's still-declining health: I record the kindly reactions of others including the phrase that carers get to know: 'Really, this is much worse for you.' The answer is: 'No, it's not. It's worse for Harold. Much worse. But it's dreadful for me in a different way.' In the meantime my Diary, with increasing gloom, lists the tiny amounts of food Harold manages to ingest. It's all much more painful than chemo.

27 August

My seventy-third birthday. I can hardly describe it. The most beautiful weather I have ever known at Bernhurst and a banquet on the front lawn, going on as in a French film, till six o'clock in the evening. Interleaved with the cricket, watched by enthusiasts indoors, a cliffhanger which ends in triumph when England wins the Ashes. But Harold is worse, really worse, eats nothing, has virtually lost his voice, coughs and splutters all night long. Back to the doctor and soonest. Oh, why is it always a Bank Holiday at the time of agonies?

An excellent emergency doctor caused Harold to be admitted to Princess Grace Hospital. It took a little time for him to be diagnosed with a rare auto-immune blood disease called Pemphigus, where 'the body attacks the body'. This is one of those diseases which you wish afterwards you had not looked up on the internet because the prognosis is so dire. Harold left me a sweet message: 'I've been listening to the *Rite of Spring* on the radio. It reminds me of you.' Actually I feel like the bleak rite of mid winter but the message is still lovely to receive.

10 September

It's so odd being alone nearly all the time and my very best friend for thirty years can't talk, really. So I moan to this Diary. Doing the Source Notes for *Love and Louis XIV* is however a marvellous distraction: normally I loathe 'the Bloody References' as I call them, but this time they are keeping me sane.

14 September

Harold came home.

15 September

New Diary, new life. This morning Harold felt very warm when I hugged him, not so much the holy man-cum-skeleton of yesterday. 'It's Paradise being here.' He said it. I agreed.

16 September

Harold went to a new doctor, Dr Chris Bunker, a dermatologist. Pemphigus is so rare that Dr Bunker, top expert, is currently treating only two people for it. And 'it can be fatal'. I think I realized that from Googling but as usual put the thought away. Anyway Harold feels great confidence in Dr Bunker. Harold's spirit is returning although steroids, doubled, make him very frail.

———

Harold remained extremely frail and extremely tense. My Diary is one long record of his inability to eat, general suffering. But there was talk of a wonder drug. He took for the first time to using a stick (one of mine left over from my knee operations, thus decorated with perky green hearts – which he removed). Also got Carter's the builders to make a wooden banister outside our front steps. Harold's feet began to swell, thanks to the steroids, and his voice became extremely croaky.

1 October

Harold managed to come and join Sofia Coppola and me at dinner at Le Caprice (to his annoyance she managed to pay the bill, which he was determined to do, by slipping deftly away and doing it un-announced). Harold feels the great charm she radiates too: 'a really nice person'. Partly it's the gentleness, the good manners with which she arms herself, perhaps, as the daughter of a genius. The editing of *Marie Antoinette* is going well. Sofia loves the 'Must you go?' story of when we first met, which Harold told her. Wishes she could get it into *Marie Antoinette*. Me: 'Maybe you can use it in your new vampire movie?'

Despite the swollen feet of a mummy (oh my God! the shoe problem), Harold gallantly said he would 'somehow' get to Dublin for a Pinter Festival to celebrate his seventy-fifth birthday. 'Somehow' turned out to be a private plane, since by now he could scarcely walk and had many medical problems arising from his many medicines. He arrived totally exhausted but 'I made it' as we used to say about our various holiday travels in the past. He was rewarded by a production of *Old Times* at the Gate Theatre, as good as this great play gets, with the utter truthfulness of Janie Dee to commend it, last seen in *Betrayal*. Then there was Penelope Wilton and Derek Jacobi in *Family Voices*.

Lastly there was an extraordinary triumph of affection – no other word will do – when *Celebration* was performed by actors who had flown in, literally, from all over the world including Jeremy Irons and Michael Gambon (from Europe and LA respectively) and Stephen Rea (from New York). But tears rushed into my eyes when Harold actually managed to get on stage for the second act, all in black, looking very noble with his stick. He seemed suddenly so frail, by which I really mean old, I suppose, albeit very, very distinguished. I thought of the dynamo, the energetic man in his forties of 1975. Then in a strong voice, miked but very clear, stronger than it has been for months, he referred to 1975, our thirty years together, and read 'Paris', the first poem he ever wrote to me. Then the tears really did flow and I had to jump up and stand by the side and applaud strongly to still my palpitations of pride and pleasure. Later, at the party, lots of wives told me they wished that poem had been written to them. All referred to the line: 'She dances in my life.'

10 October

Harold's seventy-fifth birthday. Fêted day, then fated. As Harold was walking up the steps to the VIP lounge at Dublin Airport, plus stick, he slipped. I heard a scream behind me. Harold's whole face dripping blood, down to his shoes. It was a huge gash which ultimately needed nine stitches. So it was off to Casualty in an ambulance. As I filled in the forms, about fifty times, each official said: 'But it's his birthday today!' Desperately, I thought of giving a false date of birth but realized that the whole system would then grind to a halt.

12 October

Back in London, Harold recovered very slowly and I was punch-drunk with the shock of seeing it all. To calm my nerves, in the evening I tried out Harold's denim umpire's cap on him, to distract from the enormous white patch; having originally constructed a black patch out of the tail of a black silk shirt, which looked even worse. In the meantime I hastily reread my book *The Gunpowder Plot* in order to do a dialogue with Jim Naughtie the next day for Radio 4, to commemorate the four hundredth anniversary of the Plot. The contents of the book came as somewhat of a surprise to me, given my currently addled brain, and the fact that it was nine years since I had written it.

Thus dawned the most exciting day of my life: with Harold, scarcely able to walk, heavily dependent on a stick, with a white patch over one eye and a sailor's cap lying on the hall table.

13 October

What happened was this: we both felt awful at breakfast, Harold from coughing without intermission all night, me from listening to him. I went up to the Eyrie and assembled notes re the Gunpowder Plot. Then I chatted to a friend about Dublin. About eleven thirty, Linda came in and said the odd words: 'Could you clear the line? Harold has something urgent he wants to tell you.' Somewhat crustily I did so. Now it was Harold who was engaged: I thought he might clear *his* line. Finally he buzzed me: 'I seem to have won the Nobel Prize.'

I think I cried out: 'I don't believe it!' Anyway, that was what we kept saying the whole day and night thereafter: 'I can't believe it!' 'I don't believe it!' 'I can't take it in!' So many tears recently, of joy (Gate Theatre), fear (Dublin Casualty) and now joy again. Suggested some champagne – it was 11.50 a.m., very early, but why not? – while we watched TV. Idiotically, I added: 'To see if it's true.' Actually the noon news was a long story about sick poultry and it wasn't until one o'clock that I actually saw Harold on TV.

In the meantime our two telephone lines became like mad hissing snakes. The world started to ring and bang on our door. Actual banging. Harold went out on the steps at 1.30 p.m., with his stick and wearing the cap: thank heaven for the cap, nautical in aspect, which looked great and made Harold have the air of a cheerful old salt, despite the white bandage. What a fortunate prophetic search that was! Sitting in the drawing room I heard some chuckles, so evidently Harold on the steps was in good if somewhat dazed form. Then the US woke up and Damian (in Mexico) said that while he was talking to me, he had twenty-seven messages on his BlackBerry; Natasha said she had thirty in Paris. The senior grandchild, Stella, at Yale, telephoned later to say that she had just gone walking round the University with a smile on her face, letting everyone congratulate her. I even managed to get to Bush House to talk about the Gunpowder Plot although I have absolutely no memory of what I said, I suspect I just babbled on about Harold.

It may sound odd in retrospect but it is true that neither of us had ever remotely thought that Harold would win the Nobel Prize. Occasionally people had politely suggested it, and I had always given Harold's politics as the reason why he would never win. And I meant it. That very morning we had casually hoped that our friend Orhan Pamuk, he who had escorted Harold and Arthur all those years ago, would win, to help him in his current troubles with the Turkish authorities. Harold now learned that a Nobel Prize transforms your life forever: in his opinion entirely for the better. His plays entered the stratosphere of productions. Equally dear to his heart was the fact that he would now have a political forum in his Nobel Speech.

14 October

We are living in a house full of flowers. Harold's pronouncement on the subject of his speech: 'It will be wise, lucid, sane and tolerant.' He reported that he then immediately lost his rag with a foreign TV interviewer who asked him why he wrote in dialogue, also why he thinks human rights are important.

16 October

The whole Nobel experience has sapped Harold's physical strength and he has only a month to write his speech. Me: 'Please don't forget dear old literature altogether.' Harold: 'No, I am thinking of the double theme of literature and then politics in literature.' I was even congratulated at the communion rails by Father Isidore at Mass on Sunday. I muttered 'Amen' automatically. Among messages of congratulations was one from my brother Thomas: 'Ten thousand feet up on the Chinese border with Burma I am drinking whisky to celebrate.'

17 October

Harold is inviting the whole family to Stockholm. He offers me a dress or rather dresses in which to beguile the King of Sweden and any other passing king. I haven't had a ball dress for years. Kenneth Rose told me that Lady Gwendolen Cecil, biographer of her father Lord Salisbury, used up her old evening dresses by gardening in them. I may do the same.

———

While the excitement grew, so did the weakness. There were terrifying falls including one when Harold lay for two hours outside the door of his Super-Study and I watched television in the drawing room (I did not hear his cries and thought he was having a meeting). I shuddered. Yet he still managed on occasion to make my breakfast on Sunday morning with the mantra: 'I am the luckiest man in the world.' And he did a dialogue at the Royal Court with Ian Rickson in which his love of the English language and the English countryside got stressed. The shoes were a terrible problem, his poor swollen feet, until an angel in the shape of our next-door neighbour Paul Smith came to his rescue, searching London for an adequate pair and finally offering his own shoes.

28 October

Read Harold's speech: the first draft. The beginning (Art) is brilliant, Harold at his best, writing like quicksilver. The middle is the usual stuff, all perfectly legitimate but familiar, and then it becomes Harold again. Very funny, offering to be President Bush's speech-writer. When asked, my main comment was that the synthesis was a bit spare. Harold rushed away and was last seen scribbling furiously, whether he accepted my suggestions or not.

———

Harold had numerous tests with a view to being helped by the wonder drug so as not to depend on steroids for too long. Damian arrived in London from Mexico and I asked him to be candid as to how he found Harold. Damian: 'If I hadn't been prepared by seeing the Nobel pictures when he was so terribly frail, I would have been shocked.'

7 November

The day I delivered *Love and Louis XIV* (after five years' work) was carefully chosen to be A Great Day. I am some rotten picker of Great Days. When Judy Daish rang me about six with regard to *Louis*, to say: 'How exciting . . .' I didn't even know what she was talking about. For at noon Harold had said: 'They are taking me into hospital. Now.' A test taken on Friday had come through 'bad'; I still don't know what that meant. Harold told me later that he had postponed leaving for half an hour in order to finish the second draft of his Nobel Speech. We went to Chelsea & Westminster. The Great Fear was well and truly back when I thought of the poor skeleton with its hacking cough I had held in my arms that morning. And when I returned in the afternoon, Harold was palpably worse, in a state of great distress.

A number of doctors gathered round. His throat was swelling and he couldn't breathe: there was talk of an emergency tracheotomy. The dreadful rasping breathing, the convulsions, no other word will do. Two nurses, one middle-aged white, one young black woman, were bending over Harold. Older woman as Harold rattled: 'You hear that sound? That's called Strydel and when you hear it, you send for everyone in the hospital.' Much later I learned that Strydel is the Death Rattle to you and me. Dr Bunker asked me gently what I knew about Pemphigus and gave me a lot of statistics which seemed to indicate that Harold at seventy-five had a one in two chance of survival. I looked at the book on my lap which happened to be called *The Terror* (about the French Revolution; I'd just instinctively grabbed it when I left the house).

A terrible period for Harold ensued: he was transferred to intensive care at the Royal Marsden and by degrees the immediate danger had passed far enough away for him to be able to leave the hospital. I transformed the house into an abode for a person whose legs were too weak to do anything with them. Then at the end of November he had a bad fall in the night and I couldn't get him up (later we learned this art from a South African nurse Elzanne whose cry: 'I'm with you, Mr Pinter' became a tender joke). So it was back to the Royal Marsden for a prolonged stay and treatment. Obviously in all this, the visit to Stockholm was out of the question. But it was characteristic of Harold's extraordinary spirit that he was absolutely determined nonetheless to deliver his speech: he had his forum and he was determined, intensive care or no intensive care, to take advantage of it.

9 November

Harold was declared 'out of danger' and sent for a yellow pad. Harold: 'Those are good words to hear about oneself, "out of danger".'
I wondered to myself: will Harold ever be out of danger?

25 November

Harold has a very painful infection in his poor swollen leg. Just when you think things can get no worse, at 2 a.m. I was aware that Harold was falling. Then he cried out. The next half-hour passed with two adults, seventy plus, struggling with numerous bits of equally unfit bedroom furniture to raise one of them back up. Judy Daish and Gordon, the blessed pair, came round instantly when summoned at 3 a.m. and even Big Gordon had a problem getting Harold up. So Harold went back to the Marsden in a wheelchair.

Sleepless and exhausted, I had to go and see a rough cut of *Marie Antoinette* which Sofia had brought from California, on her way to Paris to show me. Oh my God, I thought, I shall fall fast asleep in a warm dark private cinema and there is no way I can ever, ever explain that. So I rushed into the Covent Garden Hotel and drank two of the strongest coffees I could find: I was buzzing.

Then came the rock music. I had written in my Diary on this subject when I visited the set at Versailles, recording my puzzling conversation with Richard Beggs, the Sound Designer.

17 May

Richard wonders whether the sound of an aeroplane which drove the sound men mad might not be incorporated into the film as a token. Token of what? I don't get this at all. But not at all. Even odder is his reference to Rock'n'Roll when I ask him about the music. I had expected him to say Gluck, Mozart, that sort of thing – the music to which I used to listen when I researched and wrote the book. He obviously can't literally mean Rock'n'Roll. I expect the phrase has another meaning which I am not cool enough to know. I must ask Natasha.

Now I realized that Rock'n'Roll was no code ... the first blast of it nearly made me jump out of my comfortable chair in the viewing theatre at the chic Covent Garden Hotel. Although I got to love it in the wild party scene. (In the end the music was Rameau'n'Rock'n'Roll, leading to some highly original music credits.) In March, in another chic viewing theatre at the Charlotte Street Hotel, Harold also nearly jumped out of his chair at the first blast before settling down to enjoy it.

And I adored it, the whole concept, Sofia's notion of the young girl at a loss in an alien world of hostile grandeur.

27 November

Just spoke to Harold. I am in bed and so for that matter is he. Although not beside me. It is our twenty-fifth wedding anniversary. There is no doubt at all that our marriage is very, very, very ... to the infinite degree happy beyond all possible expectations. It takes something like these last months to realize the depth of love (on both sides).

Chapter Nineteen

————◆————

FORTITUDE

3 December 2005

Harold said: 'I could as easily get to Stockholm as I could climb the Andes.' He talked to Michael Kustow about going in a private ambulance to a studio and recording his speech here. Both Mike and David Hare – who will introduce it on television – think the speech is wonderful.

4 December

Harold was so amazing yesterday. In an ambulance – which took one hour from SW3 to SW1 but luckily he did not notice – we went to the Channel 4 studios. Harold had one foot in a surgical sandal (ulcer is terribly painful) and one in a cut-down shoe. He refused to wear a tie and was right about that. In the studio, he was placed in a chair in the centre, a rug of checked pale reds over his knees. He looked frail and isolated, like Methuselah's older brother. Yet on the monitor, he looked young – young and vigorous! Almost as young as the backcloth of him in an open tan shirt, at least twenty years ago. And then he went for it, coolly, huskily, no hint of a rant – he let the words convey the passion, not him – and on and on, remarkably few breaks, that is to say that the thirty-eight minutes took no more than a hour to record.

Fascinating, masterly, deceptive speech, starting exactly where you want him to go, art, the enigma and all that, and then *pow*, exactly where perhaps cravenly, many don't want him to go, the politics. 'Sometimes a writer has to smash the mirror,' says Harold. Yes, indeed. I hear smashing sounds all round me.

I would like to be able to record that that supreme effort, by a man in much pain who goes in an ambulance from a cancer hospital to issue a clarion call to the world, was followed by a rallying of Harold's health. But it was not so. The dark days of the early spring of 2006 were probably the time of greatest discomfort of all – so far. It might be nice to be like Elizabeth Bennet, who recommended her 'philosophy' to Mr Darcy at the end of *Pride and Prejudice:* 'Think only of the past as its remembrance gives you pleasure.' But that would be to ignore Harold's extraordinary fortitude – no other word is appropriate.

Back to Nobel Days:

7 December

Nobel Day. Watched Harold's speech on More4. I was quite stunned afterwards since there was far more acting than I remembered. I marvelled at the well-judged pauses, the relaxed gestures. And the strategy for the speech: I like the idea of the American Embassy gathered round and as Harold talks about his work at the start: 'So that's all right: the guy is talking about Art.' And then, Wham, Bam. After watching, I visited this rather pitiful, utterly brave creature in his cell, his skeletal appearance striking me all over again as he sat in his dark blue dressing-gown. Harold felt a bit low, he said, towards evening. A reaction? He did all that and still he was in hospital having four dressings a day . . .

31 December

Harold to Betsy Reisz and Haya Clayton, who came to play bridge: 'This is the worst year I've ever had.' Much worse than 2002 when he was only in hospital for two weeks. The Nobel Prize hardly seems to count in the field of his emotions.

2006

8 January

Harold gave me two presents to celebrate the anniversary of 'Must you go?', both alike in dignity. One was a marquise ring, a lozenge-shaped Edwardian ring of diamond tracery, which is designated the Nobel Ring. The other was a list of corrections for *Love and Louis XIV* – the latter even more heroic under the circumstances than the former. We debated the French for 'Must you go?' Me: '*Est-ce qu'il faut t'en aller?*' Harold: 'But I would have called you "*vous*".'

29 January

Tony Blair has written Harold a letter about the Nobel Prize. It's rather a good letter under the circumstances, mentioning their 'disagreement' – well, you could call Harold naming Tony Blair a war criminal a disagreement – but congratulating him all the same on what he has done for literature. It is 'Dear Harold, Yours Tony' although they have never met. Harold has replied today: 'Dear Prime Minister, Yours Harold Pinter', but referring to his 'generous' congratulation, considering their 'disagreement'. It is good to use the word 'generous' because it makes Harold, by implication, look generous too.

5 February

Jeremy King and Susanna Gross came to play bridge. Much talk congratulating me on my 'bravery'. Felt rather embarrassed as I haven't been particularly brave, to be honest, being very often in despair. In retrospect I think I was brave in 2002 but it was the bravery of ignorance. This applies to quite a lot of courage, of course, but not all.

18 February

A great day. Harold went over to the Super-Study, last seen on

7 November when he took half an hour to complete his Nobel Speech and then went to the Chelsea & Westminster Hospital.

27 March

Harold had lunch with Ian Rickson today and it looks as if *Krapp's Last Tape* is a real goer and it's my measure of hope.

———

This was a plan for Harold to play in Beckett's masterpiece of a monologue at the Royal Court, directed by Ian Rickson. Over the next six months, it became, for me, a touchstone for Harold's health, his real survival. When he felt up for it, I was encouraged, when not, cast down. And so it went on.

9 April

Harold spoke to me very tenderly and sweetly last thing at night (recently he's been going to sleep so early that we haven't talked). He thanked me as though he had thought the words out very carefully, for all the devotion, practical and otherwise, I had shown to him. Me: 'You would have done exactly the same for me.' Which is absolutely true. All this in view of the coming visit to hospital in order to deal with the ulcer on his leg, the latest extremely painful ordeal.

14 April

Good Friday. And a fine penitential day. I walked into Harold's room at the Cromwell Hospital, ready to collect him and take him home after a five-day stay. I saw the dark head in bed with the sheet more or less over it. Luckily it wasn't Harold dead: I had simply got the wrong room.

5 May

Harold's pain is worse. Nice doctor with an Indian name admits that it is rare for an ulcer to last five months. You can see the pain breaking over him in waves and he gives an involuntary groan. I can hardly bear to write about this latest martyrdom, for that is what it is, which has lasted nearly a year, since last July.

———

However Harold did come with me to Paris in late May where the French translation of *Marie Antoinette* was launched to coincide with Sofia Coppola's film. He spent most of his time holed up in our suite at the Hotel Meurice while I raced round Paris giving live interviews in French, of which I hope never to see a recording. But he came: and that was wonderfully loyal after the virtual twelve months of illness. Heroically he even made the lunch given for me at the British Embassy, to honour *Marie Antoinette* the book. Harold put on a tie and suit for the first time for – I don't know how long. The Embassy chef produced a magnificent cake, of the sort she never told the people to eat, in the shape of the Queen herself. Big pink skirts, high powdered coiffure, which I did not dare put a spoon into. Lots of ambassadorial jokes: 'Go on, lift the skirt of Marie Antoinette.' Later, in the Dark Bar, we had our now familiar argument about History. Harold's position: 'Things are getting worse and worse all the time' versus mine: 'Some things are getting better for some people some of the time.' Gut feeling versus the study of history. Jewish despair versus Catholic – what?

While he was in Paris, and in the Dark Bar, Harold wrote a little piece called *Apart from That*. It was triggered by his dislike of listening to inanities as people gossiped into their mobiles in restaurants. He decided to read it at a poetry reading held to raise money for the Patrick Pakenham Scholarships for young ex-offenders (my brother, a barrister, had recently died of leukaemia), part of the Longford Trust in memory of my father, which had also funded an annual lecture. It was a two-hander: Harold was looking for a partner and I put myself forward.

9 May

Rehearsed *Apart from That* with Harold, and contested one of his comments. Harold: 'I am the Director here.' Me: 'I am the Assistant Director.' Still, I think I won't give up the Day Job. My new project – *Queen Elizabeth I* – is beginning to obsess me because if you don't have another book on the go whenever a new book comes out, criticism can be awfully painful and stultifying. But a new book, especially with all the crises of Harold's health, gives one a separate dimension of hope.

11 May

The poetry reading. Harold, Benjie and Grey Gowrie: 'Three strong voices,' said Harold later. Matthew Burton read Harold's own poems superbly and I love all Grey's poems about heart surgery. *Apart from That* was announced by Orlando as Master of Ceremonies, as 'my mother's professional debut'.

It was not until late June that Harold told me that the Evil Ulcer was receding and we began to envisage a world without hospital visits. Harold even managed to come to *Nixon in China*, the John Adams piece we both loved, for the second time, which, whatever it cost him, was a gesture of faith. Adams is worthy to be compared with Verdi in grandeur of imagination (actually I think Harold prefers John Adams!). He also managed to speak at a Human Rights event at the Royal Court, reading 'Death' and also – what a pleasure! – encountering Václav Havel again. Interviewed by Kirsty Wark for *Newsnight*, he was accused of pessimism by the frisky Kirsty (whom by the way he likes otherwise he wouldn't do the interview, despite being furious that BBC 2 ignored his Nobel Speech). Harold replied: 'Life is beautiful but the world is Hell!' Which more or less sums up Harold's philosophy. Prompted by Kirsty, he quoted 'To My Wife': 'I was dead and now I live . . .' and listening in the box, I felt the familiar pricking of my eyes when that poem is quoted.

*

Our summer holiday at Westbrook House, an eighteenth-century house on the outskirts of Weymouth (dating from the time that George III made the town fashionable for sea-bathing). It was dominated by the question of Harold doing *Krapp's Last Tape*. I say 'the question' because it was by no means certain that someone who was in a lot of pain a lot of the time and very weak, who also had real difficulty in walking, was in a fit state to conduct a forty-minute monologue on the stage of the Royal Court Theatre Upstairs. Since there are frequent references in my Diary to Harold's 'pessimism', there also ought to be tributes to his more-or-less unconquerable will when he believed he could perform something. In this case *Krapp's Last Tape* brought together Harold's feeling for Beckett with the desire he had had since he was sixteen to be an actor. Throughout all this time Ian Rickson behaved with great sensitivity, privately assuring me that the performance didn't *have* to take place – even though it had sold out within five minutes of the short run being announced: 'Listen, we can always cancel.'

18 July

Celestial and cerulean day at Lord's. Total happiness (of eighteen people). Total cost: £8000. It was Benjie's idea that Harold should celebrate the Nobel Prize by taking a box at Lord's – 'something for yourself,' he said winningly. And of course for the cricket-loving family. The blue of the sky, the beauty of the vigorous yet serene scene, ineffable. Of the grandsons, Simon Soros and Thomas Fraser came.

25 July

Westbrook House: the most beautiful, comfortable, well-arranged house. Lots of ducks led by a long-necked one, which flock across the lawn towards the house if a door opens, asking for food. Many granddaughters staying: hard-working fathers are seen running past in some complicated game of rescue. Hard-working mothers appear to be taking the opportunity to relax.

15 August

Visit of Ian Rickson left Harold very exhausted the next day but much less depressed. Ian to me: 'He worries about whether he's good enough and I worry about whether he's strong enough.' The news from Lebanon in the meantime depresses all our spirits.

24 August

Harold's breathlessness: he pants heavily even to stretch out for a card at bridge. What is happening? Going for a walk is a thing of the past.

25–26 August

Edinburgh Book Festival. The frail figure of Harold, who was helped on stage, turned before our eyes into one, or rather two brutal interrogators as Harold did the famous scene questioning Stanley from *The Birthday Party*, as a prelude to discoursing on his own political views (he says he's bored with reading his *War Poems*). Full of force. Everyone felt privileged because most people seemed to have studied *The Birthday Party* at school . . . and here was the author himself. I spoke about *Love and Louis XIV*, which was published more or less at the same time as the Festival.

———

Through the autumn during rehearsals there were at least two episodes where Harold got chest pains and had to be rushed home from the Royal Court.

11 October

Harold's Dress Rehearsal was actually a full house of many

distinguished people in the theatre such as Caryl Churchill and Christopher Hampton. Harold stuck with his decision to use a wheelchair (despite much agonizing and counter decisions in the middle of the night) since he has terrible eczema on his palms, also the soles of his feet which makes walking the torture of Hans Andersen's Little Mermaid. He does it, despite wheelchair not always answering to his command, and sticking in the scenery twice.

12 October

Harold was amazing. No shenanigans with the chair: the stage arch was much enlarged overnight. His interaction with the tape was consummate: he laughed along with it. And thrill, thrill, Orhan Pamuk has won the Nobel Prize! Harold made a statement to Reuters: 'I expected him to win last year but somebody got in the way.'

Friday 13 October

Was Beckett born on Friday the thirteenth? Ian Rickson says not: he just pretended. Be that as it may, I was walking up the very narrow crowded stairs to the Theatre Upstairs, wondering why no one was being let in. Then a robotic announcement came: 'Due to an emergency, the theatre is closed.' Oh my God, Harold has had a heart attack, I thought. Rachel said later that she would have thought it was a bomb, but for me the bomb was Harold. Then Michael Byrne, in the queue, told me it was a technical emergency, the generator had gone wrong and it would be illegal to proceed.

14 October

The play itself was sensational! There is no other verdict: the most extraordinary experience sitting so close in the very front row of this tiny theatre so as to be able to stretch out my knee (Harold can't see me: I checked). He is there. He is not there. He is my Harold. He is not my Harold. He is Beckett's Krapp. Edward Beckett (the playwright's nephew and heir) was very friendly. He said he liked the wheelchair (not in the text and thus actually, I suppose, unlawful). His wife queried Harold's elimination of the bananas. 'Does he not like bananas?' Me: 'He's allergic to them.' Hmm . . . Actually Harold said: 'I'm not doing the bananas.' And no one seems to have queried it.

15 October

Our friend Dr John Murray has been studying ageing and how to delay it. It turns out that playing *Krapp's Last Tape* is the very best thing Harold could do.

18 October

Harold has decided not to do three more performances. 'I'm not in good health and filming it for TV seems a natural end to it.' It's true: his poor feet are appallingly blistered. Meanwhile the telephone never stops ringing with people who want tickets. Harold's mildest response: 'I am not a fucking box office.'

Harold's eczema raging in his foot. Chris Bunker instructs me how to bathe the foot in potassium solution. Bunker: 'Pale pink like a Leander tie. Do you know what I mean?' Me: 'Yes. Or a Garrick Club tie.'

21 October

Due to go to *Krapp* for the fifth time. I've given away my nightly tickets to a few deserving causes such as Edward Fitzgerald. I was tempted by an American who accosted me outside the Royal Court and said firmly: 'You must have seen this already. How about $250 dollars for your ticket?' But how could I explain it to Harold?? As it was, I did voluntarily give my ticket to Dustin Hoffman as I thought this great actor should see, as it were, another one. Had to dash backstage to explain. Harold amazed and then very pleased. Dustin and Harold had a long talk afterwards.

24 October

Last night of *Krapp*. Lucian Freud in the audience, who says he wants to paint Harold. I think it was the front-page photograph of Harold as Krapp which got his attention: an extraordinary visionary shot of a man listening to other voices. Orlando's comment pleased Harold immensely: 'Harold was like a master batsman, so utterly in control of the situation, and taking his time at the crease.' And the extraordinary thing is that Harold looks better at the end of the run than at the beginning, so maybe there is something in what Dr John said.

———

The rest of the year was dominated by the wedding of Orlando to Clemmie: an event of extraordinary happiness for everyone. To pre-empt arguments about the dress code, I sent for a pale silk Charvet tie from Paris for Harold which he consented to wear ... Immediately afterwards I set out for the US for a book tour in order to promote *Love and Louis XIV*: as the Senate fell to the Democrats, one sensed the small green shoots of hope as yet invisible to people in England. And I bought a paperback to solace me in my travels, by someone called Barack Obama, *The Audacity of Hope*.

21 November

Special lunch for Harold at the British Library to mark the purchase of his 'Archive'. This includes his collection of press cuttings. Jamie Andrews, archivist, a very nice enthusiastic man, told us that Book One was one of the most borrowed items, with those horrible early clippings about *The Birthday Party*. As we gazed at them, we marvelled over the one prophetic review by Harold Hobson in the *Sunday Times*: 'You will hear more of this man.'

2007

1 January

Harold and I both reflected on what a terrible year 2006 had been for him health-wise – with *Krapp's Last Tape* and Orlando and Clemmie's wedding as the bright spots. Harold's engagement diary last year morbidly fascinating to him: daily appointments with a nurse to dress the ulcer. But he's resolved he's better: and he's going to walk. He is determined.

4 January

This equanimity came to an end when Harold had a bad fall down some stairs when we took a break at Chewton Glen. It was a split-level apartment and it took me some time to awake to his cries: 'Help me!' He was very shaken and so was I.

Harold recovered enough to do a day's film for the director Kenneth Branagh, a little cameo with Ken himself, in the film of *Sleuth*. Jude, as co-producer, came to watch. He's been amazing, did the outside scaling-the-house scene yesterday in 'towering winds'.

17 January

Fabulous occasion! Dominique de Villepin gave Harold the *Légion d'Honneur* at the French Embassy. Harold was deeply moved by de Villepin's speech; I did not see his expression as I was standing protectively behind his chair but several people confirmed there was a tear. He looked extremely dashing in his Paul Smith suit, bought up the road on the occasion when he had to meet the Queen to receive the CH. He also wore the same pale silk tie I had had so firmly brought from Paris for Orlando's wedding.

We were greeted at the very steps of the Embassy entrance by both the Ambassador Gérard Errera and de Villepin himself. As Rebecca said: 'In Britain it would be a scrawled notice: *WE'RE BY THE POOL.*' De Villepin a marvellous apparition as we ladies were all hoping, exquisite suit, marvellous thick iron-grey hair, patrician nose and faint olive tinge to his skin. Then we were ushered into the library, an austere room full of books that looked false but probably weren't. The talk was what I used to call wide-ranging when Harold and the boys discussed nothing but cricket for the whole of a long meal but in this case was genuinely so: Venezuela where de Villepin lived for years, Cuba and Castro. De Villepin spoke intelligently and eloquently, not *quite* lecturing us, and leaving room for short answers by Harold and even shorter ones by me. (Throughout he was extraordinarily courteous in acknowledging me, referring to my works, even in the public oration, primed I am sure by the thoughtful Gérard Errera.)

Later it was intensely moving when de Villepin said: 'In the name of the President of the Republic . . .' and pinned the red ribbon on to Harold's welcoming Paul Smith lapel. Huge gathering – the children, including Natasha whom Harold wanted to come from Paris – and French-based friends such as Suzy Menkes and Laure de Gramont, Christine Jourdais from Gallimard and Jude Law who was in the midst of filming *Sleuth*. Harold had a brief encounter of the sharp kind with Mary Soames at dinner when, with huge blue Churchillian eyes blazing, she criticized Harold's views on British foreign policy expressed in his speech. 'My husband Christopher Soames would never have said that on foreign soil,' referring to the fact that we were technically on French territory at the Embassy. 'I'm not your husband,' retorted Harold. Even in her eighties, Mary was nothing if not spirited, giving as good as she got; her granddaughter Clemmie confirmed that she had enjoyed the encounter. In fact Harold also relished her company and it is good to record that they then became firm friends.

In retrospect, this evening with its magical evocations of Harold's works, his acclaim in France, and salutation for his political views, was the high point of what one might term his endgame. Medical problems continued, to be counterbalanced by a constant flow of productions, as it seemed. The National Theatre put on *The Hothouse*, the Donmar put on *Betrayal*, Matthew Burton did a brilliant production of *The Dumb Waiter* ... and so on and so on, I am glad to say. So we began to say things like: 'It's July and, rats, there *isn't* a Pinter production in town. What will people do?' Nor was this flush of success confined to the UK. In the autumn a sensational production of *The Homecoming* in New York, with Eve Best as Ruth, created a sensation and Harold, although unable to travel, felt a genuine regret for once at not being able physically (not psychologically) to go to the US.

Our lives became concentrated on the pleasures we could have together: for example we had long been fans of Anselm Kiefer since our 'discovery' of him at MOMA in New York: his work with what Harold felt was a 'literary' content as well as a poetic one, was absolutely up his street. We managed to get to the White Cube Gallery: the experience was fabulous if short, because Harold couldn't lean against the walls, which were all part of Kiefer's installation, although finally a friendly young receptionist surrendered her seat. I decide that I would take the image of the huge uprooted palm with me to Mass on Palm Sunday. Downstairs we saw battlegrounds where flowers now grew. But, as Harold said, 'for how long will they be allowed to grow?'

In general Harold spent most of his time in his chair in the drawing room reading – anything, poetry first choice, but also political works. He also spent a lot of time admiring the magnolia outside the window as it flowered, and he declined. And all the time there was the eczema, the irritations, the visits, the check-ups.

And yet:

9 March

Harold played the part of Max in *The Homecoming*, directed by Thea Sharrock on Radio 3. Gina McKee, even on radio, the slinkiest Ruth yet: I was amused to see how she swapped her trainers for high heels at

Harold's request, 'for atmosphere'. Now he should do *King Lear* on Radio 3. Oddly enough Ian Rickson, director of *Krapp* had already suggested it.

23 March

Read in a self-help column by Lesley Garner of the *Telegraph*, five things to do when you're depressed. Number One was: Do something. Don't just sit there. I was low because Harold was having a bad day health-wise so, without reading on, I dashed off to the Philip Mould Gallery to look at newly installed portrait of Queen Elizabeth I. Solaced myself admiring her pearls which were everywhere. Philip Mould had recently entertained boys from William Fraser's school and they too had admired the portrait. Philip: 'I think that object-related history is so much easier to grasp, don't you?' I entirely agree. So much of my work is in fact 'object-related history'. Decided to involve Harold in it too.

9 April

Harold came with me on my special 'Tudor tour' of the National Portrait Gallery, arranged with Tarnya Cooper. It was a success not so much because it filled Harold with a desire to be a Tudor historian (one is enough in a family) as in igniting his interest in my world. Throughout the rest of the day he kept referring to 'your world . . . the word which you inhabit'. And he actively loved the John Donne portrait of which he had previously seen a reproduction. Donne is after all among the many poets who believed in God that Harold (the *soi-disant* atheist) fervently admires, reads and is able to quote at length.

———

After Harold's death I abandoned my projected life of Queen Elizabeth I. All the same, it had served its purpose: the fascinating research had enriched my life even if I felt finally that I did not want to take the material to another stage by shaping a full-length biography.

Chapter Twenty

———

I'll Miss You So Much

In the summer of 2007 Harold wrote me a poem. As usual he worked on it not so much secretly as privately before reading it to me. Here it is:

POEM

(To A)

I shall miss you so much when I'm dead
The loveliest of smiles
The softness of your body in our bed
My everlasting bride
Remember that when I am dead
You are forever alive in my heart and my head

I burst into tears and in some ways shall always remain upset by it, as well as deeply, unbearably moved. It was written, as it turned out, about eighteen months before Harold died. But at the time, and ever after, I recognized it for what it was: a farewell. The first line in particular gave me a jolt. Rather touchingly, Harold did not seem particularly upset by my reaction since he was busy being pleased with himself for the concept of the dead missing the living rather than the other way around. He kept exclaiming over it in a contented manner: 'Isn't it an original idea, the dead missing the live?' 'Yes, but . . .'

I have the perennial spring picture of Harold in my mind, plotting with members of Gaieties Cricket Club for the greatest season ever to come — how good to record that in the summer of 2008 it actually happened. His very last season was a series of unbroken triumphs for Gaieties CC. Otherwise sitting in his chair he continued to read poetry, interlaced with politics: there was Yeats jostling with *The Future of Iraq* and similar titles, with Yeats gradually picked up more and more, *The Future of Iraq* out of exhaustion rather than lack of interest less and less.

But then I look at my Diary and see that Harold managed to get to Leeds at the end of April to attend a Pinter Festival organized by Mark Taylor-Batty. While he was there (I slogged off to the Royal Armouries and tried on the armour of the Earl of Leicester's horse as a diversion), he met the members of the Belorussian theatrical company, brought to England under the sponsorship of Tom Stoppard, always so practically effective in these matters to do with dissidents.

The end of the performance was called *Being Harold*, and featured an enactment of his Nobel Speech, seen as relative to their plight. At the end the actors lined up on the stage of the Workshop Theatre in a circle. They were of very varying physical appearance, although all young. The actor in Harold enabled him to pass slowly and with great dignity round this wide semicircle shaking each hand, providing a striking image for the press – and no doubt for them too. Later in London he actually attended the performance: the Nobel Speech, always so close to his heart because in it he addressed his 'forum' as in 'I have got my forum'. Of the Belorussian evening, Harold said, 'I felt proud of what I'd written,' even though it was a collage which he doesn't normally like.

Sunday 17 June

We were both amused by a double article about us today in the *Sunday Independent*. I am reinvented as a sort of Mitford heroine, aristo, Catholic, with the headline: 'He's grumpy, she smoothes things over.' I suggest that some role reversal might be fun in the future . . .

Then there was an evening at the Lord's Taverners' to raise funds; Derek Walcott read poetry in his fine, deep voice and Harold read his piece about a cricketing hero, *Arthur Wellard*, which got a lot of appreciative laughs. Harold and I continued to disagree about British politics, me saluting the arrival of Gordon Brown at No. 10 and refusing to give up hope of an improvement in the situation in Iraq (despite, for example, three British soldiers killed and twelve so-called 'civilians' on 28 June). We also continued to debate – politely – about religion, especially following the car bombs which exploded in the West End and Glasgow. Harold: 'People of religion must take responsibility for its crimes.' Me: 'And must people of no religion take responsibility for the crimes of those without religion?' Harold: 'Who are they?' Me: 'Stalin and Hitler.' Harold, according to my Diary which generally, I have to admit, gives me the last word, replied: 'I see the logic of what you say and acknowledge it.'

At a moment of considerable distress – physical – Harold suddenly said he would ask Tony Astbury of Greville Press to print a pamphlet of all his love poems to me, starting with 'Paris' and ending on 'I'll Miss You So Much' . . . Should it be *Six Poems for A* or *Six Poems to A*? Tony tells us that according to the poet Anne Ridler, '"For" is for the living and "To" is to the dead.' So it's 'For'. I like this distinction and find it cheering.

On another occasion, listening in Dorset to an exquisite late-night Prom of Bach Cantatas, we discussed whether Bach's belief in God validated Him. Evidently not, if God does not exist, which is Harold's position some of the time. My point however is that Bach's belief in God does mean that Harold (who worships Bach as God) can't dismiss all people who believe in God as hopeless nincompoops. At one point I declare: 'I wouldn't care if Bach voted for Mussolini, this is the most perfect music I have ever heard.' It's the old Wagner-the-anti-Semite argument: does Wagner's anti-Semitism stop him being personally great? Yes. Does it stop his music being great? No. In all these discussions Harold is careful to say that he respects my personal position. I reply by saying that I admire Jesus Christ for the social message of the New Testament and that, more than the precepts of the Church, is what guides my life, even though I seldom, if ever, manage to live up to it.

30 September

Mitsuko Uchida was like a dragonfly skimming over a lake in her gauzy attire as she played Mozart's Piano Concert No. 27 at the Barbican. We had wonderful seats from where we could see her miraculous hands. It may be the last concert Harold ever goes to (the physical strain of reaching the auditorium was so great) but *what* a concert!

———

Friendship with Mitsuko Uchida and her partner the diplomat Robert Cooper with whom we played bridge and drank wonderful wines provided by them, I note from my Diaries, were among the solaces of these years.

11 October

The day after Harold's birthday. The vengeful Gods were listening when I recorded yesterday, his seventy-seventh birthday, that Harold was really in good nick, given the weakness of his legs caused by the (essential) injections of steroids. I gave him the *Letters of Graham Greene*, one of his heroes. And there was a special showing of *Sleuth* in Soho, a film of which Harold is very proud. The next day Harold didn't feel too well, which I put down to birthday-roistering. I was wrong. In a restaurant with Kevin and Rachel, Harold collapsed in front of our eyes and disappeared to the floor. I felt his forehead: it was ice cold and clammy where it had been burning in the morning. Terrifying hours passed in Casualty at St Mary's, followed by intensive care for eight days. One 4 a.m. call from a doctor suggested that Harold might not recover (I was of course alone in the house) and if he did, he might not be in too good shape . . . The answer was prolonged internal bleeding leading to a terrifyingly low blood count. It had to be stopped. Harold did in a sense recover and so, I suppose, did I, although never totally. The Great Fear now walked with me everywhere and I guess it accompanied Harold too.

There were very few light moments during the rest of the autumn, very few beautiful ones, although the arrival of *Six Poems for A* was one of them. There was the pleasure of sending it out, not as a memorial, as had seemed likely since the pamphlets arrived on 11 October, the day Harold fell 'dead'. At least Harold retained a grim sense of humour having yet another brain scan. Harold to scanner: 'Do you know what's inside this brain?' Busy scanner: 'No.' Harold: 'Masses of unwritten plays.' I like it: a nice concept.

At times Harold issued poignant apologies along the lines: 'I know I'm not the gallant you married–' To which I would reply perfectly correctly: 'And I'm not the romantic beauty *you* married.' Both statements were true. All the same, the gallant and the romantic beauty were never quite forgotten, but seen through a prism of time and also long-lasting happiness. I tried to write a poem called 'Death v. H.P.' mentioning all the goals he had saved against Death: but 'The trouble with Death: he only needs one goal.' I read it to Harold, but it was not as good as I thought. Far better to concentrate on the words of the greatest poet of them all:

> Let me not to the marriage of true minds
> Admit impediment. Love is not love,
> Which alters when it alteration finds

The truest lines on love that Shakespeare ever wrote, and I have always thought absolutely appropriate to us in these last years.

16 December

Our pre-Christmas lunch (for those with whom we wouldn't spend Christmas) was notable for Harold presenting the grandchildren with £50 notes, to mark the British Library's completion of the purchase of his archives. I was about to say: from his lottery winnings, which in one sense he has. I watched these delightful kids waving their £50 notes at him as they sat at the table and he came in on his stick, slowly but benevolently. The notes seemed almost as bright as Atalanta Fitzgerald's beautiful Botticelli-like face. In the meantime the adults, who immediately felt like children themselves – but not children getting £50 notes – looked on disgruntled. 'Don't touch!' I cried to them. To the children: 'Don't listen to any parental schemes for keeping your money safe.'

31 December

New Year's Eve. Dinner with Simon and Victoria Gray at the Café Anglais. How many New Years have we seen in à quatre? This year however we parted before midnight.

———

Harold's friendship with Simon was precious to him and had already lasted over thirty-five years since he directed Butley with Alan Bates; altogether he directed nine of his stage plays, as well as for television and the film of Butley. Simon was one of the people in the world Harold really loved – quite apart from relishing his company as everyone did who knew him, famously 'our funniest friend'. As in any long and deeply affectionate association there were transient disagreements, as when Harold objected to Simon mocking his political views as he saw it, in a TV play (I begged Harold not to take umbrage but was ignored, which left Victoria and me to mutter, 'The men, God bless them ... ', our separate friendship unaffected). It is therefore good to record that in this coming summer, which was to be the last summer of their lives, they were closer than ever. Our last image of Simon was a photograph taken in the box Harold took that year at Lord's, smiling, a jest on his lips. Victoria was at his side smiling too.

2008

15 January

The Granta party at the Twentieth-Century Theatre, in Westbourne Grove. We talk to Ian McEwan and Martin Amis. We have to leave, so I address them: 'Could you giants of modern literature help Harold down the stairs?' Harold will have none if it. 'Out of my way, giants of modern literature,' he commands – and plunges forward. It's all right. He manages to stay upright. Symbolic or what? Harold refuses the support of the young lions.

20 January

We've been invited to Sunday lunch at Chequers by Gordon and Sarah Brown: this is because I met Sarah Brown at a ladies lunch and we discussed the Chequers portraits which I had reproduced in my biography *Cromwell*. At lunch Harold volunteered: 'I have decided I will not go to Chequers. If I went, I might ask about Guantanamo Bay, also a case of schoolgirls arrested on an American base in Gloucestershire (I hadn't heard about this). I might embarrass you.' Me, taking a deep breath: 'You could never embarrass me, but you might upset me.' Harold, sweetly: 'I don't trust myself.' And as I very much want to go, I decide hastily not to argue the point any further. After all, I needn't feel any guilt at leaving him. God bless Harold!

———

Thereafter Harold's various visits to hospitals for various procedures, were interleaved with the opening of *The Lover* and *The Collection*. I console myself by obsessing over the American election, the Democratic contest, watching endless news bulletins in between going to see Harold.

15 March

Of course being Harold, there were moments of comedy, orchestrated by him. Witness the scene at the British Library where Harold formally handed over his archive. He had said to me, innocently, a few days before: 'I've found an unpublished poem which I shall take the opportunity to hand over.' Me: 'What is it?' Harold, carelessly: 'Oh, wait and see.' And secretly I thought it might be a new love poem to me . . . Well, it wasn't exactly that. In the event, at the extremely formal ceremony, a man in an elegant suit, surrounded by other men in suits, introduced Harold with a tribute to his lyrical use of language. And Harold then proceeded to read from one of his yellow pages as follows a poem called 'Modern Love' which began: Do you fuck him / And she fucks me too . . .' going on to play with the word thereafter, with the word 'love' occasionally thrown in. I shall not easily forget that scene. The faces of the suits never moved: but after all suits do have total control of their facial expressions, don't they? Rebecca, Judy and I were shaking.

My Diaries at this time are full of good resolutions along predictable lines about taking each day as it comes, enjoying what yet remains, quotations from Browning's 'Rabbi Ben Ezra': 'Grow old along with me / The best is yet to be.' Yes, but would we really be allowed to grow old (or you might say, older) together? Nevertheless Harold did not lose all his zest despite almost intolerable physical challenges. He suddenly volunteered to accompany me to Harrison Birtwistle's opera *The Minotaur*, out of respect for and interest in Harry, when my original date fell through, a gesture of solidarity and optimism given that Covent Garden had long been deemed too physically testing. I think he identified with John Tomlinson's Minotaur.

19 May

I can hardly write about the amazing night last night at *The Birthday Party* – its fiftieth anniversary in exactly the same theatre and on the exact date in 1958. It was a Gala to raise funds for the Lyric and what a gala! All the performances excellent – Sheila Hancock a joyful Meg – but most moving of all Harold going on stage at the end to join David Farr (the director) and the actors. Looking incredibly fragile, he was led on by Justin Salinger who played Stanley, a rather odd reversal of roles. His last fall (one of two recent ones) has left nasty debilitating wounds. But he managed to speak and tell the story of the usherette at the Thursday matinee who when he told her he was the author said, surveying the empty house: 'You poor dear.' And he appealed to the usherette if still around, to come forward and he would give her a kiss.

I tried to think of some other playwright who would have attended the fiftieth anniversary of his own play, transformed from total failure to classic within his own lifetime. Chekhov? Died in his forties. John Osborne and *Look Back in Anger*? He died in his sixties; of course there was a difference because the Osborne play was a startling success, Harold's a resounding failure.

It is good to read of this glorious occasion because shortly afterwards there was a terrifying experience, when Harold collapsed and fell at 10 a.m. fifteen minutes before we were to leave for Eurostar and Europe. (I was due to talk on historical biography at the Shakespeare and Co. Bookshop festival.) The Great Fear was coming nearer, especially as he might easily have collapsed on Eurostar in the tunnel . . . At first Harold resisted the idea of going to hospital, his roar at the sound of the word 'hospital' making a Siberian tiger sound like a pussycat. He finally agreed. O Dante's Inferno! O St Mary's Casualty! We were cheered up in a highly depressing situation by the award of a CBE to Edward Fitzgerald for Human Rights and Harold vowed to give him a lunch on the day he went to the Palace.

27 July

We sat in the drawing room listening to my *Desert Island Discs*: Harold delighted by it and kept saying so throughout the day, that day and the next. He was immensely touched I chose the Beethoven String Quartet Op. 132 – his favourite piece of music – especially for him and didn't mind me telling the anecdote from 1980 of the so-called 'missing' scene from *Betrayal*. Although it was perfectly true that I suggested one scene was missing, at which he went fast round Holland Park and then wrote it (not one I had expected, however) in principle I can't bear it when artists' wives say: 'It was all me . . .'

While we were at Westbrook House enjoying our Dorset holiday in the pleasant house with the pond and ducks, the tragedy occurred which plunged Harold into a profound depression that I believe never quite lifted till the end of his life. The telephone rang and it was Victoria Gray telling me the news that Simon had died, in a small sad voice of total disbelief. I had to go upstairs and break the news to Harold, who crumpled before my eyes. He said he had a premonition when he saw my face. He put his head in his hands and wept.

With someone like Harold, it is impossible to divide off the reactions of the body to those of the mind: with hindsight, the liver cancer which was diagnosed in October (but not present in May) may have been developing at exactly that moment. But certainly Harold went into a state of depression, expressed in virtual lack of mobility, which never lifted except briefly in the next months. He struggled to read Eliot at Simon's funeral, helped up the steps to the pulpit by Matthew Burton. (I had been quite unsure that he would manage it.) And we gave the wake following the funeral in our house. It was after that that Harold gave me exact instructions about his own burial, sitting in his chair, who was to read what, the privacy of the event which he wanted. I think Harold was contemplating his own mortality from the moment of Simon's death onwards in a way he had never quite done for seven years of illness because the need for courage and endurance did not encourage reflection. I told Harold this: 'Death kept coming to grab you and you eluded him.'

One of the gleams of happiness occurred when I persuaded Harold that he was needed to go to Dublin for the opening of *No Man's Land* because it was not jollity but a 'professional engagement – your advice is wanted'. He felt better after this decision – and we won the Test Match with a six! So we went. Harold adored the production with Michael Gambon, David Bradley, Nick Dunning and David Walliams; this great play about age and memory – and death and drink – was the last play he actually saw. And we had an idyllic spree, Celtic, which covered my birthday. (A 1913 volume of Yeats, green with golden embellishments, was my present from Harold to chime with a Yeats exhibition at the National Library of Ireland.) We both enjoyed a state of elegiac happiness for a few days including a visit to a restaurant perfectly entitled (for me) Aqua, surrounded on three sides by water, for my birthday lunch.

At the end of the first night of *No Man's Land*, Michael Gambon gestured from the stage to Harold and he managed to stand up. The whole audience then stood up and clapped. Harold looked very genial, in Edward Fitzgerald's favourite word. But he was visibly moved.

7 October

Fabulous opening night of *No Man's Land* at the Duke of York's Theatre in London. We began by sitting in a box together, for ease of access for Harold, but in order to spy Gambon's second act entrance, that extraordinary sprightly tread which takes one by surprise after the weakness of his gait and the falls in the first act, I moved to an empty seat in the dress circle. Peter Stothard told me that the reason it was empty was because a big financial man had arrived and been rushed away to deal with the latest crisis in the City: 'a vast aboriginal calamity' to quote the line from the play when the financial adviser fails to arrive.

Of course in the autumn of 2008 that line got a big laugh: whereas in 1975 like most of the rest of the play it had been received in dead silence.

3 November

Arrive on foot at Essenza to find Harold sitting looking wan. I sat opposite to him, then moved to his side in order to hear his voice, which was very weak. *Et pour cause*. He's just come from seeing Jonathan Hoare at St Mary's and he must give up drink 'otherwise I won't last very long'. Jonathan Hoare said to him: 'You have survived so much. You have so much to live for.' Harold says he answered: 'And central to that is my marriage.' As I reel from the shock, I realize that Harold has chosen life. That is the thing to cling to, in what is going to be a difficult time for him, very, very difficult.

In the thirty-seven days which followed in which Harold heroically did not drink and the house flowed with elderflower wine, I had to keep reminding myself in view of his suffering that he had chosen to do this. 'In order to live. And with you,' as he said from time to time. As for me, I sneaked about swigging white wine from a silver goblet which just might contain elderflower wine ... I reminded Harold that he had valiantly and successfully given up both whisky and cigarettes in the past.

5 November

O frabjous day! Calloo! Callay! The day that Obama was elected. Spoke about the Gunpowder Plot at the House of Commons, came back and watched TV all night, Harold having gone to sleep. But when Ohio fell, I couldn't resist waking him and we rejoiced. In triumphalist mood, I point out that it is the United States of America, not England, France or Germany who has democratically elected the first black leader;

we must now salute the American Embassy as we pass it, in honour of a great people, not wave fists. Harold goes back to sleep.

9 November

Listened to the Britten War Requiem on Radio 3 (the original Peter Pears/Fischer-Dieskau recording) and as I was just finishing Sebastian Barry's awesome novel on the same subject *A Long, Long Way*, I found tears pouring down my face at: 'I am the enemy you killed, my friend.' Harold, who did not, I think, notice, wept silently at 'Let us sleep now'.

11 November

Learned from Jonathan Hoare that Harold has a cancerous tumour on his liver, when in Harold's presence and with Harold's permission I question him, to get it straight. Felt in shock. Idiotically told myself: 'It's not liver cancer but just a cancerous tumour.' As if there was a difference! I sat downstairs in the hospital waiting to be picked up to see the Babylon exhibition, of all things, at the British Museum and kept falling asleep. Shock. Jonathan Hoare is hopeful 'so long as he doesn't drink'. Harold, faintly but firmly: 'I've no intention of drinking.'

21 November

Harold is so low, so thin, with his sad, searching eyes like a sick Labrador. I pity him so much and keep thinking what I can do to help, not able to face the fact, I suppose, that basically I can do nothing.

28 November

The long-promised lunch at Lucio's restaurant which Harold gave for Edward, following his investiture at Buckingham Palace, was an enormous success, and at such a crucial moment, immensely warming for me. Superb arrangements, thanks to Lucio. I saw with pleasure that

Edward, who had said, 'No, no, I won't make a speech, just a few remarks,' had a thick pile of notes by his plate. Harold rose to his feet and quoted Yeats on Swift: '"He serves human liberty".' (Edward would later read that at Harold's burial.)

30 November

Went to Farm Street Mass and we then gave lunch to Sebastian and Allie Barry, with Dinah Wood, at Scott's. 'It's very nice to meet new people,' said Harold, a rare remark from him and a direct response to the charm of the Barrys, telling us of their Irish lives; also Harold's profound admiration for *The Secret Scriptures*. (I had written in the *Guardian* the day before commending it: 'What were the Booker judges thinking about?' So we were all off to a flying start.) Sebastian Barry told Harold how seeing the 1975 *No Man's Land* was the 'first step' towards him writing his great play *The Steward of Christendom*.

17 December

It's the original 'good news, bad news' as I said to Harold in the car outside the Cromwell as we departed. It was a feeble attempt at black humour. The good news is that Harold can drink again, the bad news is that he's dying, so it doesn't matter if he drinks. We visited Dr Westaby who had saved Harold's life once already over oesophageal cancer. Westaby said there was no point in a procedure to zap the tumour. It would – only possibly – prolong life: but there was a danger of infection, haemorrhage. Me: 'What are we talking about? Years? Months?' The answer after a silence was 'Months'. I knew the real answer was probably rather different: weeks, perhaps.

I did not guess that the real answer was 'days'. At the time I told myself there would be lots and lots of months. All the same I hated the very word 'months'. Dr Westaby kindly said there was no point Harold stopping drinking. He also told Harold that seven years ago, he never expected him to be alive for so long. I noticed that Harold left down the stairs, however, with more agility than when he had arrived. I said: 'I know just what you are going to do when we get home.' And sure enough Harold instructed me to fetch a bottle of champagne from the cellar and sat sipping: 'Oh, the enjoyment of this glass! I had forgotten how absolutely lovely champagne was.'

That was Wednesday. On the last Sunday, we had lunch at Scott's, along with the Billingtons and Honor Fitzgerald, aged thirteen, whose parents were away celebrating their wedding anniversary. Harold was convivial although possibly, with hindsight, beginning to be a little confused. We watched a DVD of *The Reader* that night and Harold admired David Hare's screenplay and Kate Winslett's vigorous, intelligent acting at length. But he refused to eat.

The next morning, Monday 22 December at about seven o'clock in the morning he collapsed. I contacted Dr Westaby and he was taken by ambulance to the Hammersmith Hospital. All round us, as we left, were the preparations for a family Christmas lunch. There was the Christmas tree in the window, and a pile of presents underneath it. In the square people were already getting their houses ready for the traditional Christmas Eve ritual of candles in all the windows. (When I returned home, the square would be in darkness except for flickering candlelight which seemed to be a salutation to Harold.) The ambulance took us through streets full of cheerful, busy people shopping urgently, holding parcels and children by the hand.

Harold to me as he lay waiting for a bed: 'What are your plans,' pause, 'generally?' It was our last real conversation. I replied: 'First of all I'm going to have wonderful support from family and friends, but by the way, you're not dead yet. Secondly, I'm going to pop home for a short while to preside over Christmas lunch.' The last word I heard him say was 'the key'. It seemed to be a question.

By the evening, and all the next day, he was unconscious, lying in a room which looked high over West London facing a clock tower as in some Oxford college.

Wednesday 24 December

Harold was very calm and still. I thought of Rilke's 'The Poet's Death', 'his mere mask, timidly dying there, tender and open'. In the late morning all the grandchildren who were in England came to visit him and give him a last kiss. Their ages ranged from twenty-one to eight, all shapes and sizes. The scene was like a Victorian painting called 'Farewell to a Grandfather'. The last to leave the room was Simon Soros, who bent and kissed Harold's hand. That night he began to write a kind of reggae poem on the subject: with the title 'Grandpa Harold'. It was exactly what this grandfather, to whom these children had brought so much pleasure, would have liked.

About twenty past seven I was sitting reading Tolstoy's *Resurrection* by Harold's bedside. He was breathing but with a strong rattling sound. The nurses were outside. The children and grandchildren had dispersed for Christmas. I was alone in the room. I was happy like that. Suddenly the rattling stopped. Harold opened his black eyes very wide, almost staring, although he didn't respond when I spoke to him as before: 'It's me, Antonia, who loves you.' Then he went quite tense, his whole body. Finally he went still and silent.

I leant forward and found no breath. He looked white and dead. I sat for a while. Then I kissed him. His dear body was already quite cool. Must you go? Yes, it was time. Before I left the room, after another, last kiss, I said: 'Goodnight, sweet prince, and flights of angels sing you to your rest.'

FAITH AND TREASON
The Story of the Gunpowder Plot

In England, November 5 is Guy Fawkes Day, when fireworks commemorate one of the most shocking moments in British history—the 1605 attempt to blow up the House of Parliament, and King James I along with it. In *Faith and Treason*, Antonia Fraser untangles the web of religion, politics, and personalities surrounding this infamous act of terrorism. Planned by a group of English Catholics in response to a history of severe penal laws against Catholicism, the Gunpowder Plot was a desperate—and doomed—conspiracy that led to torture, executions, and a high tide of anti-Catholic feeling in England that would alter the nation's Catholic community forever. Both detective story and social history, *Faith and Treason* is gripping and dramatic history.

History

MARIE ANTOINETTE
The Journey

France's iconic queen, Marie Antoinette, wrongly accused of uttering the infamous "Let them eat cake," was alternately revered and reviled during her lifetime. For centuries since, she has been the object of debate, speculation, and the fascination so often accorded illustrious figures in history. Married in mere girlhood, this essentially lighthearted child was thrust onto the royal stage and commanded by circumstance to play a significant role in European history. Antonia Fraser's lavish and engaging portrait excites compassion and regard for all aspects of the queen, immersing the reader not only in the coming-of-age of a graceful woman, but in the culture of an unparalleled time and place.

History/Biography

LOVE AND LOUIS XIV
The Women in the Life of the Sun King

Louis XIV, the highly feted "Sun King," was renowned for his political and cultural influence and for raising France to a new level of prominence in seventeenth-century Europe. And yet, as Antonia Fraser keenly describes, he was equally legendary in the domestic sphere. Indeed, a panoply of women—his mother, Anne; mistresses such as Louise de la Vallière, Athénaïs de Montespan, and the puritanical Madame de Maintenon; and an array of courtesans—moved in and out of the court. The highly visible presence of these women raises many questions about their position in both Louis XIV's life and in France at large. With careful research and vivid, engaging prose, Fraser makes the multifaceted life of one of the most famous European monarchs accessible and vibrantly current.

History/Biography

THE WARRIOR QUEENS
The Legends and the Lives of the Women Who Have Led Their Nations in War

"Cleopatra, Zenobia, Tamara, Jinga Mbandi of Angola, Catherine the Great and Caterina Sforza, England's two Matildas and Tuscany's one, the beautiful Queen Louise of Prussia and Queen Elizabeth I of England, the names roll on as these women led their countries into victory and into defeat. . . . Fraser, always a diligent historian, has . . . become a graceful writer and achieved the formidable task of winding a variety of women and countries onto one skein."

—*The Plain Dealer*

History/Women's Studies

In the popular imagination the unfortunate consorts of Henry VIII survive as feminine stereotypes: the Betrayed Wife, the Temptress, the Good Woman, the Ugly Sister, the Bad Girl, and the Mother Figure. Now one of our leading historians restores these women to human dimensions while unraveling the web of forces that raised them to the throne and sometimes brought them to the headsman's block. Under Antonia Fraser's intense scrutiny, Catherine of Aragon emerges as a scholar-queen who steadfastly refused to grant a divorce to her royal husband; Anne Boleyn is absolved of everything but a sharp tongue and an inability to produce a male heir; and Catherine Parr is revealed as a religious reformer with the good sense to tack with the treacherous winds of the Tudor court. And we gain fresh understanding of Jane Seymour's circumspect wisdom, the touching dignity of Anna of Cleves, and the youthful naïveté that led to Katherine Howard's fatal indiscretions. *The Wives of Henry VIII* interweaves passion and power, personality and politics, into a superb work of history.

History/Biography

ANCHOR BOOKS
Available wherever books are sold.
www.randomhouse.com